3 6 . 13

WMANF

- Please return items before closing time
  on the last date stamped to avoid charges.
- Renew books by phoning 01305 224311 or
  online www.dorsetforyou.com/libraries
- Items may be returned to any Dorset library.
- Please note that children's books issued on
  an adult card will incur overdue charges.

Dorset County Council
Library Service

DL/2372 dd05450

MASTERPIECES OF
CLASSICAL ART

MASTERPIECES OF
CLASSICAL ART

DYFRI WILLIAMS

THE BRITISH MUSEUM PRESS

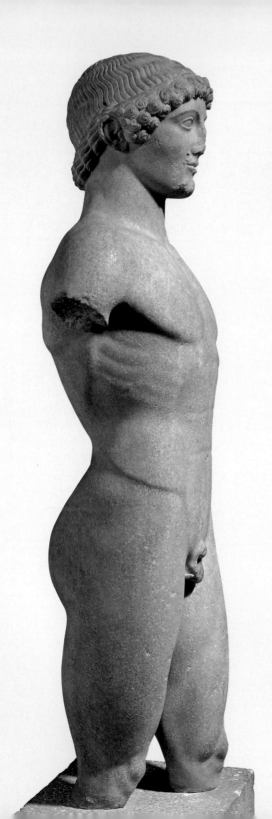

For my father
Roderick T. Williams

Half-title: Pottery drinking bowl, Etruscan, 300–280 BC (**119**)
Frontispiece: Cameo glass plaque, Roman, AD 5–25 (**133**)
Left: Marble funerary figure, Greek, 500–490 BC (**40**)
Right: End panel of ivory gaming box, Cypriot, 1200–1100 BC (**99**)

First published in 2009 by The British Museum Press
A division of The British Museum Company Ltd
38 Russell Square, London WC1B 3QQ
www.britishmuseum.org

A catalogue record for this book is available from the British Library

ISBN 978-0-7141-2254-0

Designed and typeset in Minion and Venetian by John Hawkins
and Janet James
Maps by Kate Morton
Printed and bound in Singapore by CS Graphics Pte Ltd

CONTENTS

PREFACE

This book brings together over 160 important objects from the material culture of the ancient Greek and Roman worlds, dating from the fourth millennium BC until the early fourth century AD.

Greece was for much of its early history a loose collection of fiercely independent city-states and only occasionally, and then briefly, became more coherent when faced by external threat. The Greeks travelled all round the Mediterranean, trading, sometimes settling, always curious and imaginative. When they settled abroad they retained their independent spirit and identity through their language, their gods and their customs, but they also welcomed new ideas, such as writing, and many new technological and scientific developments. Greek art was consequently fluid, searching and self-aware.

Rome, by contrast, just a single city, came to dominate a huge empire that spread across Europe and round the shores of the Mediterranean, through northern Africa and Egypt, and on into the Near and Middle East. Like the Greeks, the Romans took their language and customs with them wherever they went, but as they conquered they also offered Roman citizenship and this brought fresh blood to Rome's ruling class – the emperor Hadrian (**143**) was from Spain, Septimius Severus (**155**) from North Africa – and a thrusting, vibrant atmosphere to the capital. Virgil, Augustus' epic poet, wrote in his *Aeneid* (vi, 847–53) that 'others [the Greeks] will beat out more subtly lifelike figures in bronze, I have no doubt, and draw living faces from marble … You, Roman, remember to rule the peoples of your empire – these will be your arts – to impose the ways of peace, to spare the defeated and subdue the proud.' This may in part be a poetic paradox, but Greek artists certainly had an enormous impact on the Romans, though those artists worked within and for a Roman world. Indeed, the fusion of the long artistic tradition of the Greeks, the native Italic traditions and Roman imagination and drive were to result in such great sculptural programmes as the Actium victory monument (compare **129**), the Ara Pacis and the great victory columns and arches of Rome. Roman sculpture was eclectic, not least because of the breadth of artistic choice available.

Early Greeks did not have a concept of art, but they did value beautiful craftsmanship (*techne*). The concept of 'art' perhaps began to take shape during the Classical period, as the reputations of some sculptors and painters grew and they wrote about their own works and ideas. It was, however, only during the Hellenistic period that art as such began to be written about, and by the Roman period both writing about art (*ars*) and collecting it were important cultural activities. Today, of course, even mundane ancient objects are appreciated for their quality, artistic innovativeness and historical importance, and looked upon not only as history but also as art.

In the medieval world a 'masterpiece' was literally a product for which a craftsman received his master's patent, and hence the right to set up his own workshop and train and employ his own helpers. The world of the ancient craftsman does not seem to have been so highly structured: at least we have no evidence for similar guilds or hierarchies. Our idea of a masterpiece today is determined by our knowledge of Renaissance art combined with the impact of modern art, which has led us to think in terms of a work by a great Master, or a piece that challenges our preconceptions of the world (or even the idea of art itself). In this volume pieces of real quality or importance that engender a sense of wonder, as well as those best suited to represent their time and place, have been chosen for inclusion as 'masterpieces'. I hope that this small selection – the number could so easily have been doubled – can serve as both an introduction to the great collection of the British Museum and an overview of the worlds of Greek and Roman art, of interest to general readers and students.

Compiling this volume allows me to pay tribute to all my colleagues in the Museum with whom I have worked over many years, curators, conservators, scientists and photographers, too many to mention by name but all sharing the same deep enthusiasm for objects and the desire to make them better understood by all. In particular, however, I should like to thank Richard Abdy, Lucilla Burn, Dudley Hubbard, Ralph Jackson, Ivor Kerslake, Thomas Kiely, Ingrid McAlpine, Kate Morton, Kim Overend, Nancy and Andrew Ramage, Nina Shandloff, Alexandra Villing and Susan Woodford.

I PREHISTORIC GREECE *c.* 4500–1000 BC

The development of permanent settlements marks the beginning of the Neolithic period. We also find the first representations of the animate and inanimate world, figurines and models that are not mere tools but manifestations of an intellectual reaction to the environment and to existence. The most remarkable of these are the earliest sculptures of human beings (**1**).

The Bronze Age (from about 3000 BC) saw the gradual adoption of bronze instead of stone tools. Bronze Age Greece is traditionally divided into three cultural regions: the Cycladic islands, Crete and mainland Greece. In the Early Bronze Age (3000–2000 BC) it was the people of the Cyclades, those stepping stones between the mainland and Crete, who produced the most striking works of art (referred to as Cycladic), the series of marble figurines that typifies the period (**2**).

Around 2200 BC several settlements on the mainland and some of the neighbouring islands were destroyed in a wave of invasions that are often connected with the arrival of the first Greeks. Subsequently the Cyclades, along with the mainland, came under the influence of Crete (**3**), where from about 1950 BC a number of so-called palaces arose. These large, built structures served as storage and distribution hubs (**4**) and manufacturing and cult centres (**5**), as well as living quarters for an elite. Such centralization also acted as a spur to important social developments, including writing and new technologies.

The interests of Minoan Crete (Cretan culture is called Minoan, after Minos, the island's legendary king) spread across the Aegean to the coast of Turkey. Trading outposts with seasonal or even permanent communities grew up not only on the islands that linked Crete to the mainland but also on the coastline of Turkey. An example of the consequences of such outreach is the gold jewellery from Aigina, which was probably made there by resident Cretan craftsmen (**7**). Contacts reached further still, to Egypt and the Levant, where a document found at Mari on the Euphrates even mentions a resident from Kaptara (Crete).

At some point around 1700 BC the Minoan palaces suffered severe damage, probably caused by earthquakes, but were rebuilt on a grander scale. This second palace period (1700–1500 BC) was the time of Crete's greatest power and artistic achievement. There was much interchange with the Greek mainland, where the elite acquired Minoan objects and had them imitated (**10**). Specialist craftsmen travelled too, for Minoan-style frescos have been found in the Near East, while in Egypt a remarkable Minoan fresco has come to light depicting bull-leaping.

Linear B inscribed clay tablet recording offerings of oil to a goddess, from Knossos, Crete, 1450–1400 BC, ht 15.6 cm (GR 1910,0423.1; presented by Arthur Evans)

In perhaps about 1530 BC the island of Thera (Santorini), an active volcano, was devastated in a huge eruption and the main, Minoanized town was buried deep in ash and pumice. Although this catastrophe had an impact on Crete, it was not what brought the end of the Minoan palaces. This came some fifty or more years later. The causes remain unclear, but one might suspect a combination of natural and human action. The outcome was a growing dominance by the mainland.

The Bronze Age culture of mainland Greece (Helladic, as it is called) had, by the end of the early phase, begun to grow in wealth and contacts. At this time it was probably controlled by warrior chieftains. Those buried in a series of shaft graves at Mycenae (1600–1450 BC) were accompanied by gold death masks and vessels of precious metal (compare **9**), while their women were adorned with jewellery and one child with a suit of gold.

In about 1450 BC destructions on Crete allowed the mainland Greeks to expand their influence to include that island, where the mainland system of writing (Linear B) now replaced the Minoan script (Linear A). The Mycenaeans, as we call the people and the culture in the Late Bronze Age, also took over the Minoan trading routes through the islands to Cyprus and the east, as well as south to Egypt (**10–11**). They also began to trade with the west, where they may have set up trading posts. This was the time of the construction of great palaces with massive defensive walls, as well as huge stone-built tombs, the grandest of which, the so-called Treasury of Atreus at Mycenae, was even decorated with relief sculptures (**12**). It was a time when there was a general similarity between the products of all the Mycenaean centres, a unified cultural tradition. After the destruction of the Mycenaean palaces around 1200 BC, however, many sites were abandoned and the uniformity of Mycenaean culture disintegrated. By about 1100 BC a period of increased isolation had set in and many people fled the mainland, some migrating to Cyprus. The reason for this collapse is not clear, although theories abound.

1 THE KARPATHOS LIMESTONE GODDESS

This roughly carved, schematic figure of a female is the earliest known sculpture from Greece on a large scale. Its size and the strange unanatomical horizontal groove below the pubic area suggest that the figure served a particular role in a cult context, rather than as an offering in a tomb, perhaps even representing a goddess rising from the earth or sea.

The figure was carved from local grey limestone without the use of metal tools, only stone hammers, stone blades and abrasives. It is now heavily weathered. The arms are mere stumps and there seem to have been no legs at all, as it is unlikely that the horizontal groove below the pubic triangle was intended to indicate folded legs. The head has been reduced to a triangle dominated by a large projection for the nose, while the eyebrows have been lightly incised. The breasts are clearly rendered but most emphasis has been given to the pubic triangle and the genitalia. The light incision of the eyebrows suggests that the eyes and other details may have been painted, as is the case with later Cycladic marble figurines (**2**).

The figure comes from Pegadia (Poseidonia) on the island of Karpathos in the southeastern Aegean and was found by James Theodore Bent, the first person to carry out systematic excavations in the Cyclades. It recalls some much smaller figurines from various parts of mainland Greece and the islands that belong in the Late Neolithic (5300–4500 BC) and Final Neolithic (4500–3200 BC) periods. Nevertheless, it remains essentially unparalleled: a truly remarkable representation of what is surely a divine mediator in the human world, whether as mother-goddess or love-goddess, and a sculpture that is primitive yet sophisticated in its carefully conceptualized form.

Limestone figure

Greek, made on Karpathos, probably Final Neolithic, 4500–3200 BC

From Pegadia (Karpathos)

From the collection of J.T. Bent

Ht 66 cm

GR 1886,0310.1 (*Sculpture* A 11)

2 CYCLADIC MARBLE FIGURE

'I love and admire Cycladic sculpture', wrote the sculptor Henry Moore. 'It has such elemental simplicity.' This particularly large, well carved and well preserved figure of a naked woman typifies this special quality of Cycladic art.

The top and back of the head are modelled into an elongated and flattened projection and may represent some sort of special hat or hairstyle. The nose is long and the ears project, as they do on a number of the larger figures. Remarkable traces of paint are preserved on this figure's head and neck: almond-shaped eyes, a necklace and two rows of dots around the brow that may indicate a diadem or the lower border of hair or hat. It is not certain whether the mouth was also delineated in paint, but there is a clear, dotted pattern on the figure's right cheek, which, along with traces of paint elsewhere on the face, show that it was originally extensively covered with bright, perhaps even garish patterns. The dots on the brow and on the cheek can be paralleled on other contemporary large Cycladic figures.

The neck is solid, with a curved neck line at the front and a Y-shaped line at the back which merges into the spine. The arms are folded, as usual on such sculptures, and the fingers carefully incised. There is no indication of the pubic triangle, although this may have been rendered in paint. Thighs and legs are well carved, with a short incised line on the back to mark the division from the buttocks. The marble has been cut away to a large extent between the lower legs, leaving only a thin bridge – a piece of bravura carving, for there must have been great danger of the legs breaking off.

Analysis of the traces of paint on this figure has shown that the red is cinnabar and the black meta-cinnabar, an altered form of the same pigment. The black paint may have originally been black, or it may have changed with age from red. Colouring matter, containers and grinders for pigments have been found in Cycladic graves. This may indicate that the painting of the faces of the dead was part of the funerary ritual: the decoration on the figurines may then have deliberately echoed that to be painted on the deceased.

Marble figure

Greek, made on one of the Cyclades, Early Cycladic II, 2700–2500 BC

Ht 76.5 cm

GR 1971,0521.1

3 CYCLADIC JUGS

The potter of the jug on the right has turned a simple narrow-necked shape into something both elegant and remarkably human by tilting back the neck, adding a pair of small breasts to the upper body and painting in the midst of an abstract, moustache-like pattern a single human eye.

The tilted-back neck was already fashionable among the potters of the Cyclades in the Early Bronze Age. The matt surface of the dark paint may be the result of difficulty in obtaining a lustrous effect with the island clay, but it also probably reflects the spread of a fashion already at home in Syria and parts of Anatolia. The dark-on-light scheme of painting is found on Melos before the end of the final phase of the Early Cycladic period, when it replaced the regular dark slipped pottery with incised and stamped decoration so typical of the islands in the third millennium BC.

Cycladic pottery, like most of Cycladic art, was increasingly influenced by Cretan work. Minoan vases were imported from Crete and then imitated, as we can see clearly from the pottery found on the island of Thera (Santorini) which was buried under volcanic debris from the catastrophic eruption of the island perhaps in about 1530 BC. Some of the later Cycladic matt-painted vases introduced a matt red as well, as seen on the fragmentary larger vase of the same shape on the left. Such vases decorated with colourfully schematic birds were themselves exported both to Crete and to Mycenae on the Greek mainland, where the potters even imitated the style.

Henry Moore's comment on the complete vase is fascinatingly suggestive: 'This piece is strongly figurative with a body, neck and head, and two little breasts at the front. There is no doubt our sense of form comes from our own bodies. If we didn't have a head and a body, two arms and two legs, feet and hands, the whole basis of plastic art would be quite different.'

Pottery jugs

(*left*) Greek, made in the Cyclades, Middle Cycladic, 1700–1550 BC

From Knossos ('The Temple Repositories')

Gift of Sir Arthur Evans

Preserved ht 37 cm

GR 1906,1112.95 (*Vase* A 360)

(*right*) Greek, probably made on Melos, Middle Cycladic, 1850–1750 BC

Probably from Melos

Gift of G. Dunn

Ht 39.8 cm

GR 1920,1015.1 (*Vase* A 342)

4 MINOAN POTTERY *PITHOS*

This huge storage jar was found in 1878/9 in the third 'magazine' (storeroom) in the western wing of the so-called palace of Knossos by a Cretan antiquary from Heraklion, named Minos Kalokairinos.

Of the twelve *pithoi* excavated by Kalokairinos, the first to leave his collection was sent to the British Museum in 1884, through the agency of the British Consul on Crete, T.B. Sandwith. Two others later ended up in the Louvre, one in the Museo Pigorini in Rome, one in the National Museum in Athens, and three in the museum in Heraklion. Sandwith witnessed Kalokairinos's excavations and wrote to Sir Charles Newton, then Keeper of Greek and Roman Antiquities, encouraging the British Museum to undertake excavations at Knossos. He also 'called on the principal members of the Syllogos at Candia who are very jealous of any antiquity leaving the island, and represented to them that by allowing this curious relic of this ancient city to be displayed in our national collection, it would interest archaeologists in Cretan pottery which is so little known'.

The storage of large quantities of agricultural produce, mainly grain crops, olive oil and wine, was one of the main functions of the centralized structures or palaces of Minoan Crete. Gathered from the surrounding countryside, it was then used or redistributed by the palace administration. Through this mechanism the palaces reinforced their control of the island.

The rope decoration in relief on the vessel may reflect the way that such huge jars were transported from their place of manufacture to their locations in the storerooms. Once in place, their contents would have been accessed with the aid of smaller vessels or dippers. Such large vessels had been used in the storage areas of palaces since the Late Neolithic period. They were, however, also sometimes used as coffins, both on Minoan Crete and, in the seventh century BC, on some Cycladic islands and in cities on the west coast of Anatolia.

Heinrich Schliemann visited Crete in 1886, but his attention was drawn more to Troy and it was left to Sir Arthur Evans to begin excavations in March 1900 on the site of what he called the 'Palace of Minos', the legendary king of Crete, thus giving the culture and its people the name 'Minoan'.

Pottery storage jar

Greek, made at Knossos, Late Minoan, 1450–1400 BC

From the palace storerooms at Knossos

Gift of Minos Kalokairinos

Ht 1.13 m

GR 1884,0807.1 (*Vase* A 739)

5 MINOAN BRONZE BULL-LEAPER

Bull-jumping was frequently shown in Minoan art and no doubt formed part of a ritualized spectacle on Crete. The strength and potency of bulls lay behind their religious importance to the Minoans, just as they have done for other cultures at other times in history. Here the artist has captured not only the bucking energy of the bull but also the contrast between its massive size and the delicacy of the slight-limbed youth.

Different leaps appear to have been represented by the Minoans, although it is sometimes doubted whether all were really possible, not least because of the unpredictability of the bull's movements, particularly which way he might toss his head. Here the leaper is represented as somersaulting over the bull's head and landing with both feet on its back, whence he would have leapt to the ground. The sculptor has cleverly supported the flying acrobat by allowing his long hair to trail on the bull's forehead. As well as bull-leaping, scenes of the capture, tethering and leading of bulls are represented in Minoan art (**6**). Perhaps the Minoans endeavoured to train or even tame the bulls to some extent.

The bronze group is solid cast, in one piece, using the lost-wax technique. The arms are not represented but end in stumps: it is not clear whether this was by design or because the bronze did not flow properly into the narrow extremities of the mould. Similarly, the loss of the lower legs may be due to a casting flaw. Minoan bronzes tended to have a low tin content that resulted in a slow-flowing alloy and a bubbly surface. Examples of large pieces, like this bull-jumper, or others in the form of both male and female worshippers, are known from palace sites on Crete, but there are also smaller, simpler representations in bronze of both humans and animals from Minoan sanctuaries in the countryside, whether in sacred caves or on the peaks of mountains.

Bronze group

Greek, made on Crete, Late Minoan I, 1550–1450 BC

Said to be from Rethymnon, Crete

Formerly in the collection of Captain E.G. Spencer Churchill

Ht 11.4 cm

GR 1966,0328.1

6 MINOAN AGATE SEALSTONE

This pale, mottled agate sealstone, only just over two centimetres in diameter, has been carved with the scene of a man leading a bull by means of a rope or woollen fillet tied to his horns.

Such engraved sealstones were used to impress a unique mark on to lumps of clay attached to the fastenings of doors, jars, boxes and even bundles of inscribed clay tablets. They could indicate individual ownership or the identity of a controlling authority and were used to discourage illicit access. Seals, indeed, were part of the Minoan administrative system that served to control the movement of goods and produce throughout the island of Crete.

The idea was probably introduced from the palace cultures of the Near East. Early examples were cut from soft stones, such as steatite, and from bone and ivory: they often took the form of stamp seals, roughly cylindrical or conical in shape. In the Middle Bronze Age the introduction of fast, rotary drills meant that harder stones, such as quartzes, could be engraved. The most popular shapes became those with slightly convex surfaces, especially those shaped like lenses (as here), almonds and rectangular cushions. All were drilled right through so that they could be threaded and worn round the neck or wrist. As well as functioning as seals, the attractively coloured stones and complex scenes meant that they were also probably worn and admired as jewellery. Some were no doubt even felt by their owners to have amuletic powers.

It was the existence of sealstones, especially those with writing on them, that in 1894 attracted Arthur Evans to Crete, where he was to unearth the great palace at Knossos. Their nineteenth-century Cretan owners called them *galapetres* (milk stones), for they were thought to increase milk for nursing mothers.

Agate sealstone

Greek, made on Crete, Late Minoan, 1450–1200 BC

Probably from Crete

Formerly in the collection of Admiral T.A.B. Spratt

Ht 2.2 cm

GR 1892,0720.2 (*Gem* 79)

7 THE AIGINA TREASURE

In 1892 the British Museum purchased an extraordinary group of gold and gemstone jewellery, together with a gold cup, that had been found some ten years earlier on the island of Aigina. The circumstances of the find are shrouded in mystery, but it seems likely that the Aigina Treasure represents the precious contents of a small group of Middle Bronze Age tombs, perhaps of one male and two or three women, discovered to the southeast of the later Temple of Apollo in the island's main port.

One of the most striking pieces of jewellery is the 'Master of the Animals' pendant (above). A male figure has his arms outstretched and holds by the necks two large water birds. He stands amidst lotus flowers, perhaps on a stylized boat, and wears a tall headdress, a belted kilt-like garment with a long tassel, and boots. Pairs of ridged, curving elements with bud-like ends appear from behind him and enclose the birds. Below hang simple disks: the one on the left was repaired in antiquity.

Equally unusual is the curved pectoral ornament which has at either end a head with two long curls of hair (below). This piece is of a very high quality of workmanship and the eyes and eyebrows were once inlaid with a blue material, perhaps lapis lazuli. There is some slight evidence of wear on one suspension loop, as well as an ancient repair.

Both these pieces seem to reveal influence from stylistic traditions beyond the Greek world, in particular those of Egypt and the Levant. It is likely that the pectoral came from the burial of a male, to which we may also assign other items from the Treasure, notably a gold cup, some heavy gold rings, a bracelet and a series of 54 circular shroud ornaments. The 'Master of the Animals' pendant, however, might have come from the richest of the female burials, among which were divided the two pairs of earrings and the various decorated rings.

All the pieces from the Aigina Treasure were probably made in about 1800–1750 BC by Minoan jewellers, living and working on Aigina. Indeed, it seems very likely that there was a resident Minoan community that included both traders and craftsmen.

Gold jewellery

Greek, probably made on Aigina, Middle Minoan, 1800–1750 BC

Said to be from the island of Aigina

(*above*) Pendant

Ht 6 cm

GR 1892,0520.8 (*Jewellery* 762)

(*below*) Pectoral ornament

Length 10.8 cm

GR 1892,0520.7 (*Jewellery* 761)

8 MYCENAEAN COPPER PITCHER

The body of this large water pitcher or jar was made from four sheets of copper hammered into shape and riveted together. The horizontal handle low on the side of the vessel was to help pouring, because when the pitcher was full it would have been very heavy.

Copper and bronze vessels may have already been in use in the Greek world by the middle of the third millennium BC. They seem to have become common, however, only in the sixteenth and fifteenth centuries BC. Numerous copper or bronze vessels for domestic use have been excavated at Knossos on Crete, including cooking vessels, jugs and large basins. Most are severely functional, but some bear decoration, usually in the form of motifs taken from the decoration of vessels in silver or gold. On the Greek mainland, sets of such vessels, including pitchers, ladles and bowls, have been found in Mycenaean tombs in the Peloponnese, including the shaft graves at Mycenae itself. These mainland examples seem to have been locally produced. They are undecorated, except for a few from the richest shaft graves, which have added adornment in the form of gold or silver plating on the handles and rims.

The placing of such vessels in tombs suggests that the family of the deceased could afford to give up not just the vessel itself but also the value of its raw material. They were thus demonstrations of surplus wealth. Such vessels also probably indicate a belief that the deceased hoped to enjoy banquets in the afterlife.

Copper water jar

Greek, probably made in the Peloponnese, Mycenaean, Late Helladic, 1500–1300 BC

Said to be from the Peloponnese

Ht 54 cm

GR 1963,0705.1

9 TWO MYCENAEAN CUPS

These two cups, one of silver, the other of gold, and of different shapes, are typical of the very fine drinking vessels produced for the elite of the first Mycenaean palaces on the Greek mainland in the sixteenth and fifteenth centuries BC.

The silver drinking cup (right) was found at Enkomi on Cyprus. The shape is known as a 'Vapheio' cup, named after the pair of gold cups found in the *tholos* tomb at Vapheio in Lakonia on the Greek mainland, although the shape had been standard on Crete since about 2000 BC. This silver example is made from one thick sheet of metal, beaten up to form the truncated cone shape of the cup, with the spool-shaped handle made separately and riveted on. There are groups of incised lines by way of decoration. Aegean men carrying oversize versions of such cups as offerings are to be seen in Egyptian wall-paintings, for example in the tomb of Senmut of the fifteenth century BC. The shape was also imitated by Mycenaean potters.

The gold cup (left) is a single-handled goblet with a stemmed foot. Inside the lower part of the foot is a strengthening of bronze. The small handle is of gold-plated silver with three grooves running down the centre and a series of notches on the edge. It is riveted to the body of the cup with four gold pins. The shape of this cup appears in the repertoire of Mycenaean potters: interestingly, it is regularly found in ritual contexts, rather than in domestic or funerary ones. It is possible, therefore, that such a gold example might originally have been used in some cult practice in one of the Mycenaean palaces.

(*left*) Gold cup
Greek, probably made in the Peloponnese, Mycenaean, Late Helladic II, 1500–1450 BC
Formerly in the Forman collection
Ht 7.1 cm
GR 1900,0727.1 (*Jewellery* 820)

(*right*) Silver cup
Greek, probably made in the Peloponnese, Mycenaean, Late Helladic II, 1500–1450 BC
Miss E.T. Turner Bequest Excavations at Enkomi (Cyprus), tomb 92
Ht 6.9 cm
GR1897,0401.506 (*Jewellery* 821)

10 MARINE STYLE POTTERY

Perfumed oil and ointment were important commodities in the Bronze Age world and these two vessels, of different shapes, were probably intended to hold such exotic substances. They are both decorated in the so-called Marine Style, which takes its name from the use of sea motifs, especially octopuses, whorl-shells, seaweed and rocks.

The Marine Style was developed on Crete, where the vessels decorated in this fashion (left) seem often to have been made especially for use in cult. They were, however, quickly imitated by some fine mainland Mycenaean potters (right) and in Mycenaean contexts they occur in graves rather than in sanctuaries. In both forms the sinuous contours of such marine life regularly cover the whole vase like a living, dripping net. The painter of the tall jar has wrapped a squirming octopus around the surface of his vessel, while on the flat-bodied jar an argonaut dominates the scene, moving among rocks and seaweed. In reality the argonaut had eight tentacles, but in Bronze Age Greek art these are regularly reduced to three.

An interest in the marine world is visible in a number of arts, both minor and major, on Crete and the mainland, reflecting the importance of the sea for the Aegean peoples in the Bronze Age both as a source for food and as means of communication and exchange. Fine vessels such as these were exported, presumably with their contents, all over the Mediterranean and are known from Cyprus, Egypt and the Near East.

Pottery jars

(*left*) Greek, made on Crete, Minoan, Late Minoan I B, 1500–1450 BC

From Palaikastro

Ht 30.5 cm

GR 1907,0119.193 (*Vase* A 650)

(*right*) Greek, probably made in the Argolid, Mycenaean, Late Helladic II A, 1500–1450 BC

From Egypt

Ht 11.5 cm; diam. 20 cm

GR 1890,0922.1 (*Vase* A 651)

11 MYCENAEAN POTTERY *KRATERS*

Pottery wine bowls

Greek, probably made in the Argolid, Mycenaean, Late Helladic IIIA2–B, 1350–1200 BC

(*left*) From Maroni, Cyprus

Ht 25.8 cm

GR 1911,0428.1

(*right*) From Enkomi, Cyprus, Miss E.T. Turner Bequest Excavations, tomb 83, chamber B

Ht 27.2 cm

GR 1897,0401.1150 (*Vase* C 416)

From about 1400 BC Mycenaean potters began to make a series of large *kraters*, or bowls for mixing wine and water, which are richly decorated in a pictorial style. The earliest examples depict birds and fish, the later ones have scenes of human figures in chariots (left), hunting or in funerary processions, all aristocratic pursuits. This represents the first sustained use of human figures on the pottery of Greece, and was probably inspired by large-scale wall-paintings created for palaces.

One splendid pottery *krater* (right), in the Pictorial Style, is decorated with a bird (a cattle egret) removing a tick or parasite from the neck of a bull. The style is essentially one of outlines, with the interior space divided into zones, which were filled with simple decorative patterns, or sometimes just with solid paint. This cheerfully unassuming, decorative style has perhaps taken something from contemporary textiles, as well as from more monumental wall-paintings and perhaps even sculpture (compare **12**).

Large numbers of such Pictorial Style vases decorated with scenes of humans and animals were made in the Mycenaean heartland and exported widely, especially to the east to Rhodes and Kos, and beyond to Cyprus, where local potters also imitated them. Others found their way west to the Italian peninsula and Sardinia, and even south to Egypt.

12 GYPSUM RELIEFS FROM MYCENAE

These two fragmentary reliefs, carved in gypsum, show parts of bulls. On one fragment (right) we see the forequarters and part of the head of a bull charging to the right, while in the background there appears a leafy branch. On the other fragment (left) are the hooves and part of the belly of a standing bull facing to the left. The scenes were most probably connected with the capture, taming and display of bulls in a ritual context, as on the famous pair of gold cups from the Vapheio *tholos* tomb near Sparta in Lakonia, on engraved gems (**6**) and on frescos from Knossos. On the shoulder and back of the bull are quatrefoil ornaments, incised in the gypsum, perhaps once outlining areas of paint, for it is quite likely that these reliefs were originally brightly painted.

They were found in the so-called Treasury of Atreus at Mycenae in 1802 by Lord Elgin's team when they excavated this great, beehive-shaped *tholos* tomb. These slabs are usually associated with the decoration of the façade of the tomb, but there remains the possibility that they actually decorated the curved walls of the interior of the *tholos* itself – a huge domed space some fifteen metres high.

Unlike contemporary Egypt, or later Greece, there are few examples of large-scale sculpture from Bronze Age Crete. This stems from the lack on Crete of suitable stones. There was wood, of course, and ivory, and there are some bronze locks of hair that might have been attached to large statues made from several materials. On the mainland, however, the situation was different and we find not only the decorative carving of stone and marble for architectural details of tombs but also a series of grave markers decorated in low relief from the shaft graves at Mycenae (1600–1500 BC) that are no doubt of local production. Both the subject and the style of the gypsum reliefs from Mycenae, however, reveal strong Minoan influence, while the material itself was probably imported from Crete. It is thus possible that these sculptures were carved by visiting or even resident Minoan sculptors, using their native stone.

Carved gypsum panels

Greek, made at Mycenae, Minoan or Mycenaean, Late Bonze Age, *c.* 1350–1250 BC

From Mycenae, Treasury of Atreus

Formerly in the Elgin collection

(*left*) GR 1816,0610.224 (*Sculpture* A 57); width 73 cm

(*right*) GR 1816,0610.204 (*Sculpture* A 56); width 72 cm

2 THE EARLY GREEK WORLD
c. 1000–500 BC

After a century of isolation and cultural stagnation, in about 1000 BC the Greeks began to look abroad again and a new beginning was made. In artistic terms, this renaissance began in Athens and is marked by the appearance of so-called Protogeometric pottery (**13**). This fine Athenian pottery also began to attract distant buyers, including those in northern Greece, in Crete and on the coast of Turkey. Protogeometric pottery has also been found on Cyprus and along the Levantine coast, but much of this may be of Euboean rather than Athenian origin, for the Euboeans seem to have expanded their trading horizons to the east very early, with the result that many Near Eastern imports have been found at Lefkandi on Euboea.

Around 900 BC there was a change in the repertoire of decorative motifs that heralded the beginning of what we now call the Geometric period (900–700 BC). Of these new rectilinear motifs it is the maeander, or Greek key pattern, that typifies the Geometric period. By about 770 BC Athenian potters had also begun, rather hesitantly, to paint human figures as well as animals, in an essentially conceptual manner – the painter drew what he knew to be there rather than just what he could see. These schematic silhouettes mark a new beginning for figure painting in Greece. They are first found in substantial numbers on a series of monumental vessels that served as grave-markers and are combined with the most carefully drawn geometric patterns. The best of these were products of one workshop that we call the Dipylon Workshop (**15**). In succeeding decades there was an explosion in the number of pottery workshops, and during this time not only narrative scenes appeared but also the occasional, seemingly mythological subject is first found (**17**).

The Euboeans, who had traded early with the eastern Mediterranean, seem to have also looked west, for by about 750 BC they had established a trading post on the island of Pithekoussai (Ischia), off the coast of Etruria. It must have been in such a context of interchange that late in the eighth century BC through contact with Phoenicians, whether in the west or in the east, there occurred the momentous adoption of the Phoenician alphabet to write the Greek language. This crucial development was followed in the next century by an influx of Near Eastern curvilinear decorative motifs in art that opened up the rigidity of Geometric art. In the transmission of such contacts between Greece and the Near East, the Greek cities on the coast of Asia Minor and the neighbouring islands,

such as Rhodes, played an important role. From this cultural milieu we find both rich gold jewellery with oriental-looking goddesses (**20**) and bronze work with oriental mythical beasts (**21**). This period is often referred to as the Orientalizing period.

In the world of pottery, if the ninth and eighth centuries BC had belonged to Athens, then the seventh century was Corinth's. Its pottery was becoming the import item of choice across most of the Mediterranean, including in the numerous colonies now planted by the adventurous Greeks, both east and west. It was at Corinth that a new painting technique was developed, the black-figure technique, which combined black silhouettes with the addition of a purplish red and the use of incision, done with a fine point that scratched through the painted surface to the clay below. This technique was brought to perfection in the middle of the seventh century BC, and some of its finest scions are the ubiquitous Corinthian perfumed oil vases (**22**).

The last decades of the seventh century BC also saw the rise of monumental sculpture, in particular the development of the standing nude male youth or *kouros* (**24**, **38** and **40**), the standing draped female and seated figures of both sexes (**27**). The sources of inspiration for these developments included both Egypt and the Near East, where monumental sculpture had a long history, although there the statue types and style were more formalized and static.

Athens reasserted its dominance in the craft of pottery-making in the sixth century BC. We now see a rise in the self-confidence and importance of both potters and painters, as they occasionally sign their work (**26**, **30**, **32**, **35** and **36**). Their very names are also an important key to understanding the role of these craftsmen in society: they comprised citizens, foreigners and slaves. In addition, their products, because they concentrated on figured scenes, provide important insights into the society and culture of ancient Athens.

Egyptian limestone statue of the priest Tjayestimu, from Memphis, Egypt, 664–610 BC, ht 1.25 m (EA 1682)

13 PROTOGEOMETRIC POTTERY *PYXIS*

This large, tub-shaped vase was made in Athens in the last quarter of the tenth century BC. The shape is a very rare alternative to the small globular form of *pyxis* (trinket box) without handles that is typical of Attic pottery of the time. Furthermore, the form has here been enlarged to match the largest contemporary *kraters* (bowls from which wine mixed with water was served).

The decoration is very finely delineated and carefully structured over the broad surface of the vessel. The scheme is essentially dark ground. On the upper body, between two rows of dogtooth pattern, there is a broad zone with three tall panels of chequer pattern, alternating with columns of vertical zigzag and solid paint. The lower body is black save for a third row of dogtooth.

There are traces of burning inside the vessel, on the floor, indicating that it was used as a burial urn and once held the ashes of the deceased. We do not know for certain where Lord Elgin's men excavated this vase, but it was most probably to the south of the Acropolis between Mouseion Hill and the river Ilissos, where in recent years an important burial plot, later surrounded by an enclosure wall, has been found (Erechtheion Street). The grave probably took the form of a trench with a pit at the end. The vase, containing the ashes, would have been placed in the pit and covered either with its lid (not preserved), another vessel or a bronze bowl. In Athens at this date it has been claimed that women's burials did not contain gold jewellery, in contrast to the situation on Euboea where rich women were accompanied in death by both jewellery and foreign imports. This may well not have been the case, as the Elgin collection includes several rings and other gold items that should date to the Protogeometric period. One of the burials from the Erechtheion Street site in Athens had the remains of a seventeen-year-old young woman and an eighteen-year-old youth in a single urn. This may have been the result of simultaneous death from disease, but the suggestion has been made that it might reflect a ritual *suttee*, a practice that seems to be attested at Lefkandi.

Pottery box

Greek, made in Athens, Late Protogeometric, 925–900 BC

Probably from Athens

Formerly in the Elgin collection

Ht 44.5 cm

GR 1950,0228.3

14 THE ELGIN GOLD BROOCHES

These two pairs of gold brooches or safety pins for holding together pieces of clothing are of extraordinary quality. They must have come from an exceptionally rich tomb in Athens and may well have been found with some of the other early jewellery in the Elgin collection.

On one pair (right), the catch-plate (which holds the pin in place when closed) is engraved with the figure of a horse on one side and a lion on the other; its mate has a horse and a ship. The other pair (left), however, has matching designs – a grazing deer on one side, a swastika on the other. Each brooch has been hammered from a single piece of gold, a considerable feat of craftsmanship. For the extremely delicate, engraved decoration two related decorative techniques have been used: the animals and ship have been made with a regular sharp-pointed graver producing a furrow-like gouge, but the tremolo border patterns have been produced by using a scorper or chisel-like blade, rocked as it was 'walked' across the surface to leave a cut, zigzag trail.

The shape and form of early Greek brooches can be seen to develop from ones with small catch-plates (mostly of bronze) to ones like these pairs, and finally to those with greatly exaggerated catch-plates, which are all of bronze and seem to have become something of a speciality in Boeotia, where they were often engraved with elaborate mythological scenes.

In a rich tomb at Anavyssos, southeast of Athens, were found, in a large belly-handled *amphora* typical of a woman's burial, two pairs of gold brooches just like the Elgin ones and probably produced by the same jeweller. Two are decorated with a swastika on one side and a bird on the other; two with a swastika and a scorpion. In addition there were two gold finger rings, part of a sheet gold diadem embossed with animals, and a gold chain necklace with clasps in the form of snake's heads. The belly-handled *amphora* is of Middle Geometric II date, thus providing a date for the Elgin brooches of 800–750 BC. The depiction of animals and a ship might suggest a moment late in this period.

Gold brooches

Greek, probably made in Athens, Middle Geometric, 800–750 BC

Probably from Athens

Formerly in the Elgin collection

Length (*right*) 4.5 cm; (*left*) 5.6 cm

GR 1960,1101.44 and 45, 46 and 47

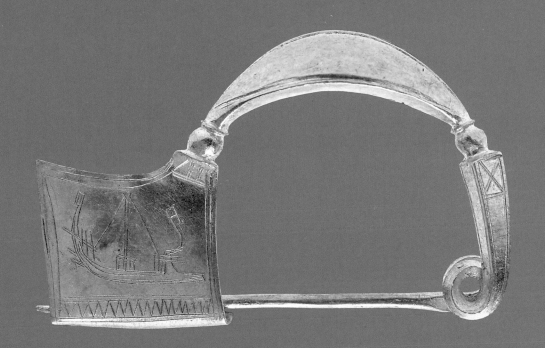
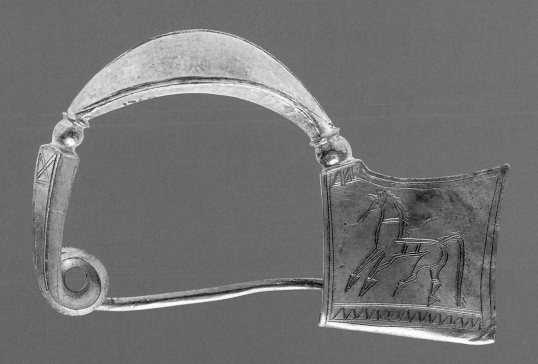

15 THE ELGIN GEOMETRIC *AMPHORA*

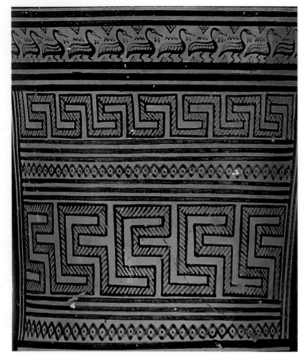

Pottery wine jar

Greek, made in Athens, Late Geometric Ia, 760–750 BC

Attributed to the Workshop of the Dipylon Painter

Probably from Athens

Formerly in the Elgin collection

Purchased with the aid of the Art Fund, the British Museum Friends, the Dilettanti Society and the Caryatid Fund

Ht 67 cm

GR 2004,0927.1

Despite the fragmentary condition of this large Geometric *amphora* (wine jar), its outstanding quality is clear. It is, indeed, a product of the workshop of the Dipylon Painter (named after the double gates leading from the city of Athens into the Kerameikos cemetery). This extremely important workshop produced some of the very finest and largest Geometric vessels, many placed as offerings in rich tombs, some even being used as monumental grave-markers above ground.

The Dipylon Painter's workshop took the geometric decoration that gives its name to the period to its highest level, spreading it out across the surface of vessels like a continuous, perfectly woven textile or tattooed skin. Carefully worked out patterns such as the complex 'tapestry' that dominates the upper body of this vase and the combination of dotted lozenges set between rows of cross-hatched triangles pointing up and down are typical of the Dipylon Painter's work. He was also the first to develop a consistent figured style, although on this vase we see only a fine frieze of birds below the lip of the vessel and a highly stylized snake on the handle.

In the Geometric period the neck-handled *amphora* shape was associated with the burials of men. On the basis of contemporary graves in the Athenian Kerameikos, we can presume that this *amphora* probably held wine at the funerary feast of the deceased and was a mark of his wealth and status. It would then have been placed in the tomb with some smaller vases and a bronze *dinos* (cauldron) that contained his ashes, as well as a gold sheet diadem. The fragments of this *amphora* were excavated in Athens by Lord Elgin's team. It is the finest of all Elgin's Geometric vases. It is quite possible that some of his other Geometric vases, and even gold ornaments, in the British Museum's collection were offerings in the very same tomb of an ancient Greek aristocrat.

16 BRONZE GEOMETRIC HORSE

This small, solid cast figurine of a horse dates to the late eighth century BC and is a masterpiece of miniature sculpture, its form highly stylized but packed with power.

Small Geometric bronzes, intended for offerings in sanctuaries and tombs, take the form of horses, stags, cattle, birds and, occasionally, humans (**18**). Here the horse, a symbol of wealth and status among the aristocracy, has been given massive shoulders and rump with a very short intervening body, angular joints, a large mane merged with the neck, and a tubular muzzle. This stylization, together with the details of muzzle, eyes and ears, link the piece with a workshop that was most likely based in Lakonia in the Peloponnese.

Under the stand is the sunken design of two figures back to back, each holding some sort of stick or staff. They have sometimes been interpreted as ancient conjoined twins, whom we seem to find on a number of Late Geometric vases. These twins are regularly identified as the sons of Molione and her mortal husband Aktor or Poseidon, god of the sea: in Homer they fought Nestor, but according to other sources they were killed by Herakles.

Such elaborate designs under the stand are very rare in the Laconian series (they are more common in Argos), but a figure of a stag (now in Munich), clearly by the same craftsman, has two birds in a similar sunken relief under the stand. They are arranged back to back, with their heads bent back – a symmetrical, mirror image. This is the same idea as on the underside of the London horse and suggests that we should see the two figures as being simply back to back and not joined in any way. As such they might have been intended to represent the Dioskouroi, Kastor and Polydeukes, the twin sons of Zeus and Leda, whose cult was particularly favoured at Sparta in Lakonia.

Bronze figurine
Greek, probably made in Lakonia,
Late Geometric, 740–720 BC
Said to be from Phigaleia, Arcadia
Ht 9.8 cm
GR 1905,1024.5

17 GEOMETRIC POTTERY SHIP *KRATER*

The spouted *krater*, a bowl for mixing and pouring wine, is a rare hybrid shape. This example was created by a bold innovator working in the tradition of the Dipylon Painter and his workshop (cf. **15**).

The front of the vase is dominated by a ship, facing to the right, with two rows of oarsmen and a helmsman equipped with two large, striped steering oars. It seems most likely that the artist intended to show the rows of oarsmen on both sides of the ship at one and the same time, much as other Geometric painters showed chariots with two wheels side by side instead of only one wheel, the other being invisible.

Pottery wine bowl

Greek, made in Athens, Late Geometric IIa, 735–720 BC

Attributed to the Sub-Dipylon Group

Said to be from Thebes, Boeotia

Ht 30.9 cm

GR 1899,0219.1

To the left of the ship a man begins to climb aboard while holding the wrist of a woman at the far left. She has long, loose hair and a cross-hatched skirt and holds a circular wreath or garland: she is the earliest woman to be distinguished as such by shoulder-length hair and a decorated skirt, the prototype of all later Geometric representations of female mourners and dancers. The scene may be taken from everyday life – a man bids a woman farewell or perhaps is taking her with him. Although most Geometric scenes are generic and timeless, the painter of this *krater* may have had a more specific occasion in mind and in this case the circular wreath or garland that the woman holds would play a role. There are a number of possible interpretations but the most widely accepted is the one that sees the man as Theseus and the woman as Ariadne. The wreath would then be the garland of light that helped Theseus find his way through the Cretan Labyrinth to kill the Minotaur. The water bird on the ship's ram might even refer to the 'Crane Dance' on Delos with which Theseus' party were later to celebrate their deliverance from Crete.

A warrior in conical helmet and collar is seated on a low stool. His arms are out in front of him as he bends slightly forward. His hands are joined together to hold a dagger or short sword that is turned towards his abdomen. These elements all point towards the scene being the earliest known representation of the suicide of Ajax, and at the same time the earliest certain representation in bronze of a mythological theme.

The great Ajax, after carrying the dead body of Achilles from the battlefield before Troy, had been forced to compete with Odysseus for possession of the slain hero's arms. The loss of this contest sent Ajax mad and he slaughtered the cattle of the Greeks, thinking them to be his fellow Greek warriors. When he came to his senses, out of shame, he put an end to his life by falling on his sword. We know the moment from Sophokles' great tragedy where he also poignantly remarks on the fact that the sword used by Ajax was that of his old enemy, Hektor. Despite its small scale and simple design, this bronze evokes something of the hero's inner tension and the drama of the moment.

The great Athenian black-figure vase-painter Exekias (32), in the middle of the sixth century BC, chose to show Ajax with furrowed brow preparing a little mound of sand to support the sword, while other painters, Athenian and Corinthian, earlier and later, showed the deed already done and Ajax transfixed by the sword. A superb Hellenistic bronze in a private collection, however, has a tormented Ajax seated as he decides his last act. This small Geometric bronze alone seems to show the actual moment, a precursor almost to the Japanese *hara kiri*.

Bronze figurine
Greek, perhaps made in the Peloponnese, Late Geometric, 720–700 BC
Formerly in the collection of G. Witt
Ht 6.5 cm
GR 1865,1118.230

19 THE GRIFFIN JUG

Pottery jug

Greek, Cycladic, made on Thera or Paros, 670–650 BC

Said to be from Aigina

Ht 41.5 cm

GR 1873,0820.385

This extraordinary creation is part vessel, part mythical beast. The neck and spout take the form of the head and neck of a griffin, a lion-eagle hybrid.

The griffin's beak seems to have been given teeth; between beak and neck is a dotted throat sack; on top of the head and between the upright ears is a small knob; and two tresses in relief curl down the side of the neck to end in small palmettes. The front of the neck is decorated with a scale or feather pattern, the back with ringed dots. The shoulder zone is dominated by three panels: in the centre, on the front, a lion is shown dragging off its kill, a stag, while in two panels either side, and to the back, is a grazing horse.

The griffin is a mythical beast that was adopted and adapted by the Greeks from the Near East. Griffins were thought of as beasts of prey that acted as guardians and helpers for the gods. According to one particular story they lived in the far north where they guarded heaps of gold, and in art they are shown fighting off the local people, the one-eyed Arimasps. Orientalizing too are some of the decorative motifs, such as the palmette and the curls added to the triangles.

The idea for a spout in the form of a griffin head might have been borrowed from metalwork, in particular the series of bronze cauldrons with griffin heads produced in East Greece from the first half of the seventh century BC onwards (cf. 21). But, as with the Corinthian oil bottle with a lion-headed spout (22), there was also a tradition of, on occasion, giving pouring vessels animal-headed or even human-headed spouts.

The different centres that produced pottery on the islands of the Cyclades in the seventh century BC are not well understood, although the earlier, Geometric styles are somewhat easier to distinguish. The Griffin Jug is clearly an exceptional object, produced by an imaginative and excellent potter. It has been associated with a number of other lesser pieces under the sobriquet of the 'Linear Island' Group. The most impressive of these have been found on Thera (Santorini) and it is possible that this was the home of the Griffin Jug, too, although the clay seems somewhat finer than the earlier products of that island.

20 RHODIAN GOLD PLAQUES

These two gold pectoral ornaments are both made up of a series of seven rectangular gold plaques. They were found in a very rich tomb at Kamiros on the island of Rhodes together with a scarab of Psammetichos I (pharaoh of Egypt, 666–612 BC), a gold ring with Phoenician designs, two thin sheet-gold bands and 180 tiny gold ornaments that would have been sewn on to the deceased's clothing or shroud.

Each of the smaller plaques has two frontal female heads in relief, while the larger plaques are decorated with the relief figure of a winged goddess, presumably Artemis as the Mistress of the Animals, an idea borrowed from the Near East. The goddess wears a long sleeveless garment, richly decorated with patterns in fine granulation (miniature applied spheres of gold), a diadem and a pair of armlets. Her elaborate hairstyle is also ornamented with granulation, as are her wings. Her arms are stretched out low on each side over a small lion, which stands on its hind legs, with its near forepaw resting against the dress of the goddess, and its head turned back. The two large, terminal plaques are surmounted by a large rosette and have a hook at the back instead of the threading tubes of the other plaques. All of the large plaques have five loops attached to the bottom edge from which hang chains ending in a pomegranate, a symbol of fertility (cf. **97**); the smaller plaques have simpler pendant beads.

This unusual class of ornament was quite common on Rhodes in the seventh century, perhaps from about 660 BC onwards. It occurs in gold, electrum (a natural alloy of gold and silver) and silver, and was probably worn by women strung along the top edge of their clothing – the end plaques of the larger series could have been hooked into the fabric. The idea for such plaque pectorals may have come from Cyprus or Syria. The smaller, simpler examples were formed either by working sheet gold over a core or into a mould, but in the case of the very elaborate ones the figures were embossed separately and then soldered in place on a backing sheet.

Gold pectoral ornaments

Greek, probably made on Rhodes, 650–630 BC

From a tomb at Kamiros, Rhodes

Ht of large plaques 4.2 cm

GR 1861,1111.1–4 (*Jewellery* 1103 and 1128–30)

22 THE MACMILLAN *ARYBALLOS*

Pottery oil-bottle
Greek, made in Corinth, Middle
Protocorinthian II, about 640 BC
Attributed to the Chigi Painter
Said to be from Thebes, Boeotia
Given by M. Macmillan
Ht 6.8 cm
GR 1889,0418.1

This little jewel of an oil-bottle (*aryballos*) with a lion's head spout was made in Corinth in about 640 BC. The lion-headed spout is, of course, rather impractical for a bottle meant to deliver scented oil and the piece was no doubt intended as a special vase for dedication in a sanctuary or as an offering for the dead.

The body of the vase has three zones of figured decoration. Into the upper and largest one are packed some seventeen struggling warriors, pushing and thrusting with their spears, their shields decked with vivid blazons. The second zone has a horse race, each jockey driving his steed on with a stick. The lowest zone represents a hare hunt – the hunter hides behind a stylized bush as the hounds chase the hare towards him. There is much use of added red both on the tiny figures and on the lion's head, as well as on the floral chain on the shoulder of the vase. Details of the figures and their shields are also picked out with delicate incisions. This is miniaturist black-figure painting at its finest.

This vase, like the other similarly complex fight scenes by the same painter – known as the Chigi Painter, after a superb, and much larger, *oinochoe* once in the Chigi collection and now in the Villa Giulia Museum in Rome – belongs to a time in Corinth's history when a long-established aristocracy was suddenly replaced by a tyranny, and when a new method of fighting began to gain widespread acceptance. This method involved lines of heavily armed infantry (hoplites) fighting, as the seventh-century poet Tyrtaios described it, 'foot to foot, shield to shield, crest to crest, helmet to helmet, chest to chest, grasping your sword or long spear'. The battle scenes on these vases may reflect this period of violence and change, while the horse race and hare hunt were aristocratic pastimes.

23 THE EUPHORBOS PLATE

Within the shield-like frame of this large plate, the painter has given us a combat from Homer's *Iliad*. Greek Menelaos, on the left, has killed the Trojan Euphorbos, who lies dead on his back, and Hektor presses forward to try to retrieve the body. Menelaos is seen from the front and we are shown the interior of his shield; Hektor is represented in back view thus revealing his shield's fine blazon in the form of a black-figure eagle, Zeus' bird – and Hektor was favoured by Zeus. According to Homer, Euphorbos was the first warrior to wound Patroklos when he came out to battle in Achilles' stead. Indeed, it was after this initial wound that Hektor pressed forward and killed Patroklos. Euphorbos tried to secure Patroklos' armour, but was driven back by Menelaos and in his turn killed and stripped of his armour.

Suspended between the figures is a complex floral ornament, originally probably a borrowing from the Near East. Surprisingly, a pair of eyes and eyebrows has been painted on either side of the chequer-board triangle, as if it was a nose. It is almost as if some divinity is watching the battle, echoing Homer's vision of the gods on Olympos.

The figures are painted in outline, but exceptionally with an unusually realistic colour scheme: the bare flesh has been given a rosy red wash, while dilute brown has been used on two of the helmets and for the short *chitons* worn by all the warriors. Hektor's shield device relies on incision in the black silhouette. The names of the heroes are written in a Doric dialect, such as that used on Rhodes, yet the letter forms seem for the most part more at home in Argos. Perhaps the vase-painter copied some other work of art, both figures and inscriptions. It is intriguing to remember, therefore, that, in the middle of the second century AD Pausanias saw in the temple of Hera near Argos a shield that was said to have been the one taken by Menelaos from Euphorbos.

Pottery plate

Greek, made in the East Dorian region, probably on Rhodes, about 600 BC

From Kamiros, Rhodes

Diam. 38 cm

GR 1860,0404.1

24 BOEOTIAN *KOUROS*

Marble statue
Greek, made in Boeotia, 570–560 BC
From Greece (probably Boeotia)
Ht 77 cm
GR 1878,0120.1 (*Sculpture* B 474)

Towards the end of the seventh century BC contact was made with the Egyptian Nile Delta and beyond by adventurous Greek traders and by Greek mercenaries employed by the Egyptians. One result was the beginning of the production of large-scale sculpture and the use of hard marble instead of soft limestone.

The creation of the Greek *kouros*, a naked standing youth, drew directly from the large-scale sculptures of standing males in Egypt, usually represented with one leg forward and arms by their side (see p. 35). Greek craftsmen, however, rendered their figures nude, instead of wearing a short kilt-like garment. They also omitted the artificial support at the back and thus were able to distribute the weight evenly on both legs, instead of just on the rear leg.

This fine, small example of the *kouros* type is made from local Boeotian marble, not the more popular whiter island marbles of Paros or Naxos. The nude youth stands stiffly, arms (originally) to his sides and left leg slightly forward. Collar bones, pectorals and the lower boundary of the thorax are lightly modelled and, in the manner of early Archaic art, form a rather stiff symmetrical pattern that seems to lie on the surface of the body rather than appearing to be connected with the underlying muscles and bones. The youth's belly is smooth, his hips slim. His knees are gently outlined, as are the thigh muscles. His long hair is arranged in waves and flows down over his shoulders.

Such statues functioned either as dedications in sanctuaries or as funerary monuments, representing members of the aristocracy in an idealized and impersonal manner. Some were created on a truly monumental scale, such as that found in recent years on Samos which was about five metres tall, or one on Delos known since the fifteenth century (but now preserved in only a few battered fragments) that must have stood some ten metres high. Greek sculptors also created a fine series of draped female statues, *korai*, which served similar purposes, although they are rarer in Boeotia than the *kouroi*.

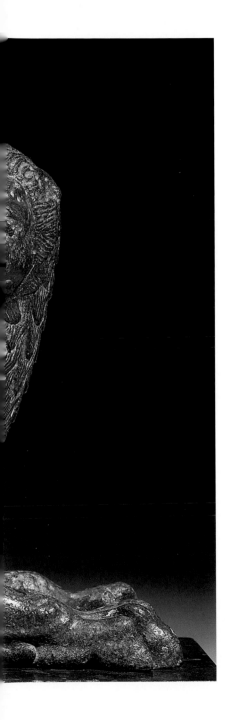

25 BRONZE LIONESS

This superb bronze lioness is solid cast and unusually large for a statuette. Her front legs are stretched forwards with shoulders down near the ground; her rear legs are straighter and her rump is raised. Her small head is turned to her right; her tail, probably once outstretched, is now lost. Her mane takes the form of a thick cape, covered with a flame-like pattern. Legs and body are powerfully modelled.

The ancient Greeks did not know much about lions. Firstly, there is combined here in one beast the mane of a male and the dugs of a female. Secondly, the pose is that of a dog about to spring, not that of a lion, which as a member of the cat family keeps its whole body close to the ground before leaping forward.

There are no remaining traces of a base or means for attachment to one. The head is turned to the side on which the ribs are fully modelled – on the other side, the ribs are omitted. This suggests that the lioness was not intended to be seen from her left side. The fact that the legs are aligned straight, with no hint of curvature, would seem to indicate that the bronze may have been a fitting from a piece of furniture rather than a circular vessel.

The misunderstanding of the pose of the lioness is something that, interestingly, seems to have passed into Greek literature, and even custom. In the women's oath in Aristophanes' comedy *Lysistrata*, they swear 'not to stand like a lioness on the cheese-grater'. This is thought to be a reference to the woman's posture in making love which resembles that of a lion crouching with its bottom in the air, a pose that is often seen in scenes of lovemaking between men and courtesans on Athenian vases (compare **100**), and explains why so many 'ladies of the night' were give the nickname Leaina (lioness) in antiquity.

Bronze furniture attachment

Greek, probably made in Corinth, 580–560 BC

From Corfu

Formerly in the Woodhouse collection; bequeathed by James Woodhouse

Length 17 cm

GR 1868,0110.371 (*Bronze* 232)

26 THE SOPHILOS *DINOS*

Sophilos, the first Athenian vase-painter whose name has been preserved for us, decorated this large pottery *dinos* (serving bowl for wine) and its stand. His signature is written on the uppermost zone, next to one of the white pillars of a house façade – *Sophilos megraphsen*: 'Sophilos painted me'.

Pottery wine bowl with stand
Greek, made in Athens, about 580 BC
Signed by Sophilos as painter
Formerly in the collection of the
Hon. Robert Erskine
Ht 71 cm
GR 1971,1101.1

The *dinos* and its separately made stand are covered with friezes of animals, both real and fantastic, very much in the Corinthian manner. The uppermost frieze, however, is decorated with a procession of human figures, some forty-four, all named. The Olympian gods have come to celebrate the marriage of mortal Peleus to immortal Thetis. In the hands of Sophilos this procession is filled with a naive charm and unaffected vigour.

Peleus stands on the extreme right of the front of the vase, outside his palace with its red door, white pillars and black *antae* (projecting wall-ends). He is waiting for the gods as they arrive, holding out a *kantharos* (high-handled cup) of wine as a sign of welcome. Iris, the messenger goddess, heads the parade and behind her come four goddesses who are all connected with marriage in general and this one in particular; indeed, Demeter's open arms may be for the bride, Thetis, who is hidden behind the closed doors of Peleus' palace. Beyond these goddesses comes Dionysos, the god of wine, one hand grasping a vine branch laden with grapes. Dionysos is, in fact, positioned over the centre of the elaborate floral in the frieze below, and so stands right in the middle of the front of a vase that was made for the mixing and serving of wine at a feast.

Behind Dionysos come three more important figures on foot. First is Hebe, the goddess of youth, in a beautifully decorated *peplos*; then Cheiron, the wise centaur, part man, part horse, with his catch over his shoulder, a welcome gift for the feast; and finally the majestic figure of Themis with her sceptre. Themis was the goddess who revealed the secret about any son that Thetis might bear – namely that he would grow up to be stronger than his father. This prophecy led Zeus to marry off Thetis to a mortal. Cheiron was to be foster father to their offspring, the great Achilles.

27 STATUE OF CHARES, GOVERNOR OF TEICHIOUSSA

This powerful, over life-size marble statue of a seated man is perhaps the earliest portrait from the Greek world. It was never a portrait in the modern sense of the word, but rather it is a statue of a man who is identified through the inscription on it, not through any attempt to create his likeness. Inscribed on the edge of the right leg of the chair are the words, 'I am Chares, son of Kleisios, *archon* of Teichiosa' and 'a gift to Apollo'.

The statue of Chares was discovered about five hundred metres to the northwest of the great temple of Apollo at Didyma in southwestern Turkey. It was found beside the Sacred Way as it led to the sacred port of Panormos, whence it continued on to the city of Miletos. This was not the original location: it must have been moved to line the Sacred Way at a later date, after the abandonment of the sacred enclosure that it had once adorned.

An important cult text, essentially of the end of the sixth century BC, describes the New Year's procession from the sanctuary of Apollo Delphinios at Miletos down the Sacred Way, eighteen kilometres long, to Didyma and notes seven places where it stopped for ceremonial songs to be sung. The last stopping place, close to the gates of Didyma, is referred to as the 'statues of Chares'. No doubt these included this statue: they would have been displayed in a sacred enclosure celebrating Chares and his family.

Teichioussa, of which Chares was *archon* (governor), was a fortified settlement in the southeast corner of Milesian territory: it protected access to the peninsula. Chares had perhaps performed some heroic deed in defence of the area that led to his posthumous heroization. He is shown sitting on a cushion on an elaborate throne. He wears a short-sleeved *chiton* over which is draped a *himation* (cloak). The pleats of the garments are rendered in a series of neat and simple verticals and diagonals. His body is massive, broad and rounded – characteristics of East Greek Archaic sculptures, especially those of Miletos. The whole figure was once painted, and traces of patterns survive on the drapery and the cushion. The idea for such large-scale seated figures may have come from Egypt, like the standing male statues (**24**), or from the Near East.

Marble statue

Greek, made in Miletos, about 560 BC

From the Sacred Way near Didyma, Ionia

Ht 1.49 m

GR 1859,1226.5 (*Sculpture* B 278)

28 WINE COOLER PAINTED BY LYDOS

Athenian potters were extraordinarily inventive. This vase looks like an ordinary *amphora* (wine jar) of elegant curving form but it is really much more. The potter has made a vessel within a vessel – the normal inner chamber accessible through the top of the vase; the invisible outer chamber through a round spout or funnel in the side and a hole in the base (stoppered when the vase was in use). This sort of vase (a *psykter amphora*) was used for cooling wine: the ice-cold water or melted snow was poured into the outer chamber, the wine into the inner. Some five examples are known in Athenian pottery, this being the earliest; there are also a further five from South Italy, Chalcidian vases perhaps produced in Rhegion, modern Reggio (compare **31**).

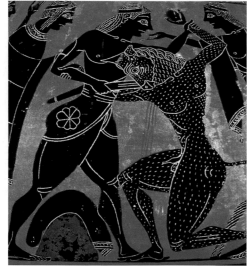

Pottery wine cooler
Greek, made in Athens, about 560 BC
Painting attributed to Lydos
Probably from Vulci, Etruria
Ht 40.2 cm
GR 1848,0619.5 (*Vase* B 148)

The scene on the front of the vase emphasizes its function. To the right of the spout, we see Dionysos, the god of wine, holding a drinking horn. He is accompanied by his regular entourage of satyrs (part man, part horse) and maenads (wild women). Here we find a maenad with an animal skin tied round her waist, three dancing satyrs and a young hairless satyr, who bends down to play with a hare. The other side shows the Athenian hero Theseus killing the bull-headed Minotaur who inhabited the Labyrinth on Crete.

The lively black-figure painting has been attributed to the vase-painter Lydos. The name Lydos (Lydian) clearly marks him out as a foreigner, as might his imperfect Greek (on an early work he wrote *ho ludos egrsen*, 'the Lydian painted', misspelling *egraphsen*). Lydos' name and writing remind us of the welcome offered in Athens to foreign craftsmen from the beginning of the sixth century BC and of other potters and painters whose names suggest foreign birth, including Skythes (the Scythian), Kolchos (the Colchian), Mys (the Mysian), Sikellos (the Sikellan, from Sicily), Thrax (the Thracian) and Syriskos (the little Syrian). Some of these craftsmen were probably what the Athenians called *metoikoi* (foreign residents), but others may have been slaves.

29 THE ARMENTO RIDER

Bronze statuette

Greek, probably made in Taranto, 560–550 BC

Said to come from Armento, Lucania

Formerly in the G. Fejérváry and F. Pulszky collections

Ht 23.6 cm

GR 1904,0703.1

This bronze horse and rider is one of the earliest pieces of Greek sculpture known from southern Italy. The group is full of vitality, pride and power. The horse and rider are both solid-cast and made separately – a locating pin in the bottom of the rider fits into a hole in the horse's back, keeping him in his seat.

The rider wears a Corinthian helmet (as **42**) and a short, belted *chiton*. His right hand is turned horizontally to hold the horse's reins, now lost (there is a corresponding hole through the horse's mouth), while his left is turned up, probably to hold a spear, with a shield over his forearm. The horse is very long in the body and has a stylized head with huge eyes and bold cheek markings. Its mane is simply modelled, but the division at the front so that it curls around each ear is very effective. Muscles are lightly incised on its forelegs and rump.

The helmet worn by the rider is particularly interesting, with a carefully incised floral pattern on the front, between the curving eyebrows, and traces of an unusual crest. Two cuttings in the top of the helmet run sideways rather than from front to back: these probably once held two flat, cut-out bull's horns, perhaps complete with ears. A similar, but earlier, actual bronze helmet has been found in South Italy.

This proud image of a rider on parade vividly brings to mind the frequency with which the Greek colonies in southern Italy (Magna Graecia, Great Greece as it was called) went to war, with both their native neighbours and their fellow Greeks (compare **47**). It also symbolizes the aristocratic, land-owning families of the Greek colonies of South Italy and Sicily, families that produced not just heroes in battle but also victors in the ritualized competitions of the great Hellenic festivals.

It is said to have come from Armento. A number of important later bronzes have come from this part of the interior of Lucania, many of them from rich chamber-tombs. There was, however, a sanctuary of Herakles in the neighbourhood and this bronze may have been a dedication there.

30 DRINKING CUP POTTED BY TLESON, SON OF NEARCHOS

One of the most graceful shapes produced by Athenian potters was the drinking cup. Here we see the shape taken to an extraordinary degree of refinement, while the decoration has been reduced just to three words: *Tleson Nearchou epoiesen* – 'Tleson son of Nearchos made [me]'.

Tleson is a typical member of the group of potters and painters who produced such cups, the Little Masters, as they have been dubbed by scholars, in recognition of both the extraordinary fineness of the potting and the wonderful miniaturistic black-figure painting on some of their products. Many of Tleson's cups, however, have little or no decoration beyond the signature in the zone at handle level.

The handle zone is bordered above by a thin black line, stressing the slight articulation of the wall of the cup above, the offset lip, as it is called. At the handles themselves, fine miniature palmettes sprout from curling tendrils. Below the handle zone all is black, save for a narrow relieving band at the mid-point of the bowl and on the edge of the tall, trumpet-shaped foot.

The signatures on such cups provide precious insights into the organization of the potters' workshops in Athens in the third quarter of the sixth century BC. We know the signatures of some 28 potters and only four painters. This, combined with the frequently reduced level of decoration, suggests that the potters were the leading figures. Furthermore, the names reveal a number of foreign ethnicities, including names indicative of people from the east, Mysia and Lycia in Anatolia, and from the north in Thrace. As with Lydos (compare **28**), these may have been free resident foreigners or slaves. There were, however, also citizens at work in the potters' quarter of Athens, the Kerameikos, as is indicated by signatures such as this one (and **56**).

Pottery cup
Greek, made in Athens, about 540 BC
Signed as potter by Tleson, son of Nearchos
From Kamiros, Rhodes
Ht 16.5 cm
GR 1867,0506.34 (*Vase* B 411)

31 CHALCIDIAN COLUMN *KRATER*

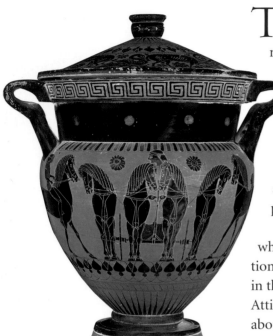

Pottery wine bowl

Greek, perhaps made in Rhegion, about 540 BC

Chalcidian, attributed to the Inscription Painter

From Vulci, Etruria

Formerly in the Canino collection

Ht 46 cm

GR 1843,1103.38 (*Vase* B 15)

This majestic black-figure *krater* (bowl for mixing wine and water) with stirrup-like handles is all about horses, whether harnessed to a chariot, ridden or led, and, of course, their aristocratic owners. It celebrates the horse-owning elite of wealthy Rhegion (modern Reggio), the Greek colony at the very tip of the toe of Italy, where the vase was very probably made.

One side of the *krater* is dominated by a frontal, four-horse chariot. The other side has the meeting of two youths, each with a spear, each accompanied by his hunting dog. To the left a boy sits on a horse, perhaps the youth's squire with his horse, while to the right it is a woman on foot who accompanies a horse, perhaps the other youth's mother. There seems to be no precise narrative.

The vase was decorated by the first painter of the so-called Chalcidian school, whom we refer to as the Inscription Painter. He takes his name from the inscriptions that appear on some of his works. Their interest lies in the fact that they are in the script of Chalkis, a city on the island of Euboea off the northeastern coast of Attica. This has given rise to the name for the fabric as a whole, which dates from about the middle of the sixth century BC until its end. The script first suggested to scholars that such vases were actually made in Chalkis on Euboea, but later study indicated that they were actually of Italian manufacture. Latest research indicates that they might have been made at Rhegion, a Chalcidian colony. Other groups closely connected with this workshop may have been based at Taranto and perhaps in Campania to the north.

The style of the Inscription Painter is essentially very Athenian and it seems most likely that his artistic heritage lay in Athens. He might have been trained in a strongly Athenian workshop on Euboea before emigrating to South Italy, but it is equally possible that he learnt his writing only when he got to Rhegion and that he arrived direct from Athens, as did another artist, the Eyre Painter, who went to live in Etruria and established a workshop there (**111**). But while such more northerly Greek settlers quickly lost touch with their Greek roots, Chalcidian pottery remained completely Greek in style and idiom.

32 ACHILLES AND PENTHESILEA PAINTED BY EXEKIAS

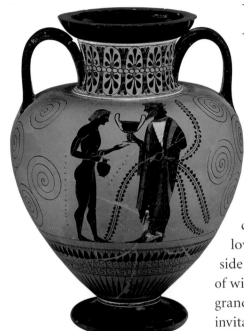

Pottery wine jar

Greek, made in Athens, 540–530 BC

Signed on both sides by Exekias as potter, and attributed to him as painter

From Vulci, Etruria

Ht 41.6 cm

GR 1836,0224.127 (*Vase* B 210)

Exekias was perhaps the finest of all vase-painters to use the black-figure technique. His name is known from several signatures, both as potter and as painter. His painting combines monumentality with delicacy; his potting is crisp and perfectly balanced.

On one side of this *amphora* (wine jar) Exekias has created a bold, triangular composition with Achilles, the Greek hero of Troy, thrusting down with his spear into the throat of Penthesilea, queen of the Amazons. She has sunk to the ground as blood gushes from her throat. Their eyes seem locked together in this last moment of violence, but also perhaps the first of something more. Exekias achieved this kind of psychologically potent moment on a number of his other vases, and one need not dismiss as the creation of a later and more melodramatic age the story that Achilles fell in love with Penthesilea at the very instant in which he killed her. On the other side the mood is very different. The calmly majestic figure of Dionysos, the god of wine, faces his young son Oinopion. Dionysos holds three ivy branches and his grand *kantharos* (special drinking cup); his son holds out his hand in a gesture of invitation to his father, ready to refill the Olympian drinking vessel from his jug.

Exekias' mastery of the incised line for the markings on armour, animal skin and cloth, his restraint in the use of added colours, the sheer calligraphy of his inscriptions and the unerring precision of his subsidiary ornaments are simply breathtaking. His potting too is extraordinarily fine. The added elements, foot, handles and neck, all have the same clarity and perfection, while his preparation of the surface and the quality of the shiny black glaze are consummate. The contour of the body of the vessel is so tight that it seems as if just touching the vase might cause it gently to lift off like a balloon.

In addition to the names of the figures and the signature of Exekias, to the right of the heroic group are the words *Onetorides kalos* – 'Onetorides is beautiful'. The idea of praising the beauty of such golden boys of the Athenian upper class seems to have begun around 550 BC and lasted into the second half of the fifth century.

33 LACONIAN *HYDRIA*

This monumental *hydria* (water jar) has a white slip on which has been painted a series of cheerfully colourful friezes, using the regular black-figure technique with added purple. The two chief friezes are filled with animals. In the centre of the upper one, at handle level, is the head of the monstrous Gorgon Medusa (decapitated by the hero Perseus); round the back are roosters and birds. In the lower frieze is a parade of guinea fowl.

The repertoire of shapes produced by Laconian potters is dominated by drinking cups, but there are some more monumental pieces, including *hydriae*, such as this one, *amphorae* and *kraters*. There was clearly much interaction with other Greek craftsmen, in both the pottery and metalworking traditions. Laconian pottery was widely exported and it is found in southern Italy (especially in Sparta's daughter colony of Taranto), Sicily and Etruria, in East Greek centres like Samos and Miletos, and even on the coast of Africa in Cyrenaica (eastern Libya) and at Naukratis on Egypt's Nile Delta.

This superbly preserved *hydria* has been associated with the works of the so-called Hunt Painter: it is probably one of his late works. The Hunt Painter (*c.* 560–530 BC) was a rather original artist, sometimes isolating just part of a scene in the circular interior fields of his cups, adopting almost a 'porthole' view of a scene. He was also one of the few Laconian painters to write the names of some of his figures on his vases with mythological scenes.

It used to be thought, based on our mostly fifth- and fourth-century BC Classical literary sources, that ancient Sparta, which dominated the region of Lakonia in the southern Peloponnese, was but a rather brutal and austere military state. Excavations at the beginning of the twentieth century, however, revealed that this was a mirage and that in the seventh and sixth centuries BC the Spartans led a more pleasure-loving and creative life similar to that of other Greek cities, their craftsman producing fine pottery, impressive metal vessels and wonderful bronze figurines, as well as some marble sculpture.

Pottery water jar

Greek, made in Lakonia, 540–530 BC

Attributed to the Hunt Painter

From Vulci

Formerly in the Pizzati, Blayds and Campanari collections

Ht 39.3 cm

GR 1849,0518.14 (*Vase* B 58)

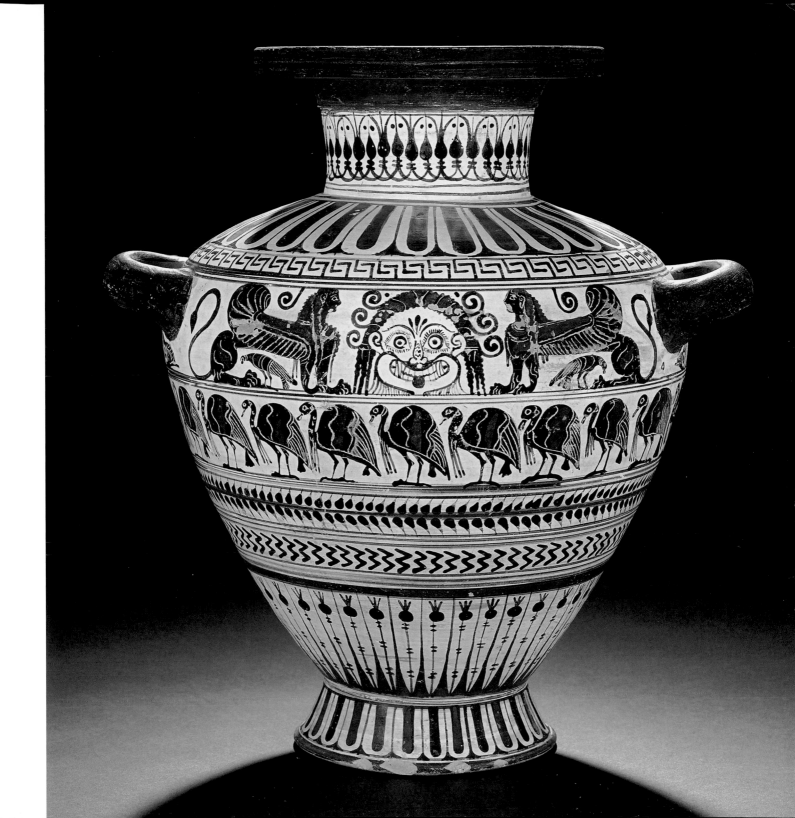

34 AGATE SEALSTONE DEPICTING A SATYR

The device on the flat side of this agate sealstone is that of a satyr with horse's tail, hooves and ears. His large head is frontal, as is his chest, but one leg is shown in three-quarter view. He holds a deep cup in one hand, while in the field appears a round-bodied *krater* (wine bowl) with volute-shaped handles. It is a very striking pose: he almost dances as he dips his cup over the *krater* of wine.

The back of this agate sealstone takes the form of a large scarab (or dung beetle), the gem cutter's favourite shape, one borrowed from Egypt and Phoenicia; the device is cut into the flat under-surface. The stone has also been drilled lengthwise so it could be worn as a movable bezel for a ring, or as an ornament on a chain or cord, round neck or wrist.

The style of the carving of this gem is Greek, and more specifically probably East Greek, but it is possible that the gem was actually made in Etruria in Italy, where many Greek craftsmen seem to have moved from East Greece and elsewhere around the middle of the sixth century BC. The question of the place of manufacture and origin of the craftsman is very difficult to resolve when the material is imported, the workshop equipment minimal, and the craftsmen so mobile.

By the middle of the sixth century BC gem engravers were using a drill to carve out curved depressions, a technique that enabled them to attempt more ambitious poses and greater naturalism in their figures. The skill of gemstone carving was taken to extraordinary heights in the following centuries (compare **64, 83** and **128**).

Agate sealstone

Greek, made in an East Greek city, or in Etruria, 530–500 BC

Name-piece of the Master of the London Satyr

Formerly in the Mertens-Schaffhausen collection

Length 2.2 cm

GR 1865,0712.106 (*Gem* 465)

35 THE ANDOKIDES *AMPHORA*

The special shape of this *amphora* (wine jar) was probably the invention of the potter who has signed it on the rim, *Andokides epoie* – 'Andokides made [me]'. There are only three other known examples of this shape, all similarly decorated solely on the neck, and all painted with black-figure scenes.

Here the god Dionysos is accompanied by two satyrs, a suitable scene for a wine *amphora*, and one that is repeated on two of the other examples of the shape. On the opposite side is a frontal four-horse chariot, the white-robed charioteer obscuring all but the warrior's helmeted head. Who the warrior is intended to be is not made clear, although one imagines he is a Homeric hero. The almost miniature painting of the figures is extraordinarily delicate and may be attributed to the vase-painter Psiax. He was a highly accomplished painter in the black-figure technique who also worked in the new red-figure technique, where he showed considerable interest in ambitious poses.

All four vases of this special shape were probably potted by Andokides; the other three were decorated by Psiax's close stylistic companion, the so-called Antimenes Painter; and all four were found in Italy. It seems likely that Andokides produced this unusual shape specifically with export to Italy in mind, for it resembles a number of bronze vessels from the Greek colonies of southern Italy.

The potter Andokides has left his signatures on a number of *amphorae* and cups that span the period 540–510 BC. His name, together with that of Mnesiades, also appears on a large marble base for a bronze statue, a dedication on the Athenian Acropolis. Mnesiades, too, is known as a potter, although only from a single signature. He may well have been the senior figure in the partnership, the dedication marking perhaps the transfer of ownership or direction of the business from Mnesiades to the younger Andokides.

Pottery wine jar

Greek, made in Athens, 530–520 BC

Signed by Andokides as potter, and attributed to Psiax as painter

From Vulci, Etruria

Formerly in the Northampton collection

Ht 39.5 cm

GR 1980,1029.1

36 PLATE PAINTED BY EPIKTETOS

On this perfectly preserved plate two garlanded revellers fill the circular field: one plays the pipes, the other bends to lift a large *skyphos* (deep cup) from the ground. The languid vertical of the young piper as he gently rocks on to his toes, the supple arched back of the bearded man with one boot-clad foot balancing the heavy *skyphos*, together with the neat letters of Epiktetos' signature as painter, all combine to produce a superb composition. The piper's vertical is further enhanced by the flute-case that hangs over his left shoulder, while the folds of the man's cloak that cover his back and fall down in front act as a counterpoint to his arched form, gently lining his back like ripples etched in the sand by the receding tide.

These revellers are presumably to be thought of as setting out from one party to go on to the next, the man determined to take his outsized drinking cup with him. Such a procession, the ancient equivalent of a pub crawl, was called a *komos*.

Epiktetos worked in both the black-figure and red-figure techniques. In his black-figure work it is clear that his teacher was Psiax (**35**), but his best work was done in red-figure, especially on cups, some of which are 'bilingual' (both black- and red-figure on one vessel), and on plates. He worked for the potters Hischylos, Nikosthenes, Pamphaios, Python and Pistoxenos, but he also potted for himself, for many of his late cups are signed simply with the word *epoiesen* (made). Indeed, one of his plates, a special piece with the image of Athena, given as a dedication on the Athenian Acropolis, bears his signature both as painter and as potter.

This plate was found in a tomb at Vulci in Etruria together with five other plates also all signed by Epiktetos as painter. They must have been exported as a set and specially placed in the tomb. Another example of a tomb containing a very large number of plates (all the work of the so-called Bryn Mawr Painter) has been found in Etruria in recent years.

Pottery plate
Greek, made in Athens, 520–500 BC
Signed by Epiktetos as painter
From Vulci, Etruria
Formerly in the Canino and Blacas collections
Diam. 18.8 cm
GR 1867,0508.1022 (*Vase* E 137)

37 BRONZE BANQUETER

Bronze attachment for a vessel

Greek, probably made in the Peloponnese, perhaps at Corinth, 530–510 BC

Said to be from Dodona, Epiros

Purchased with the aid of the Art Fund

Length 10.2 cm

GR 1954,1018.1

This beautiful bronze with its dark patina takes the form of a bearded reclining banqueter. He lies on a thin, plain mattress, with his left elbow resting on a cushion that is propped up against the simple curved end of the couch (*kline*), the vertical legs of which are not represented. His right knee is slightly raised under the cover of his plain *himation* and his right hand rests on top. His left leg is turned frontally so that the toes point over the end of the mattress.

He holds a full *phiale* (libation bowl) or stemless cup in his left hand. His lips seem to be parted and this, together with the proud carriage of his head, his intense gaze and the tension in his left arm, suggests that he should perhaps be thought of as declaiming a ritual prayer. In a Greek symposium the first *krater* (bowl for mixing wine and water) of wine was dedicated to Zeus and the Olympian gods, the second to the Heroes and the third to Zeus Soter (Saviour). We might well take this imposing little figure as the *symposiarchos*, the leader of the party, who controlled the ratio of wine to water and the number of *kraters* to be drunk.

For the modern world wine is often a 'medicine for misery', but the Greeks perhaps understood it better, considering it a *pharmakon*, both a poison and a medicine. It had to be drunk mixed with water and then it could bring happiness and sociability. As Aeschylus wrote, 'bronze [i.e. a mirror] reflects the appearance, wine is the mirror of the soul'.

This figure was solid cast and cold worked. The precision of the marking of his moustache and beard and the elaborate treatment of his long hair are quite remarkable. His drapery, by contrast, is extremely simple; his body and musculature are only slightly modelled, except for his prominent collar bone, an idea that the artist may have had from nature, the result of leaning on one elbow. Together with a number of companions, he must originally have been attached to the rim of a large *krater* or to its tripod stand. He is said to have been found in the great oracular shrine of Zeus at Dodona in northern Greece and we can well imagine the presence of such a vessel at a ritual feast in honour of the great god.

38 THE MARION *KOUROS*

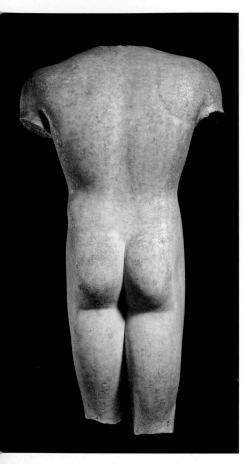

Marble statue

Greek, perhaps made on Paros,
520–510 BC

Excavated at Marion, Cyprus
(Ohnefalsch-Richter excavation,
Necropolis II, tomb 92)

Ht 72 cm

GR 1887,0801.1 (*Sculpture* B 325)

'Look how taut it is, how this young boy is drawing in his stomach, and, from the back, see how the buttocks are nipped in like nutcrackers. It is motionless and yet it oozes with energy', noted the sculptor Henry Moore.

This marble torso of a naked standing youth, a *kouros*, was found at Marion in the far northwest of Cyprus. It is slightly under life-size and is missing its head, arms and lower legs, but the treatment of the pectorals, shoulders and back give us a real sense of the vital force within the slim figure – they are so much more naturalistic than on the Boeotian *kouros* (**24**).

The marble is from the island of Paros and the figure was surely carved by a Parian sculptor. Very few marble statues were imported to Cyprus at this time and this is the only example of a Greek *kouros*. It was excavated in 1886 in the *dromos* (entrance passage) of a tomb at Marion. This *dromos* was nearly 23 m long and ran down to a chamber of 'four irregularly shaped caves communicating with each other' that were cut into the bedrock. The *kouros* was found 'set up like a stele in front and over the door of the tomb'. The tomb, which contained only a single burial, yielded a silver coin of the city of Idalion dating to 510–500 BC, part of a Persian gold bowl decorated with acorns, parts of an ornamental silver belt, an Egyptianizing gold ring, a bronze cauldron and a bronze sarcophagus ornament (perhaps Late Assyrian), as well as imported Athenian black-figured pottery, Cypriot pottery and alabaster *alabastra* (perfume bottles). The date of the burial was thus probably about 510–500 BC and it was one of the richest in the cemetery. The contents clearly point to the wide range of contacts and connections that the deceased and his family enjoyed.

Judging from its findspot underground, the *kouros* does not seem to have served as a grave-marker, as he would have in Greece, although he may in some way have been thought to have guarded the tomb. At the time of the sculpture's discovery a minute search was made for the missing parts, but they were not found. Did the figure, then, have an earlier function in another place; and was it deliberately broken up before being placed in the tomb?

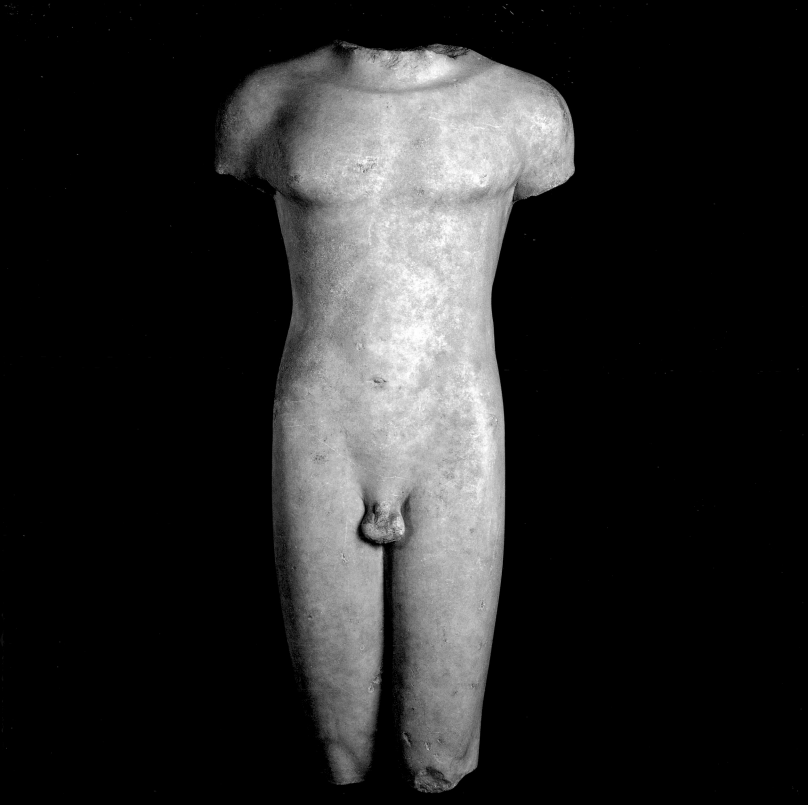

39 *HYDRIA* PAINTED BY PHINTIAS

Pottery water jar

Greek, made in Athens,
about 510 BC

Signed by Phintias as painter

From Vulci, Etruria

Formerly in the Canino collection

Ht 54.1 cm

GR 1843,1103.8 (*Vase* E 159)

Painted on the body of this red-figured *hydria* (water jar) we find three youths at a fountain accompanied by a bearded man. The youth on the right stoops to hold his *hydria* under a lion-head water spout. Behind him a second youth stands in the queue, his empty *hydria* still on his shoulder; he turns back to the left, his attention caught by the bearded man who leans on a stick. At the far left, a third youth holds his *hydria* out in front of him.

These youths, drawing water for use in the *palaistra* (wrestling ground), are all studies of the human body in movement. Two exemplify how weights are lifted, one low and heavy, the other high and lighter. In the turning second youth the painter has tried to show the way that such a twist affects the whole body, from profile legs in one direction to head in profile in the other: one might note too the way he has carefully posed the left arm, which has turned round with the upper body.

On the shoulder of the vase are two male banqueters. The man holds two cups, but the youth on the right seems to have just finished playing on the lyre, his left hand still holds its strings, but his right hand now rests on his knee. His head is turned down to the right, emotion and concentration spent. Above these two figures is written *Phi[n]tias egraphsen*. Phintias was a member of a small group of exceptional early red-figure vase-painters whom we call the Pioneers, after their pioneering explorations of complex movements. This group included Euphronios and Euthymides, as well as lesser artists such as Smikros and Sosias. They clearly were all friends, and rivals, since we find them writing toasts to each other on their vases. Euphronios was perhaps the most successful of the group, for he went on to pot a very fine series of cups (compare **48**): he even made an expensive sculptural dedication on the Acropolis, the base of which has been preserved. Phintias, however, has left us his name as potter on only three vessels, all small scent-bottles. A second Phintias, however, perhaps a member of the same family, is known as the potter of an acorn-shaped *lekythos* (oil-bottle) of the last quarter of the fifth century BC.

3 THE CLASSICAL GREEK WORLD
c. 500–323 BC

The massive Persian campaigns against Greece were defeated at Marathon in 490 BC by the Athenians virtually single-handed, and then again in 480/479 BC by the united city-states of Greece. One of the consequences of these victorious struggles in which Athenian citizens of all classes shared was the acceleration of political change. Power was increasingly transferred from the aristocrats to the citizen body as a whole, eventually resulting in a radical democracy. Similar developments also took place in other Greek cities.

An enhanced self-confidence also permeated all aspects of Greek life and art. In the hands of some of Athens's finest vase-painters (compare **41**, **43** and **44**) we see the melding of hitherto separately patterned areas of the human body into a unified and naturalistic whole. This was greatly helped by the new red-figure technique, developed in Athens late in the sixth century BC, which offered greater fluidity of line, with harsh incised lines replaced by two new types of brush line, the black line in high relief and the diluted, light brown line.

There were similar developments in sculpture, superficial pattern giving place to structural understanding. From this time we also find cities, rather than individuals, making large sculptural dedications in major sanctuaries, such as the Tarentines at Delphi, the work of Onatas of Aigina (compare **47**). Other sculptors who similarly preferred bronze to marble now begin to be known by name, including Myron (about 460–440 BC), one of his most famous creations being an athlete throwing the *diskos* (**144**), and Polykleitos, who produced many bronze sculptures of athletes (compare **150**) that were now imbued with a sense of organic balance and the potential, it would seem, to move.

After the defeat of the Persians the Greek city-states formed a defensive alliance, the Delian League, against any further eastern threat. In 454/3 BC its treasury was transferred from Delos to the Acropolis, in effect turning the League into an Athenian empire. Perikles, the popular leader of Athens, soon drew on the city's new wealth and began an elaborate building programme on the Acropolis. At the heart of this project was the Parthenon (**52**) with its gold and ivory statue of Athena by Pheidias. In 432/1 BC, however, the Peloponnesian War broke out, the culmination of a long-festering conflict between Athens and Sparta. Then in 430 BC plague struck Athens, overcrowded with refugees from the Attic countryside. In an attempt to rally the Athenians Perikles

Marble portrait of Perikles,
Roman, second century AD, from
Hadrian's villa at Tivoli, ht 58.5 cm
(GR 1805,0703.91; *Sculpture* 549;
formerly in the Townley
collection)

delivered a speech honouring the dead of the first year of the war, declaring with foresight that: 'Mighty indeed are the marks and monuments of our empire which we have left. Future ages will wonder at us as the present age wonders at us now.'

Sculptors working on the Acropolis projects may well have found work in periods of inactivity producing tombstones (**54**). Some eventually left Athens for employment elsewhere, they or their descendants working on such grand funerary monuments as the so-called Nereid Monument in Lycia (**61**). The dreadful conditions in Athens may similarly have led potters to leave the city, for in the 430s BC we find the reinvigoration of red-figure vase-painting elsewhere around Greece and the development of new workshops, especially several particularly important ones in southern Italy.

Finally, in 404 BC, after twenty-seven years of hardship, the Peloponnesian War ended with Sparta victorious and Athens forced to pull down her own walls. It was not long, however, before the Greek cities were once again embroiled in internecine conflict until, ultimately, the northern kingdom of Macedonia under Philip II emerged as the leader of Greece.

Art nevertheless continued to flourish throughout the Greek world. A number of sculptors came to prominence, working now in both bronze and marble. Praxiteles (about 375–335 BC) introduced the female nude as a major sculptural type, imparting a new sense of femininity to the body and pose; his male statues were also languidly posed (compare **72** and **78**). Leochares (about 365–325 BC), who collaborated late in his career with Lysippos on the bronze lion-hunt group for Delphi (compare **90**), has also been associated by modern scholars with the Demeter of Knidos (**66**), while ancient sources name him as one of the team responsible for the sculptural decoration of the Mausoleum (**65**).

Other crafts, including gem cutting (**64**), die engraving (**50**) and bronze casting (**51**), prospered in the major Greek centres. Increased wealth also made gold jewellery much more widespread from the late fifth century BC (**59** and **69**). Although red-figure vase-painting had ended in Athens by about 350 BC, in southern Italy it continued until at least 280 BC. Of these South Italian schools, Apulian (**62** and **67**) was the most important, its ornate pieces vying with the best of the Athenian (**63** and **70**). Although there are rare glimpses of free painting (**60**), it is only with the great Macedonian painted tombs at the end of the fourth century BC that we can sense what has been lost of the large-scale painting of earlier times.

40 THE STRANGFORD *KOUROS*

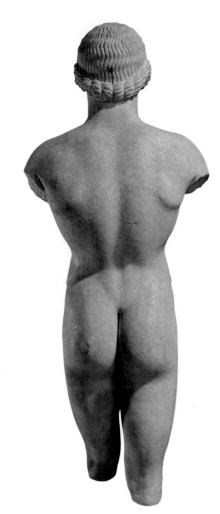

The Strangford *kouros*, an under life-sized statue of a naked youth, has been carved from marble quarried on the island of Paros. It probably stood as a grave-marker over the tomb of a wealthy man, not a portrait of the deceased but rather an idealized representation of the values and virtues to which the dead laid claim, such as youthful beauty, athleticism, honour and aristocratic bearing (compare **24** and **38**).

The youth's hair is worn long, but is braided around the back and has a formal arrangement of curls across the forehead. The hair above is waved and swells and falls so that a real sense of volume and texture is achieved. There are also holes for a bronze wreath or ribbon around the head. The stylization of the stomach and groin is rather flat, and the hips impossibly taut and slim, but the shoulders are powerfully rendered and the back and buttocks well modelled. Indeed, this contrast between the power of the shoulders, upper back and chest, and the slim sleekness of the lower abdomen and hips make one think of some well-honed swimmer. Certainly the Greeks had a preference for the combination of speed and stamina, rather than heavy musculature.

This sculpture stands right on the boundary between Archaic and Classical art. The structure of the youth's frame, especially his shoulders, back and ribs are well understood, but the treatment of the stomach muscles, the hips and the groin remains very stiff and pattern dominated. The sculptor has not yet learnt to bring this area of his figure to life or link it convincingly to the upper torso.

The *kouros* was acquired by the Sixth Viscount Strangford (1780–1855), who was British Ambassador to Constantinople between 1820 and 1824. When it was sold to the Museum by the Eighth Viscount, it was said to have come from the island of Lemnos in the northeast Aegean, but Charles Newton later associated it with the island of Anaphi in the Cyclades (east of Thera), which is perhaps more plausible.

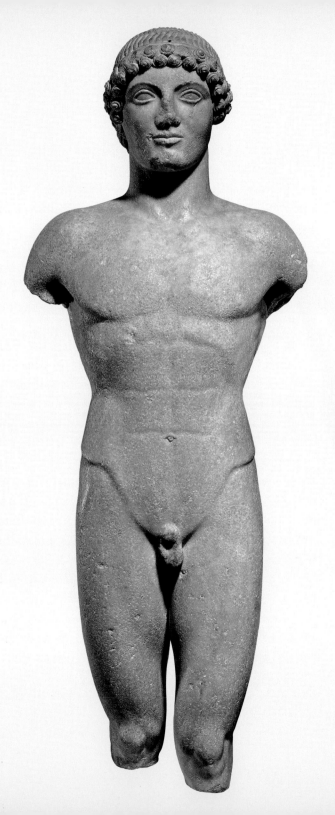

Marble funerary figure

Greek, probably made in the
Cyclades, 500–490 BC

Said to be from Anaphi (or
Lemnos)

Formerly in the Strangford
collection

Ht 1.01 m

GR 1864,0220.1 (*Sculpture* B 475)

Pottery wine bowl

Greek, made in Athens,
about 490 BC

Attributed to the Berlin Painter

From Cerveteri, Etruria

Formerly in the Alibrandi collection

Ht 63.5 cm

GR 1848,0801.1 (*Vase* E 468)

This monumental *krater* (bowl for mixing wine and water) with volute-shaped handles is decorated only on the neck; the body has been left completely black. The upper level of the neck is filled with an immaculate double chain of alternating lotus and palmette; below this is a figured scene filled with the graceful forms of gods and heroes.

The red-figure scenes on either side are linked by the figure of Achilles, the greatest Greek hero of the Trojan War. On one side he is in combat with Memnon (left), on the other with Hektor (right). While Memnon charges forward recklessly to meet his end on Achilles' spear, Hektor is already wounded and is falling back, his shield slipping inexorably from his grasp. Achilles seems, at first, virtually identical on both sides, but on closer inspection he appears tense and alert meeting Memnon, while against Hektor he has bent his leading leg more and is already moving forward in the final attack.

In each scene the heroes are supported by a deity. In the duel between Achilles and Memnon, it is their mothers, Thetis and Eos, who attend them and react to the action with foreknowledge. In the death of Hektor, Achilles is supported by Athena who seems to shake her snake-fringed *aegis*, perhaps to terrify Hektor. By contrast, Hektor's divine second, Apollo, already moves away, the battle lost. The god, however, does turn round to wave an arrow threateningly in the air, alluding no doubt to the fashion in which Achilles will himself eventually meet his end, through an arrow in his heel.

The splendid artist who created these dramatic images has not left us his name, but he has been named the Berlin Painter after a very large and beautifully decorated *amphora* now in that city. He was a prolific pupil of the Pioneers, Phintias (**39**) and Euthymides. A master of clean, elegant contours and perfectly formed inner details, his figures all seem heroes, their veins filled with the elixir of immortality. The potter, too, was a master of his art and as anonymous as the painter, but once no doubt an important presence in the Athenian potters' quarter, the Kerameikos.

42 BRONZE HELMET OF CORINTHIAN TYPE

There is every reason to believe that this type of helmet was called 'Corinthian' in antiquity. The fifth-century BC Greek historian Herodotos mentions the name and we see the type represented first and most frequently on Corinthian pottery. Such a helmet, however, soon became the most conspicuous possession of any Greek hoplite (heavily armed warrior) and over the three hundred years during which the type was produced it was made not only in mainland Greece but also in the Greek colonies of central and southern Italy. Indeed, in Athens in the fifth century this type of helmet came to symbolize the role and status of general (cf. Perikles, p. 91).

The beautifully stylized form of this helmet from the last phase has a strong articulation running all round the skull, rather like the lower edge of a cap, which also added strength, especially over the brow where the bronze tended to be very thin. However, the type had one particular drawback, namely that, once pulled down over the head, it was hard to hear words of command. As a result, it was often shown pushed up on the head when battle was not actually under way (compare p. 91 and **44**).

The art of hammering out a helmet from a single disk of metal with the aid of a rod anvil was particularly celebrated in the Greek world and we see craftsmen producing such feats of smithing on vases and on engraved sealstones, as well as very occasionally even in the round, as with a small bronze figurine.

Many bronze helmets have been found in Greek sanctuaries, particularly Olympia, where they were regularly dedicated, often as part of a complete panoply or set of armour, seized from the conquered enemy (compare **64** and p. 225).

Bronze helmet

Greek, probably made in Corinth, 500–480 BC

Said to be from Corinth

Ht 21.8 cm

GR 1873,0910.1 (*Bronze* 2818)

43 WINE COOLER PAINTED BY DOURIS

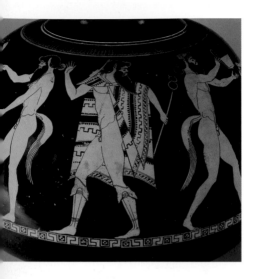

Pottery wine cooler

Greek, made in Athens,
about 490 BC

Signed by Douris as painter

From Cerveteri, Etruria

Ht 28.7 cm

GR 1868,0616.7 (*Vase* E 768)

This mushroom-shaped vessel is a masterpiece of both potting and painting. It served to hold wine for the symposium and was set to float in a large *krater* filled with ice-cold water or ice. This sort of wine cooler (*psykter*) may have been the invention of the potter Nikosthenes, an easier and perhaps more practical alternative to the earlier, multiple vessel versions (compare **28**).

The potter of this *psykter* is unknown, but the decoration is the work of the vase-painter Douris, for he has signed it *Doris egraphsen*. Some 250 of his works, mostly cups, have been recognized. Here the decoration takes the form of a frieze around the bulging wall of the vessel and is directly related to its function, for we see a troop of satyrs, part-man, part-horse, the companions of the wine god Dionysos. They cavort wildly in a boisterous ballet, led by one of the younger members of their number who is dressed up as the messenger god Hermes. As the satyrs process, they dance, do handstands, and one performs a prodigious feat of balancing, made even more remarkable by the imminent addition of wine into the *kantharos* (special, high-handled drinking cup) so precariously poised.

Douris' red-figure painting is very elegant and controlled. His earlier works, like this *psykter*, have fire as well as elegance, but his later vases tend to become more academic. The method of attributing vases to particular painters is based on, among other things, a close observation of all the lines that go to make up the painting, for every line is personal to its painter, part of his own individual 'handwriting'. Two typical features of Douris' style can be seen clearly here: the W-shaped hip line and the small arc at the junction of the lines marking the lower boundaries of the pectorals.

Although it is clear that a potter called Python fashioned most, if not all, of the cups that Douris decorated, Douris did himself occasionally turn his hand to potting, for he has left us his signature on two vessels that were no doubt intended to be special pieces. One also bears an owner's name, that of Asopodoros, and must have been made as a special commission; the second is of a very rare shape.

44 DRINKING CUP POTTED BY BRYGOS

Pottery drinking cup

Greek, made in Athens,
485–480 BC

Signed by Brygos as potter;
attributed to the Brygos Painter

From Capua (the so-called Brygos
Tomb), Campania

Ht 12.3 cm; diam. 27.5 cm

GR 1873,0820.376 (*Vase* E 65)

The potter Brygos proudly signed this perfectly preserved cup on the edge of the foot. We know his work from some fifteen other signatures on cups. He seems to have learnt his craft from Euphronios, but went on to establish his own workshop, which was staffed by a number of red-figure painters, among whom the anonymous painter now referred to as the Brygos Painter was the finest – he was the painter of this superb piece.

The scenes on the exterior of the cup are linked. They are set in a sanctuary of Dionysos, the wine god, which is represented by an altar, to the left of which stands Dionysos himself, holding a black *kantharos* (high-handled drinking cup), and by the block on the far left on which the painter sketched, but then omitted, a folding stool covered with an animal skin – the placing of a stool or chair was a means of calling for a deity to appear. The messenger goddess, Iris, equipped with her messenger's staff (*kerykeion*), has been sent by the goddess Hera to interrupt the sacrifice that the satyrs are making to Dionysos. Two of their number, however, have caught her, while, on the other side of the cup, four others are threatening Hera herself. Before Hera stands Hermes, the messenger god, who seems to be trying to reason with the satyrs, while Herakles, in the outfit of the Scythian police force of Athens, rushes up to counter the physical threat.

The painter has given his figures names, including the satyrs, who bear, on the side with Hera, names connected with their characters or attributes (Reveller, Joyful, Lust, Erect) and, on the other, names connected with the chase and capture of Iris (Rushing, Holding, Catching). One other, unusual feature deserves to be noted: the use of raised clay for Herakles' club and the bracelets worn by Iris and Hera – these would originally have carried gilding on top, added after the firing of the cup.

This splendid cup gives its name to a tomb found in the winter of 1870/71 at Capua. The tomb had a single interment but had been plundered in antiquity. The spectacular vases that remained were all Athenian (including **49**) and of the highest quality, prompting the suggestion that the deceased might himself have been from Athens.

45 WHITE-GROUND JUG BY THE BRYGOS PAINTER

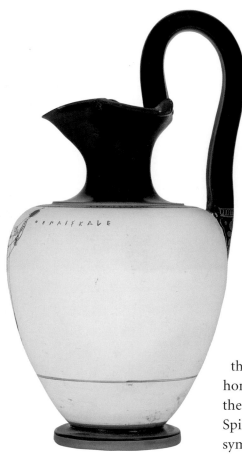

Pottery jug
Greek, made in Athens, about 490 BC
Attributed to the Brygos Painter
Said to be from Locri
Ht 21.5 cm
GR 1873,0820.304 (*Vase* D 13)

On a perfectly preserved and masterfully potted wine jug, the statuesque figure of a woman spinning stands alone in a bright, white space.

She is dressed in a long, fine *chiton*, a heavier cloak and sandals. Her hair is held up behind in a bun and further adorned by a red fillet; she also wears earrings and bracelets. In her left hand she holds up a distaff with an elaborately turned handle. The upper part of the distaff has been wound with dyed roves of wool that appear as a solid red ball. Out from this projects, both right and left, a loop of thread which the woman has drawn from the main ball. The thumb and index finger of the right hand hold the thread while the spindle whirls below. The thread has been attached to a hook at the top of the spindle which is clearly visible, as is the conical weight at the bottom, which helps to hold the thread in tension. The woman's spindle has almost reached the ground and she will soon have to stop and wind up the thread, adding to the already visible lump in the middle of the spindle. Her head is slightly bent as she carefully watches the thread, a model of serious concentration.

In fifth-century Athens well-to-do freeborn women, and perhaps many of the less well off, too, seem to have lived secluded lives, segregated within the home, especially when visitors came, and were seldom permitted to pass beyond the threshold of their own front doors unless to attend religious festivals. Spinning and weaving were their chief pastimes and the distaff itself came to be a symbol of the dedicated housewife: 'Distaff, friend of spinners, gift of grey-eyed Athena to women, who are mindful of their duties as housewives' (Theokritos).

The Brygos Painter, to whom this jug has been attributed, was the finest painter to work for the potter Brygos in the first decades of the fifth century BC (compare **44**). His figures have energy, passion and sometimes, as here, a certain monumentality. We do not know the potter of the jug, but he was a master not just of shape but also of the white slip: he may even have been Brygos himself.

46 THE HARPY TOMB

The so-called Harpy Tomb stood some nine metres high and consisted of a huge rectangular pillar of grey-blue limestone that weighed about eighty tons topped by a funerary chamber and closed above by a three-stepped capstone. The outside of the marble chamber walls were carved with relief friezes, removed by Charles Fellows in 1842 and since replaced by casts on the site.

The winged female 'Harpies' on two of the sides are now identified as Sirens (shown carrying off diminutive female figures that must be personifications of the souls of the deceased), while the occupant of the tomb has been identified as Kybernis, son of Kossikas and the ruler of Xanthos in Lycia between about 520 and 480 BC.

In 480/79 BC the Lycians were conscripted into the Persian armada being assembled by King Xerxes for his invasion of Greece. Kybernis (meaning 'helmsman') was the leader of the Lycian contingent of forty or fifty ships. He may have died in the sea battle of Salamis in 479 BC or subsequently from his wounds. He is presumably the seated figure that dominates the north side. He holds a staff and beneath his chair is a dog of unusual breed. He seems to be helping in the arming of a young man, who stands before him, handing perhaps his helmet over to him. This younger figure should be his son Kuprlli, who succeeded him and, following a retaliatory Athenian invasion led by Kimon, rebuilt the acropolis of Xanthos (Kuprlli ruled until about 440 BC). The Sirens shown on either side of the group, given their connection with the sea (they lured sailors to shipwreck), would be suitable soul-carriers for the funerary monument of Kybernis. Behind his chair another small female figure sits on the ground, mourning.

The sculptural style of the reliefs from this tomb seems to be linked to southern Ionia, in particular perhaps the city of Miletos. Indeed, it is possible that Milesian craftsmen took refuge at Xanthos following the Persian sack of Miletos in 494 BC.

Marble tomb reliefs
Lycian, made at Xanthos, about 480 BC
From Xanthos (Lycia), Turkey
Removed by Charles Fellows
Ht of friezes 1.02 m
GR 1848,1020.1 (*Sculpture* B 287)

47 THE TARANTO BRONZE RIDER

Bronze sculpture (leg of a rider and drapery)

Greek, probably made in Taranto, 480–460 BC

Said to have been found at Taranto

Ht of leg 82 cm

GR 1886,0324.1 (*Bronze* 265); GR 1886.0324.3,4,7e and 7g (drapery)

Reconstruction sketch (by Susan Bird)

Large-scale Classical bronze sculpture is all too often only known in fragments, but even fragments can carry a sense of the power and importance of the whole. This spectacular right leg from an over life-size bronze statue is such a piece.

A detailed study of the leg and the associated fragments of drapery has revealed that all came from an armed rider. The wonderfully modelled leg is equipped with a bronze greave decorated with a *gorgoneion* (the grinning, decapitated head of the Gorgon Medusa) over the knee. It must have hung by the side of the horse, as the down-pointed foot and the relaxed thigh suggest. The drapery fragments come from a thick cloak (*chlamys*) with an elaborate maeander border (the decoration done with inlaid strips of copper), and the play of its folds reveals that the figure was in lively action or motion. The scale and the material of the sculpture indicate that the group was a public monument that involved gods or heroes, set up either in a sanctuary or in the public marketplace, while the presence of greaves and the lively pose suggest a complex martial subject rather than a simple divine image.

In the early decades of the fifth century BC the Tarentines defeated a number of groups of neighbouring native peoples, as they sought to secure their borders. From Pausanias' description of the sanctuary at Delphi, and from actual inscribed blocks on the site, we know that the Tarentines set up two multi-figure bronze dedications there following their successes.

The probable date and what can be determined of the style, together with an analysis of the bronze alloy, suggest that the Tarentine Rider may have come from a group set up in Taranto to match the later of the two groups at Delphi, celebrating in particular the defeat of the Peucetians and the death of the leader of the Iapygians, King Opis, the work of Onatas of Aigina. The reconstruction drawing gives us some idea of how part of the whole might have looked. It is even possible that the sculptor may have been Onatas of Aigina.

48 APHRODITE ON A GOOSE

The interior of this delicate drinking cup shows Aphrodite, the goddess of love, sailing serenely through the bright heavens on the back of her goose. She wears a cloak over a thinner garment (*chiton*), sandals, bead necklace and a hair net. Most of the painting is done with golden brown lines, but her cloak has been given a matt red slip, with darker fold lines. Her *chiton* has a similar matt red border at neck and ankles, decorated with a continuous white maeander on top. She holds a long-stemmed flower in her right hand. Her name is painted behind her head – *Aphrodites*, [image] of Aphrodite – while to the right of the bird's body is *Glaukon kalos*, 'Glaukon is beautiful'.

There are a number of faint lines visible on the white surface that are remains of preliminary sketch work. In addition to changes to details of the wings and the flower, the most significant change is that to the pose of the head. The painter first drew Aphrodite with a frontal head, only to change his mind and give her a wonderfully delicate and serene profile.

The painting has been attributed to the so-called Pistoxenos Painter, who was one of the last important painters in Euphronios' workshop (see **39**). This cup is the painter's latest great cup and is remarkable for the new softened lines: the hard black relief lines of earlier pieces have been replaced with diluted glaze lines that fired a golden brown colour. The other new feature is the way that the eye has been drawn, for it is now properly in profile with the corner opened to let the eye take its natural form.

Glaukon was the son of Leagros, who had similarly been praised on vases in his youth at the end of the sixth century BC. The family was resident in the Kerameikos, the potters' quarter, and both Leagros and Glaukon went on to take the role of *strategos* (general) in the army. It is very likely that the family patronized a number of potters and painters, in particular the workshop of Euphronios.

This cup was discovered in a rich tomb on Rhodes. There were two chambers: one was empty, but the other, presumably that of a woman, contained, together with this Aphrodite cup, several pairs of Athenian vases and a pair of alabaster *alabastra* (perfume bottles).

Pottery drinking cup

Greek, made in Athens, 470–460 BC

Attributed to the Pistoxenos Painter

Excavated at Kamiros, Rhodes (Fikellura cemetery tomb 43)

Diam. 24.3 cm

GR 1864,1007.77 (*Vase* D 2)

49 SPHINX POTTED BY SOTADES

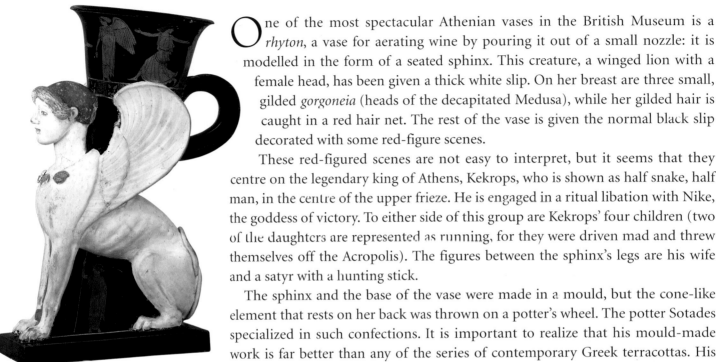

Pottery vessel in the form of a sphinx

Greek, made in Athens, 470–460 BC

Attributed to Sotades as potter and to the Sotades Painter

From Capua, Campania (the so-called Brygos Tomb)

Ht 29 cm

GR 1873,0820.265 (*Vase* E 788)

One of the most spectacular Athenian vases in the British Museum is a *rhyton*, a vase for aerating wine by pouring it out of a small nozzle: it is modelled in the form of a seated sphinx. This creature, a winged lion with a female head, has been given a thick white slip. On her breast are three small, gilded *gorgoneia* (heads of the decapitated Medusa), while her gilded hair is caught in a red hair net. The rest of the vase is given the normal black slip decorated with some red-figure scenes.

These red-figured scenes are not easy to interpret, but it seems that they centre on the legendary king of Athens, Kekrops, who is shown as half snake, half man, in the centre of the upper frieze. He is engaged in a ritual libation with Nike, the goddess of victory. To either side of this group are Kekrops' four children (two of the daughters are represented as running, for they were driven mad and threw themselves off the Acropolis). The figures between the sphinx's legs are his wife and a satyr with a hunting stick.

The sphinx and the base of the vase were made in a mould, but the cone-like element that rests on her back was thrown on a potter's wheel. The potter Sotades specialized in such confections. It is important to realize that his mould-made work is far better than any of the series of contemporary Greek terracottas. His products were, indeed, highly prized and have been found in rich tombs in Italy and even in far-off Meroë in the Sudan; they were also dedicated in a number of sanctuaries in Attica, on the northern Greek island of Thasos, on Cyprus and in Italy; and they have even been found in settlement contexts at Gordion in Phrygia and at Susa in Persia.

The Capua tomb that preserved this sphinx *rhyton* also contained six other superb Athenian vases. Four of these were probably purchased for the funeral, but the two earlier vessels, one a *skyphos* (deep drinking cup) potted by Hieron and painted by Makron, the other the great Brygos cup that has given the tomb its name (**44**), were probably owned by the deceased during his lifetime.

50 SILVER TETRADRACHM OF NAXOS

This coin, a silver four drachma piece, is one of the great masterpieces of Greek coinage. It was produced a few years after the fall of the Deinomenid dynasty on Sicily, when the Naxians were able to return to their old city: Hieron (478–466 BC) had forcibly transported them, together with the Catanians, to Leontini.

The new coinage initiated by the Naxians was created by the finest die cutter of the day. The obverse bears the head of Dionysos, traditional for the city, but here modelled with extraordinary power. The god's head, with its thick neck and full beard, seems to burst out of the bounds of the circle, while under the vine wreath that surrounds his head the waves of his delicate hair are cut to different depths on the die to give a real sense of the hair's thickness.

On the reverse, enclosed by the letters NAXION (of the Naxians), a satyr sits holding a stemless *kantharos*, a wine cup of a special shape that we know from Athenian vases of just this period. His legs are splayed apart and his right leg and foot effectively foreshortened. The muscles and structure of his torso are superbly rendered with a real sculptural sense of volume and three dimensions. His left hand is flat on the ground, taking some of his weight as he turns to the side. The impact of his pose on his chest and shoulder are well understood. His tail curls under him, its spikiness echoing his wild hair and jutting beard.

The pose is known from Athenian vase-painting from about 500 BC and, perhaps a little later, from cast bronze figures under the handles of bronze vessels. In three-dimensional sculpture, one might compare the boy near the corner of the east pediment of the temple of Zeus at Olympia, a figure that must be roughly contemporary with the coin. The die engraver has taken something from all of these traditions to create this glorious image of the Naxos satyr.

Silver four drachma coin

Greek, made at Naxos (Sicily),
about 460 BC

Diam. 2.7 cm; wt 17.44 g

CM *PCG* II C.48

51 THE CHATSWORTH APOLLO

Bronze head from a statue

Greek, made in Greece or on Cyprus, about 460 BC

From Tamassos, Cyprus

Formerly in the collection of the Dukes of Devonshire, Chatsworth House

Acquired with the aid of the Art Fund

Ht 31.6 cm (total ht of figure perhaps 2 m)

GR 1958,0418.1

An over life-sized bronze head from a statue of the god Apollo was discovered in 1836 by peasants digging for water in the dry bed of the river Pidias between the villages of Pera and Episkopi in central Cyprus.

The peasants apparently discovered the statue complete, but, in dragging it off, the sections from which it had been made up came apart. They described the statue as standing with the left leg slightly forward and the arms hanging down at his sides, and noted a wide belt around his waist, a feature sometimes to be found on early statues of the god Apollo. For fear of the Ottoman authorities, the peasants disposed of most of the pieces of the sculpture as scrap. The head, however, was preserved and was purchased in 1838 by the Sixth Duke of Devonshire. It seems that the right leg also survived, being taken to France by Edmond Duthoit in 1862/3 and then presented to the Louvre. Later excavations identified the actual find-spot within the sanctuary of Reshef and Apollo, about one kilometre north of the city wall of ancient Tamassos.

The statue would have been cast in several sections – head, torso, arms and legs. Some of the long curls of hair were also cast separately and soldered on. The god's long hair hangs in ringlets free from the head, reaching almost down to the shoulders. The long locks over the ears have been combed forward into long undulating strands and tied at the front in a so-called Herakles knot (compare **81**). The eyes were originally inlaid – sheets of bronze ending in cut-out eyelashes (remains of these are still in place) once held an ivory or marble core for the whites of the eyes and perhaps coloured and black glass inlays for the irises and pupils.

The date of this statue of Apollo, somewhere around 460 BC, is just the time when there were the strongest ties between Greece and Cyprus and when, indeed, Athenian forces actually occupied the island. The setting up of a statue of Apollo, at about the time that the Athenians transferred the funds of the Delian League from Apollo's sacred island of Delos to a treasury in Athens, may have been significant.

52 THE PARTHENON SCULPTURES

Marble architectural sculptures
Greek, made in Athens, 445–432 BC
From the Parthenon, Athens
From the Elgin collection

(*left*) South Metope IV: GR
1816,0610. 3 (*Sculpture* 307),
Lapith and Centaur (heads in
Copenhagen). Ht 1.2m

(*centre*) Computer reconstruction

(*right*) East Pediment: GR
1816,0610.97 (*Sculpture* 303,
figures L and M), Dione and
Aphrodite. Length 2.33 m

The Parthenon was the centrepiece of the great building programme set in motion by Perikles (p. 91) around 450 BC. It was erected on the site of an earlier temple, begun soon after 490 BC to celebrate the defeat of the first Persian invasion, but never finished. The purpose of the temple seems to have been twofold: to house the colossal gold and ivory statue of the goddess Athena specially created by Pheidias, and to hold the treasures of the goddess. The architects are said to have been Iktinos and Kallikrates.

The temple was richly decorated with sculptures, some of the finest ever made, in three locations: the triangular pediments at either end were filled with large scale sculptures carved fully in the round; the square panels, or metopes, above the external columns were carved in high relief; and the continuous frieze which ran within the colonnade at the top of the walls that formed the core of the building, was in low relief.

The 92 roughly square metopes were the first sculptures to be finished (*c.* 445–440 BC), for they had to be inserted into the structure before the roof could be begun. They encircled the superstructure of the building. On the short east end, the gods fought the Giants; on the west, Greeks fought Amazons; on the long north, was the sack of Troy; on the south, the Lapiths fought the Centaurs, who had become drunk at the wedding of the Lapith king (in the centre the theme may have been different). From this southern series of metopes comes one that shows a centaur rearing over a stricken Lapith who sinks to the ground in the corner of the metope (far left). The main action is dramatically centred in the lower corner of the composition as the Centaur delivers the final blow with a huge metal water-jar. Added colour and metal attachments must have added greatly to the drama of the scene and its ability to be understood from the ground, some 12m below (left).

The East Pediment showed the birth of the goddess Athena. The story was that she sprang fully formed from the head of Zeus, released by the god Hephaistos with the aid of his axe. The figures from the centre of the pediment were largely destroyed when the Parthenon was turned into a Christian church and an apse pushed out at the east end in perhaps about AD 1500.

Only some of the figures on either side of the central group are preserved. From the right hand side comes a group of two goddesses carved from one huge block (p. 117). These two elegant figures are regularly identified as the goddess Aphrodite reclining in the lap of her mother, Dione. The goddess of 'limb relaxing love' is an extraordinary study of a full, highly sensuous form enveloped in drapery, for only the flesh of her right shoulder is bared, recalling Homer's description in the *Iliad* of 'her marvellous throat, her desirable bosom'.

Much of the West Pediment survived until the explosion of 1687 that ended the Venetian siege of the Acropolis and the attempt by Morosini (soon to be Doge) to remove much of the centre of the composition as spoils for the Serene Republic of Venice. The subject was the struggle between Athena and Poseidon for patronage of the city of Athens and its countryside. From the extreme left-hand corner of the composition comes a reclining youth (right), who probably represents one of the rivers of Athens, either the river Ilissos or the Eridanos. His left hand once rested on the bank of the river; his left thigh may be imagined as still slightly submerged in the shallows. The torsion of his powerful shoulders and chest is superbly captured, while his hips and legs seem as yet not to carry any weight or exhibit any strain – they are supported by water.

(*below*) West Pediment:
GR 1816,0610.99
(*Sculpture* 304, figure A),
Ilissos. Length 1.56 m

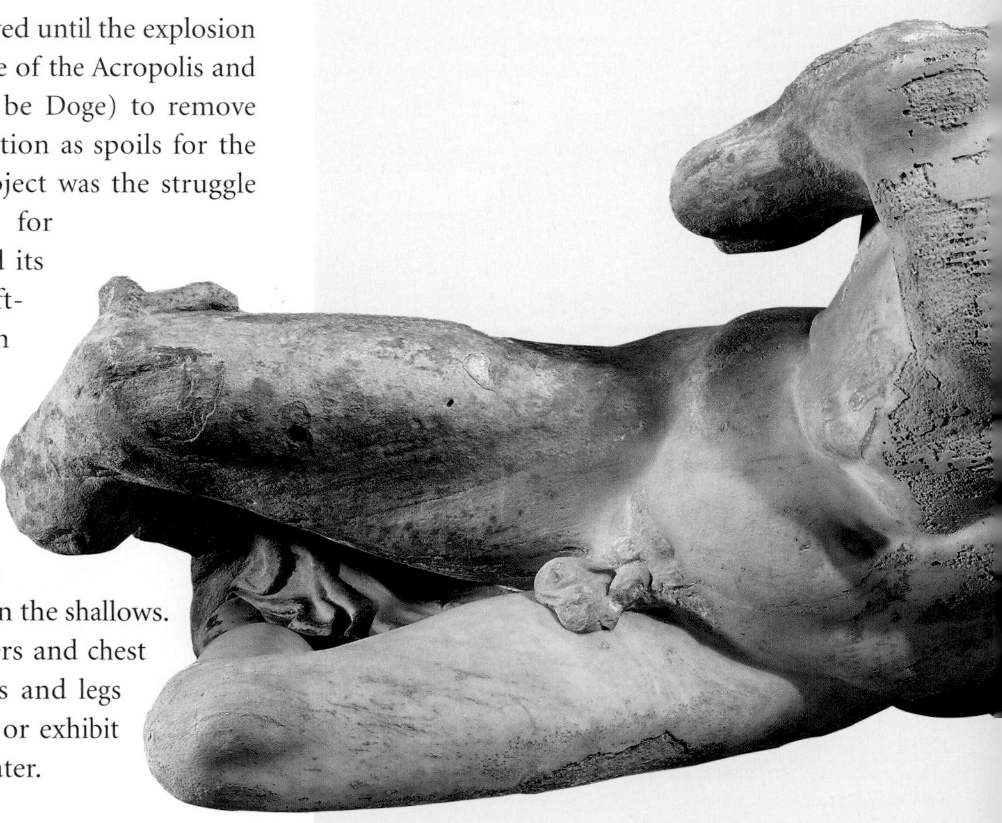

(*below*) West Pediment:
GR 1816,0610.93
(*Sculpture* 304, figure N),
Iris. Ht 1.34 m

(*left*) East Frieze V; GR 1816,0610.19 (*Sculpture* 324, v), Handing over the *peplos*. Ht 1 m

(*right*) North Frieze XLVII: GR 1816,0610.46 (*Sculpture* 325), Preparations for procession. Ht 1 m

From the other side of the pediment comes the fragmentary figure of Iris (p. 119), which was excavated by Lord Elgin's team at the west end of the temple in July 1801. Iris, the winged messenger goddess of Zeus, who heralded the arrival at the contest of Poseidon, is to be thought of as just landing on the rock of the Acropolis. Her short *chiton* is shown clinging to her youthful form, some of the folds or creases in the fabric are suggested by nothing more than a slight incision in the marble, while its ends flutter free. She is the personification of youth, speed and air.

The shallow-relief frieze measured some 160 m in length and is little short of a miracle of carving. The theme is a grand procession making its way from the west end of the temple, in two branches round either long side, to the east end, where the gods are shown seated and a large textile is handed over to the officiating magistrate (above left). It seems most likely that this procession was the central act of the Panathenaia, a festival held in honour of Athena every summer and in

every fourth year with special splendour, which culminated in the presentation of a new richly decorated garment, a *peplos*, for the goddess. A slab from the northwest corner (left) shows the beginning of the procession that runs up the north flank of the temple. A youth holds his nervous steed and turns back to his companions as he adjusts the garland in his hair (once rendered in paint). His body is superbly delineated in only a few centimetres of relief; the turn from profile right leg to frontal left is wonderfully achieved through the three-quarter views of hips, chest and face. Nearer the front of the procession we find animals being led to sacrifice (above). Although most of the animals are docile, one nervous beast tries to rush forward. While the youths turn round in alarm, the heifer in front responds by lifting its head – Keats' 'heifer lowing at the skies'. Here all is tension and bustle, as even the noise and smells of the parade seem to be brought to life; elsewhere there is calm acceptance of the sacrifice to come.

On the north side of the Acropolis, balancing the Parthenon to the south, stands the small, complex temple known today as the Erechtheion. It housed the primitive image of Athena Polias, goddess of the city, and was referred to in antiquity simply as 'the temple in which the ancient statue is'. In addition, however, the temple served a number of other gods and heroes. Here, too, were Athena's olive tree, the marks of Poseidon's trident and the salt spring he created – all connected with the contest between these two great gods for the favour of the city.

It seems likely that the decision to build a new temple was taken in 421/20 BC, during a temporary lull in the Peloponnesian War. The project was interrupted, however, by further hostilities, as is revealed by the report and accounts carved on a marble stele of 409 BC. This date marked the resumption of work on the temple; it was essentially finished by 404 BC when Athens capitulated to Sparta, thus bringing an end to the ruinous Peloponnesian War.

The most unusual feature of this complex temple is the porch at the west end of its south side. It was formed by six statues of women who stand on a low parapet wall and support a coffered ceiling above their heads. It was almost complete in 409 BC and the *korai* (maidens), as they are called in the contemporary report, were already in place – indeed, their style suggests they were carved early in the project. The modern name Caryatid, taken from the first-century BC Roman writer Vitruvius, is incorrect and we should probably think of these *korai* as eternal ministrants of Athena.

The second *kore* from the west was removed by Lord Elgin's men early in 1803 (another was already partially destroyed; the remaining four were removed in 1973 to the Acropolis Museum). She wears a *peplos*, pinned at either shoulder, with a shoulder mantle hanging behind. Like her sisters, one of her hands clutched her drapery, the other may have held a jug or a libation bowl. Her long thick hair is braided round her head with a thick, rope-like tress down her back. Her weight, and that of the building, is taken on her straight right leg; her left leg is flexed, with the drapery clinging to it.

Marble architectural sculpture

Greek, made in Athens, 430–420 BC

From the north porch of the
Erechtheion, Athens

From the Elgin collection

Ht 2.31 m

GR 1816,0610.128 (*Sculpture* 407)

A bearded man sits on a high-backed chair (*klismos*): his name, Xanthippos, is carved on the pediment above. He holds up a shoemaker's last or model of a foot, the symbol of his profession as a shoemaker, and wears a *himation* (mantle) round his waist and over his left shoulder. Gathered about him are the diminutive figures of his wife and daughter. At his knees stands his wife, wearing a hairnet and earrings, the details once added in paint, as well as a thin *chiton* and over it a heavier *himation*. She holds a bird in her right hand and looks up at him, but his little daughter at his side holds her hands up towards the model foot. She is dressed in a simple *peplos* and her father's left hand protectively encompasses her back.

Xanthippos's head and drapery strongly recall figures from the Parthenon frieze and it seems very likely that the sculptor was part of the large team of highly skilled sculptors who were previously employed on the temple. After that great Periclean project had finished there was a change of fashion in respect of the tomb monuments erected in Athens, perhaps connected with the desire by the Athenian people to honour the first casualties of the war with Sparta. Rules against elaborate monuments were relaxed, and the highly skilled sculptors could continue their craft in Athens – some, however, clearly also moved abroad to work for other cities and wealthy patrons (compare **61**).

The erection of such a fine tombstone for a shoemaker is of significance not just as a record of the likely success of the man in his trade but also in the acceptability of such a worker being thus celebrated. Under the democracy every citizen could aspire to such a memorial.

This relief was acquired by Dr Anthony Askew in Athens in 1747, either from the church of the Agii Asomati near the ancient Kerameikos or that of Panagia stin Petra near the river Ilissos to the southwest: in both areas there were ancient cemeteries. It later passed into the collection of Charles Townley, whose collection of sculpture came to the British Museum in 1805.

Marble funerary relief

Greek, made in Athens, 430–420 BC

Said to be from Athens

Formerly in the Askew and Townley collections

Ht 83.7 cm; width 50.7 cm

GR 1805,0703.183 (*Sculpture* 628)

55 THE FRIEZE FROM THE TEMPLE OF ATHENA NIKE

Marble architectural sculpture

Greek, made in Athens about
425–415 BC

From the Temple of Athena Nike,
Athens (south frieze)

From the Elgin collection

Length 1.26 m; ht 45 cm

GR 1816,0610.159 (*Sculpture* 424)

The temple of Athena Nike, goddess of victory, stood on a podium-like bastion built round a rocky spur on the southern side of the approach ramp to the Acropolis of Athens. It was decorated, above the height of the columns, with a sculptured frieze on all four sides.

In the early 430s BC the cult of Athena Nike was reorganized and a priestess elected by lot. It was further decreed that a new temple should be built by the architect Kallikrates (compare **52**).

The east frieze shows a gathering of the gods, perhaps at the birth of Athena. The north and west friezes however, show Greeks fighting Greeks. These may depict scenes from mythological conflicts, such as the Trojan War, but the south frieze depicts a pitched battle between Greeks and Orientals, which can really only be interpreted as the Greeks and the Persians at the battle of Marathon. The

Greeks are shown with helmets, shields and cloaks; the Persians in long garments and trousers, with crescent moon-shaped shields (*peltai*) and bows. The central group is particularly powerful with a Persian on horseback rearing over a crouching Greek who has just slain a Persian footsoldier.

In the seventeenth century this little jewel of a temple was dismantled and incorporated into an Ottoman fortification. Four of the frieze blocks were left visible and vulnerable to abuse until Lord Elgin's men had them removed in 1802. After the birth of the modern Greek state in the 1830s, the temple was reconstructed from the remains on its original base. The temple was again dismantled in 1935–40 and restored, but using iron pins and clamps, which soon corroded, so that in 2002 it had to be restored once again – it is now a testament to the skill and genius of Greek architects and archaeologists.

56 BELL *KRATER* POTTED BY NIKIAS

Pottery wine bowl

Greek, made in Athens, 420–410 BC

Signed by the potter Nikias, attributed to the Nikias Painter

From Greece

Formerly in the Tyszkiewicz collection

Ht 37.5 cm

GR 1898,0716.6

This bell-shaped *krater* (bowl for mixing wine and water) is particularly remarkable as it bears the signature, painted in white around the foot, of Nikias, the son of Hermokles, of the *deme* (ward or district) of Anaphlystos in Athens. This form of name means that Nikias was a citizen.

The scene on the vase is remarkable too. It is connected with a torch race, a relay competition that formed part of the athletic events at several Athenian festivals. In the centre a bearded athlete holds his torch over an altar, while a winged Nike, goddess of victory, flies in to tie a victor's fillet around his arm. Two younger athletes are also present, the one on the left seemingly warming up. To

the right of the altar stands a white-haired man, who might be thought of as the officiating priest.

The torch race was organized by tribe and the inscription on the headband of the older athlete's headgear clearly reads *Antioch…*, for Antiochis. It thus labels the team as that of the tribe Antiochis. However, the racer with the torch is bearded when he should be a youth, which suggests that he is actually Antiochos, the eponymous hero of the tribe. It would be unusual for a priest to have white hair, so this may actually be Prometheus, the god in whose honour one of the most important Athenian torch races was held. Prometheus would be there to witness the lighting of the torch from his altar near the Academy. The race into the city then symbolized his theft of fire from Olympos and his gift of it to mortals. The way he looks upwards might even suggest he was calling on Zeus to witness the reconciliation that was eventually achieved after his terrible punishment at Zeus's hands.

57 THE BASSAI FRIEZE

The Temple of Apollo Epikourios is situated in the wilds of southwestern Arcadia in the Peloponnese at Bassai, high on a rocky ridge of Mount Kotylion. Pausanias explained the cult-title 'Epikourios' by reference to the help that Apollo gave the Arcadians against the plague of 429 BC, but Thucydides stated explicitly that the plague never reached the Peloponnese. It has, therefore, been suggested that Epikourios is connected with *epikouroi*, the name the Arcadian mercenaries gave themselves: they helped both the Athenians and the Messenians against Sparta.

Pausanias recorded that the architect of the temple was Iktinos. It seems most likely that he began the project soon after his work on the Parthenon, perhaps leaving Athens to escape the plague. Work, however, was interrupted in 421 BC when the Spartans sacked nearby Phigaleia, and was not resumed until about 415 BC. The plan and design of the temple, built of local limestone, is very unusual. It

faces north, instead of east, and, although the exterior is in the Doric order, inside there is a continuous Ionic sculpted frieze. Furthermore, there is an exceptional rear chamber, which has a side door to the east and was screened off from the main room by one or more Corinthian columns.

All twenty-three blocks of the interior marble relief frieze have been preserved. Twelve show a battle between Amazons and Greeks, among whom we recognize Herakles (left); ten depict the conflict between the Lapiths and the Centaurs, and one the gods Apollo and Artemis in a chariot drawn by stags. Frustratingly, the precise arrangement is uncertain, but the scenes are filled with drama and action, as the muscular figures lunge and twist amid swirling drapery.

Marble architectural relief sculpture
Greek, made in Arcadia,
c. 415–400 BC
From Bassai, Arcadia

(*left*) Detail of Herakles
GR 1815,1020.18 (*Sculpture* 541)

From the fight with the Centaurs, who became drunk at the marriage of Perithoos, king of the Lapiths, one block is particularly remarkable (below). Two women have taken refuge in a sanctuary, marked by a small cult statue of Artemis. A Centaur has gripped the garment of the woman on her knees at the foot of the statue and is attempting to tear her away from its protection, but a Lapith, perhaps Perithoos, has leapt on to his back. A second woman spreads her arms wide in an extraordinary gesture of despair aimed directly at the viewer.

(*below*) Fight with the Centaurs
Length 1.35 m; ht 64 cm
GR 1815,1020.10 (*Sculpture* 524)

58 *HYDRIA* POTTED BY MEIDIAS

Pottery water jar

Greek, made in Athens, 410–400 BC

Signed by Meidias as potter; attributed to the Meidias Painter

Formerly in the Hamilton collection

Ht 52.2 cm

GR 1772,0320.30* (*Vase* E 224)

This large *hydria* (water jar) was the pride of Sir William Hamilton's collection, acquired by the British Museum in 1772 as the Museum's founding collection of Greek vases. The body of the vase is divided into two zones by an ornamental border. The lower zone depicts Herakles in the Garden of the Hesperides (daughters of the Evening Star), who, together with a dragon, guarded a tree on which grew golden apples, the target of Herakles' final expiatory labour. The key section shows three of the Hesperides around the tree and, to the right, Herakles seated. The mood of the scene, however, is not that of a life or death struggle for immortality, the idea behind Herakles' labours, but rather one of idyllic repose in a garden full of delights, a spirit that invests most of the Meidias Painter's compositions.

The upper zone shows the Dioskouroi, Kastor and Polydeukes, twin sons of Zeus, carrying off the daughters of Leukippos. The two daughters of the king have been surprised, together with their companions, as they gathered flowers in the sanctuary of Aphrodite. The goddess sits beside her altar at the bottom of the scene, while higher up is her stiffly Archaic cult statue. To the left of the scene, Polydeukes has got his girl and is already speeding away in his chariot; to the right, and lower, Kastor is having some difficulty.

The composition, with the chariots pulling away from the centre and the fleeing women, is boldly centrifugal. In addition to the various ground levels in the manner of the famous fifth-century wall-painter Polygnotos, there are grasses, flowers and bay trees, representing the grove of Aphrodite. The richness of the scene is further increased by the use of gilding on the cult statue and for the necklaces and armbands worn by the women, as well as by the decorative quality of the painter's drawing. Just as the great wall-painter Parrhasios was said to have achieved the impression of volume through line, without the use of shadows, the painter of this vase, whom we call the Meidias Painter after the signature of the potter Meidias that it bears, has used lines to suggest volume, the fine folds of garments enveloping and modelling the forms beneath.

59 GOLD EARRINGS FROM ERETRIA

Gold earrings

Made in Greece, probably Athens,
420–400 BC

Said to be from a tomb at Eretria

Ht 5.6 cm; wt 11.4 g

GR 1893,1103.1 (*Jewellery* 1653–4)

(*left*) Ivory stylus: GR 1893,1102.1

Pottery *pyxis*: GR 1893,1101.1
(*Vase* E775)

These splendid gold earrings take the form of a large rosette from which hangs a boat-shaped element with the tiny figure of a Siren on top. The boat-shaped elements are themselves decorated with tightly packed filigree designs, including rows of double spirals. The tiny figures of Sirens are constructed from a die-formed front sheet and a plain back sheet. Suspended from the bottom of the boats are chains ending in cockle-shells made from die-formed front and back halves. The large, two-tiered rosette above has outer convex petals and smaller inner ones that are concave and filled alternately with green and pale blue glass enamel.

The mythical Sirens, part woman, part bird, sang relentlessly to unfortunate sailors who passed by, luring them to their deaths on the rocks below their perch. As magnets for men, they are thus particularly suitable creatures for a woman's (man-made) jewellery. Similarly, the cockle shell was a popular attribute of Aphrodite. Much of the iconography of Greek jewellery is naturally connected with Aphrodite and the world of women.

These earrings are said to have been found in the same tomb as a fine Athenian red-figured *pyxis* (cosmetic box), which shows Aphrodite about to mount her chariot pulled by winged Erotes (the playful companions of Aphrodite), and an ivory stylus or writing implement (left). The tomb may thus have been that of a wealthy and educated woman, perhaps the wife of one of the Athenians sent to Eretria as colonists to keep control of it during the time of the Athenian empire.

60 PAINTED WOODEN PANEL

The preservation of an ancient painting on wood is little short of a miracle. This painted panel was found at Saqqara in Egypt, one of the ancient cemeteries of Memphis. It shows a woman, probably a goddess, seated on an elaborate throne and holding a sceptre.

Underneath a white garment over her legs (and perhaps left arm) she wears a long *chiton* of a slightly greyer hue with yellow folds that may indicate that the fabric was shot with gold thread. Her feet are visible below its hem. On her head is a hairnet formed of grey bands crossed by finer yellow lines (perhaps suggesting gold). She is also dressed in fine jewellery: her necklace and armband are done in yellowish brown, so presumably of gold; the complex earring seems darker with a few grey dots. In addition, she holds a long, black sceptre, striped with white, close to her left side (her hand is bent up near her shoulder, her elbow rests on the throne's arm-rail). In her right hand she probably held a *phiale* (libation bowl). These attributes suggest that she is a goddess, possibly Persephone, the daughter of Demeter.

Her white throne is decorated with red palmettes and, on the back piece, a red star-like decoration – perhaps an ivory veneer and amber inlays. A fringed red cloth is laid over the seat of the throne. Finally, there is a yellowish brown form rising above the arm of the goddess that may be part of the back of another figure. At the top of the panel is written in black letters the end of a name, ...*modkles*, with two dots above the delta. The remaining form of the name and its ending indicate both that it must have been of a male and that it cannot have been of a deity. It was perhaps the painter's name, or rather that of the dedicator.

The panel was found in a rubbish dump between some houses and a religious building that served those who looked after the vast necropolis of Saqqara. Mercenaries from Greece and Caria were based at Memphis from the seventh century BC until the third, and the cemetery at Saqqara has yielded many Carian tombstones of mercenaries and their families. This entirely Greek panel was perhaps a mercenary's offering: it may have shown a frieze of Underworld deities.

Painted wooden panel
Greek, 420–380 BC
From Saqqara, Egypt
Given by the Egypt Exploration Society
Ht 18.4 cm; width 6.8 cm
GR 1975,0728.1

61 THE NEREID MONUMENT

Marble funerary monument
Greek, made at Xanthos,
c. 390–380 BC
From Xanthos (Lycia), Turkey
Excavated by Charles Fellows
Total ht of monument (as restored
in the gallery) c. 10 m
GR 1848,1020.34 etc. (*Sculpture*
850 etc.)

(*below*) Detail from upper podium
frieze: Erbinna

The Nereid Monument, an extraordinarily grand funerary monument in the form of a temple on a high podium, takes its name from the draped female figures that were placed between its columns, on at least three sides. They are traditionally identified as Nereids, the daughters of the sea god Nereus, because of their wind-blown drapery and the marine creatures (dolphin, fish, crab and seabird) beneath their feet, although it is more likely that they are Lycian water nymphs known as Eliyāna.

The tomb was probably built for Erbinna, the last of the great rulers of Xanthos in Lycia (c. 390–370 BC). Originally some fifteen metres high, it once dominated the approach to the walled city of Xanthos. The monument is replete with sculptural decoration: in addition to the nymphs, there are pedimental sculptures, figured groups on the corners of the roof, a frieze above the columns, another around the outside of the central chamber and two tiers on the podium.

In the sculptural programme and style we see not only many deliberate echoes of the great monuments of Classical Athens but also an admixture of both Persian dynastic and local Lycian elements. The sculptors were probably Greek. The larger frieze on the podium seems to show the first Greek expedition against Troy, since one figure is equipped with a lion-skin helmet, identifying him as Herakles, and a few wear oriental dress. The smaller podium frieze shows a siege of a Lycian city on each side. These may record exploits of Erbinna, who is probably to be seen on one slab in the guise of a Persian potentate under his parasol receiving a petition for surrender (left). The frieze around the columns has scenes of combat, hunting and tribute, while the frieze inside the chamber includes a banquet. Finally, the pediments, also carved in relief, show, in the east, Erbinna and his wife enthroned among their family, as if they were Zeus and Hera on Olympos, and, in the west, a battle scene to celebrate the king's prowess as a warrior.

62 VOLUTE *KRATER* BY THE ILIUPERSIS PAINTER

Pottery wine bowl

Greek, made in Apulia *c.* 370–360 BC

Attributed to the Iliupersis Painter

Formerly in the Pizzati and Blayds collections

Ht 68.8 cm

GR 1849,0518.4 (*Vase* F 283)

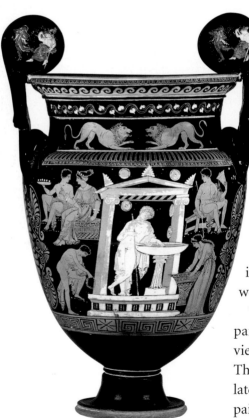

Dominating this large volute-handled *krater* (bowl for mixing wine and water) made in South Italy is the representation of the tomb of a youth. It was no doubt specifically designed for a tomb, where it would probably have been the most important of a number of such red-figured vessels.

Within a temple-like tomb (*naiskos*) of contemporary, grandiose Tarentine form stands the stone (here painted white) statue of a youth. He leans on the rim of an elaborate basin, sorrowfully trailing his fingers in the water and thereby disturbing the reflection of his face in a metaphor of death. On either side of the steps of the monument a youth and a woman approach to place offerings. Further up the vase sit a youth and a woman in intimate conversation, while opposite them sits another youth with his walking stick and *pilos* (travelling hat). They may have been intended as leisured occupants of the Fields of Lethe (Forgetfulness), to which the dead youth was now thought to have passed.

Athenian potters seem to have settled in southern Italy following the establishment of a colony at Thurii in Lucania in 443 BC or soon after. In the last quarter of the century, however, another workshop was established in Apulia, probably at Taranto, which proved particularly successful. Its craftsmen were inspired by elaborate Athenian vessels that continued to be imported. The so-called Iliupersis Painter was the first to introduce funerary iconography to match the specifically funerary function of such monumental works in South Italy.

The sophisticated three-quarter view with a low angle of vision of the upper part of the monument and the seated youth's stool, together with the high viewpoint of the basin, may suggest an attempt to unify perspective viewpoints. The idea of perspective was explored by a number of artists and writers in the later fifth century BC, especially Agatharchos, who used perspective in his scene-painting for dramatic productions.

63 *PELIKE* BY THE MARSYAS PAINTER

Pottery jar

Greek, made in Athens,
360–350 BC

Attributed to the Marsyas Painter

Found at Kamiros, Rhodes

Ht 43.3 cm

GR 1862,0530.1 (*Vase* E 424)

On the swelling surface of this spectacular *pelike* (storage-jar) is shown the mortal Peleus attempting to catch his bride-to-be Thetis, the daughter of the sea god Nereus, as she bathes herself in the company of three of her sisters, the Nereids. In a paradigm of ancient Greek marriage, watched over by the seated figure of Aphrodite and her standing companion, perhaps the goddess Peitho, the reluctant bride resists, changing herself into a serpent, into water and into fire. But Peleus holds tight, and their son, destined to be greater than his father, will be Achilles, the hero of the Trojan War.

Thetis is painted with added white and is shown in a crouching, turning pose that recalls later sculptures of Aphrodite bathing. This twisting action, which occupies space so well, can brilliantly evoke depth and volume even in the two dimensions of painting. Thetis' legs are in profile, although the slightly higher left thigh helps to suggest depth, as does her stomach, but it is her breasts, one virtually in profile, the other nearly frontal, and her head turned round in three-quarter view towards her attacker, that really pull the figure out into the third dimension. The fleeing sister up in the right-hand corner of the scene is of similar design, only the twist goes in the other direction – near-profile legs, three-quarter buttocks, frontal back and, most remarkable of all, three-quarter back view of the head (*profil perdu*). This Nereid's contorted pose and that of Thetis are probably derived from contemporary wall-painting, although elements of both are to be found much earlier, even in vase-painting.

There is much added colour: white for the naked skin of Aphrodite and Eros, blue for the wings of Eros, perhaps green for the garment that Thetis clutches, and gold for Peleus' travelling hat and for the jewellery worn by several of the women.

This vase was a found in the tomb of a woman at Kamiros on Rhodes together with a circular cosmetic box carved from marble and probably once painted, and a pair of superb gold ear-discs with tiny reliefs showing, on one side, Eros playing with a *iynx* (a love charm), and, on the other, very appositely, one of the daughters of Nereus carrying new armour for Thetis' son, Achilles.

64 CHALCEDONY SEALSTONE WITH NIKE, GODDESS OF VICTORY

This beautiful, and unusually large, blue-grey chalcedony sealstone carries the masterfully engraved image of the winged goddess of victory, Nike, who is stooping slightly to arrange a victory monument on a tree stump. Her powerful and exquisitely detailed wings rise above her head, while her mantle slips down around her legs. It is one of the very finest Classical Greek gems known.

Nike's victory monument is a trophy, made up of the captured arms of a vanquished enemy, and includes a helmet of either Chalcidian or Athenian type, as they are conventionally known, with feathers rising from its sides and a cross-ways plume, a linen corselet and under-tunic, a short sword (*kopis*), and a small round shield with central boss. From a lower branch hangs a cloth, while to the lower side of the stump has been nailed a single greave. In addition, a large round shield leans against the tree and next to it is set a spear from which flies a pennant or fillet on which we can make out some letters. These have often taken to be from the name Onatas, who would be the engraver, but the letters do not correspond. The spear and large shield are presumably those of the goddess Nike herself.

The elaborately decorated helmet and the small round shield to be seen on the trophy might suggest that the vanquished was one of the cities or peoples of South Italy, where such equipment was at home (compare **29**). It is certainly quite possible that the gem was carved in that region where the related art of coin die engraving was so highly developed (compare **50**).

The back of the sealstone is domed and plain. The stone has been vertically drilled, probably for a gold rod with a loop at either end, to which would then have been attached a gold chain bracelet or neck cord.

Chalcedony sealstone
Greek, perhaps made in South Italy, *c.* 370–350 BC
Excavated at Kamiros, Rhodes
Ht 3.3 cm
GR 1865,0712.86 (*Gem* 601)

Mausollos, ruler of Caria in southwest Turkey, died in 353 BC and was buried in a huge tomb that came to be counted as one of the Seven Wonders of the World. It also came to be known as the Mausoleum, thus giving its name to all grand funerary monuments.

It stood within a large precinct in the centre of the city and was probably planned before the death of Mausollos and not completed until after the death of his sister and wife, Artemisia, in 351 BC. It was intended not only as a tomb but also as a building sacred to Mausollos' dynasty and the new city of Halikarnassos.

On a huge rectangular podium was set an Ionic colonnade with a stepped pyramidal roof topped by a colossal statue of Mausollos in his chariot. The other chief elements of sculptural decoration were a relief frieze at the top of the podium (left) and numerous sculptures carved fully in the round, on three different scales.

From the series of standing figures of colossal scale, which probably stood on the podium between the columns, comes a figure (right) dressed in a long Carian tunic of thick material with a Greek *himation* (mantle) on top and elaborate Asiatic sandals. His face is particularly distinctive, with wide straight forehead, deep-set and heavily hooded eyes, full lips and thick, drooping moustache, short beard, and heavy mane-like hair. Yet this is no portrait in modern terms, rather a classical, idealized head on to which the sculptor has brilliantly imposed an immediate sense of a personal likeness.

Pliny, writing in the first century AD, preserves the names of four famous Greek sculptors, each said to have been responsible for the sculpture on one side of the tomb – Timotheos (south), Bryaxis (north), Skopas (east) and Leochares (west). The Mausoleum stood intact throughout antiquity and probably collapsed only in the medieval period.

Marble tomb sculpture

Greek, made in Caria, *c.* 350 BC

From the Mausoleum,
Halikarnassos

(*left*) Slab from the podium frieze
(Anatolian marble): Greeks
fighting Amazons

Presented by Sir Stratford Canning

Ht 90 cm

GR 1847,0424.5 (*Sculpture* 1006)

(*right*) So-called Mausollos (head
of Parian marble, body of Pentelic)

Excavated on the north side of the
tomb, by Charles Newton

Ht 3.01 m

GR 1857,1220.232 (*Sculpture*
1000)

66 THE DEMETER OF KNIDOS

This serene statue of Demeter, the goddess of grain and fertility, was the cult image in Demeter's sanctuary at Knidos and perhaps the work of the famous sculptor Leochares.

The goddess sits in a fully frontal pose on a cushioned throne – the back part and the arms have broken off and are lost. Her lower arms and hands are also lost, although one may presume that she once held a libation bowl or a torch. She is wrapped in a heavy mantle, the mass of close, crumpled folds and thick swags concealing her form. This mantle is pulled up over the back of her head like a veil. She is at once majestic, matronly and modest.

Her head, which is turned slightly to the left, was carved separately from the body and socketed into the shoulders. It is more finely worked and highly polished. As for the rest of the statue, the back and, to some extent, the sides are rather roughly finished, suggesting that the Demeter occupied a niche, perhaps with standing figures of her daughter Persephone on one side and Hades on the other.

The sculptor Leochares was active from the 360s to the 320s BC. Statue bases bearing his signature are known from Athens, but we are also told that late in his career he worked for the Macedonian royal family, collaborating with Lysippos on the bronze lion-hunt group for Delphi, and making chryselephantine statues for the family group in the Philippeion at Olympia. His name is also linked with the Mausoleum and there are some connections between the seated Demeter and the colossal family portraits from that monument (compare **65**).

The sanctuary of Demeter at Knidos was laid out at about the same time as the re-founding of the city, around 350 BC. The sanctuary consisted of a long platform terraced into the side of an acropolis, with spectacular views of the city below and the sea beyond. Many votive sculptures were once displayed there and they suggest the worship of other Underworld deities, in particular Hades and Persephone, his part-time consort.

Marble cult statue

Greek, probably made in Halikarnassos, *c.* 350 BC

From Knidos; excavated by Charles Newton

Ht 1.47 m

GR 1859,1226.26 (*Sculpture* 1300)

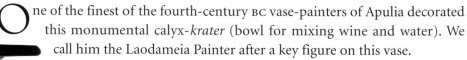

One of the finest of the fourth-century BC vase-painters of Apulia decorated this monumental calyx-*krater* (bowl for mixing wine and water). We call him the Laodameia Painter after a key figure on this vase.

There are two registers of figured decoration, with different but perhaps related scenes. The lower register shows the tragic outcome of the wedding feast of Perithoos, king of the Lapiths, and his bride Laodameia. One of the Centaurs invited to the feast has drunk too much wine (suggested by the overturned bucket between his legs) and seizes Laodameia. She appeals to Perithoos on the left while, from the right, Perithoos' friend, Theseus of Athens, raises his club. On either side other Lapith women flee in terror.

The upper register, however, is much more enigmatic. The centre of the scene is dominated by a large and richly decorated couch complete with a long footstool, very probably a wedding couch. Before it stand two women: on the left a servant with a fan and on the right a woman in a provocative pose, with her hands behind her head, attending to her hair. This group is flanked on the left by an old nurse who raises her arms in horror or dismay. She stands behind a woman with a veil over the back of her head who sits cross-legged and with both hands clutching her knee. To her right, Eros hovers above, holding a garland or fillet. On the extreme right of the scene an old man with stick, *chlamys* (cloak) and boots talks to a woman who puts her hand to her mouth in dismay. All these characters and their actions suggest a scene from a tragic drama. If this were perhaps Euripides' *Perithoos*, we could connect the two registers: the upper scene could then be the preparations of the bride before the fateful feast.

The painting is exceptionally fine, employing eloquent poses and additional colours. There are also attempts at advanced painterly techniques: the shading of the metal vessel on the ground and the perspective views, from above and below, of pieces of furniture. In addition, white dots have been painted in the corners of the eyes. All of this points to contact with monumental painting.

Pottery wine bowl

Greek, made in Apulia,
c. 350–340 BC

Attributed to the Laodameia
Painter

Said to be from Anzi, Apulia

Formerly in the Fittipaldi and
Napoleon I collections

Ht 68.6 cm

GR 1870,0710.2 (*Vase* F 272)

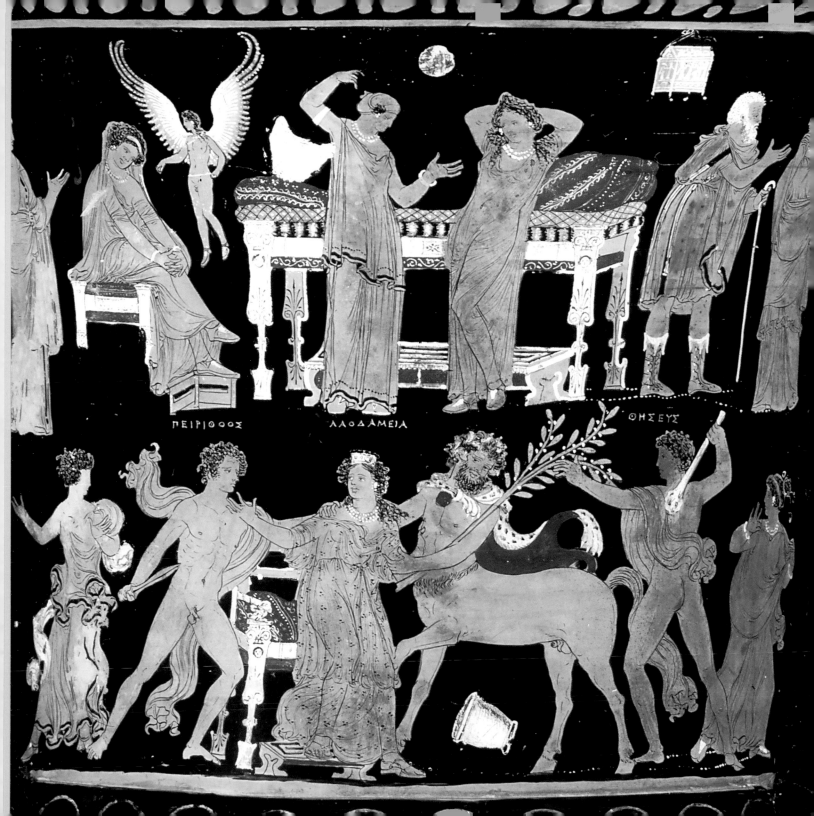

ΠΕΙΡΙΘΟΟΣ   ΛΑΟΔΑΜΕΙΑ   ΘΗΣΕΥΣ

70 PANATHENAIC PRIZE *AMPHORA*

This perfectly preserved *amphora* (jar) was made during the archonship (magistrate) of Niketes at Athens in 332/1 BC as a prize for the winner of the *pankration* contest at the Panathenaic Games. It would have been filled with olive oil pressed from the sacred olive trees, the *moirai*, and stored for presenting as a prize at the Great Panathenaia of 330/29 BC, the gymnastic events of which were held in the new marble stadium built by Lykourgos.

On one side stands Athena (left), facing right, flanked on either side by a column, each topped by a Nike standing on a ship's prow. Next to the right column is an inscription naming Niketes as *archon*. On the other side (right), a *pankration* contest is under way – an all-in fight that knew only two rules: no biting and no eye-gouging. In the centre one athlete has caught the other's head in a tight head-lock, while he pounds the back of his neck. The scene is framed by a vigilant umpire with his special stick and the next contestant.

Although the black-figure technique went out of fashion in the early fifth century BC, it was retained for the Panathenaic prize vases. Here the advanced stylistic details employed by the painter clearly reflect those of contemporary red-figure vase-painting. These details include three-quarter faces, for the umpire and the winning pankratiast, and the pairs of lines for the folds of his *himation* (mantle) that are intended to increase a sense of the shadow in the folds of drapery. There is even a line of shading that runs down from his thigh in an area of especially deep shadow. The representation of Athena, by contrast, is deliberately old-fashioned to emphasize the vessel's traditional function.

Lykourgos, during his tenure of financial control at Athens, built a new marble stadium and completed the building of the Arsenal and ship sheds around the harbour. It was probably the latter, together with the build-up of the Athenian fleet, that is celebrated by the statues with naval connections that appear on the tops of the columns flanking Athena at this time. Here the vivid figure of Nike on a ship's prow might refer to the success of the Athenian admiral Diotimos against the Aegean pirates, as well as being a pun on the archon's name, Niketes, with Nike the goddess of victory.

Pottery oil jar
Greek, made in Athens, 332/1 BC
From Capua
Ht 77.5 cm
GR 1873,0820.370 (*Vase* B 610)

71 PORTRAIT OF ALEXANDER THE GREAT

Alexander the Great (356–323 BC) was all too conscious of the importance of image, and in three great artists he is said to have found just the men to create an image of himself with the right combination of hero and ruler, a man with great aspirations and equally capable of great deeds. These were Lysippos the sculptor, Pyrgoteles the engraver of gems and coin dies, and Apelles the painter.

As Plutarch wrote, it was Lysippos 'who captured exactly those distinctive features ..., namely the poise of the neck turned slightly to the left and the melting glance of the eyes' and only he who 'brought out his real character ... and gave form to his essential excellence. For others, in their eagerness to imitate the turn of his neck and the expressive, liquid glance of his eyes, failed to preserve his manly and leonine quality.'

None of Lysippos' portraits survives, but their essential characteristics, as mentioned by Plutarch, may perhaps be recognized. The London portrait is an example of what might be called a 'divine type', projecting a serene image, transcending all human limitations. This is the Alexander of the Alexander 'legend' that was developed after his death, and the head conveys this image through its dreamy, horizon-less stare. It lacks, perhaps, the leonine quality that Plutarch notes in the earlier, Lysippan portraits. In this, however, it might come closer to the images that were developed by Apelles late in Alexander's life.

The London head is said to have been found at Alexandria, the city founded by Alexander in 331 BC, and the location of his tomb. This city was also the capital of the longest surviving Hellenistic dynasty, the Ptolemies, where Alexander was worshipped as a god and ancestor.

Marble portrait

Greek, perhaps made in Alexandria, Hellenistic, probably late second century BC

Said to be from Alexandria, Egypt

Ht 37 cm

GR 1872,0515.1 (*Sculpture* 1857)

72 THE TEMPLE OF ARTEMIS AT EPHESUS

Marble architectural sculpture
Greek, made at Ephesus,
Hellenistic, about 340–320 BC
Excavated at Ephesus by J.T. Wood
Ht 1.84 m; diam. at base 1.97 m
GR 1872,0803.9 (*Sculpture* 1206)

In 356 BC the great temple of Artemis was deliberately destroyed by fire. The Ephesians began rebuilding on a grander scale, but at the time of Alexander's progress through Ionia the temple was still unfinished and he, mindful of an opportunity for glory, offered to pay for its completion. The Ephesians, however, uncertain of Alexander's future, returned the diplomatic reply that they did not think it proper for one deity to pay for the temple of another.

The columns at the front of the new temple were elaborately decorated with square sculptured pedestals surmounted by a circular sculptured drum. There were perhaps thirty-six such *columnae caelatae*, as Pliny called them, providing a total length of relief sculpture of some five hundred metres, a colossal undertaking.

In 1871 J.T. Wood discovered the temple buried under some six metres of river silt. Almost all but this sculpted column drum had been burnt for lime in the medieval period. Parts of seven figures are preserved. A woman is being escorted by the winged god of Death (Thanatos) and Hermes the messenger god and guide of the dead. Further to the right is a standing woman (left) and a seated male: they may well be Persephone and Hades, gods of the Underworld. A number of identifications have been offered for the woman between Hermes and Thanatos. She may be Alkestis, who offered to die in her husband's stead and was rescued from the Underworld by Herakles, or Eurydike, for whom Orpheus descended to Hades. A third possibility is Iphigenia, who was sacrificed to Artemis by her father Agamemnon in order to secure a favourable wind for the Greek fleet on its way to Troy.

There is much life and pathos in these statuesque figures and a pleasant eclecticism in the style. The soft rounded forms of Thanatos recall the works of Praxiteles, while the muscular physique of Hermes echoes the earlier works of Polykleitos. The drapery of Persephone (?) imitates a statue by Praxiteles' father Kephisodotos, while the upturned head of Hermes might make one think of Skopas, who was credited by Pliny with the carving of one of the columns.

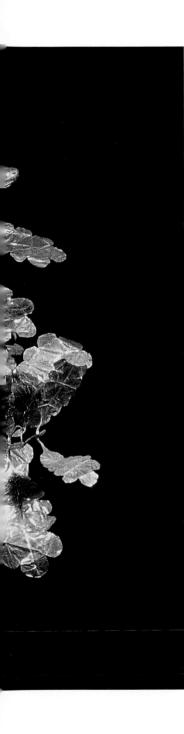

73 GOLD OAK-WREATH

This spectacular gold oak-wreath was said to have been found with a long, undecorated sheet-gold funerary band or belt, in a tomb somewhere on the Dardanelles, the narrow strait that leads from the Aegean to Istanbul and the Black Sea.

The wreath consists of two oak branches made of sheet-gold tubes. At the back, the stems have obliquely cut end-plates with relief circles that imitate the natural internal rings of the stems. At the front, the two branches are held together with a split-pin fastener that has a small bee as its cap. Each branch has six sprays with eight leaves and seven or eight acorns; in addition there are about a dozen single leaves set directly into the stem of each branch. Perched on either branch the jeweller has added the delightful conceit of a cicada made from sheet gold.

Gold wreaths of oak, olive, ivy, vine, laurel and myrtle are known from burials in Macedonia, South Italy, Asia Minor and the northern Black Sea region. The trees and shrubs selected by the Greek jewellers all had their place in Greek cult: the oak was sacred to Zeus, the olive to Athena, the ivy and vine to Dionysos, the laurel to Apollo and the myrtle to Aphrodite. Vast numbers of such wreaths are listed in the inventories of Greek temples and sanctuaries. They are of greatly varying weights (in the Parthenon they ranged from 26 to 300 drachmai, i.e. *c.* 100 g to 1300 g) and could be dedicated by private individuals (men, women and foreigners), by officials at the end of their term of office, and by the state or even by a foreign power. Gold wreaths were worn in festival processions and could also be presented as prizes in competitions.

Gold wreath

Greek, probably made in an East Greek
city, Hellenistic, 350–300 BC

Said to be from the Dardanelles, Turkey

Diam. as restored *c.* 23 cm

GR 1908,0414.1 (*Jewellery* 1628)

74 MONUMENTAL BLACK-GLAZED *KRATER* WITH GILDING

The production of plain, black-glazed vases at Athens began early in the sixth century BC. In the second half of the fourth century BC, however, these humble vessels were elevated to works of extraordinary sophistication. This very large *krater* (bowl for mixing wine and water) is decorated with gilded wreaths, necklaces and earrings and is a masterpiece of potting.

Such large, special black-glaze vessels all have delicate decoration, usually in the form of jewellery, especially necklaces and wreaths, with raised clay that was gilded after firing. Here we see twin gilded sprigs of myrtle that intertwine at the centre and, below, a gilded strap necklace with beechnut pendants. Over the handles are gilded earrings and, on the back, the myrtle wreath is replaced with a flowering grapevine.

The production of these black-glazed vessels coincides with a remarkable nexus of information about potters and their lives. The first is a funerary monument from Athens (about 330 BC) with the following inscription: 'Of those who blend earth, water and fire into one by skill, Bakchios was judged by all Hellas first for natural gifts; and in every contest appointed by the city he won the crown.' We know a Bakchios as a potter of Panathenaic prize *amphorae* in 375/4 BC, as well as a Kittos as potter of such vessels in about 367 BC: they were probably brothers. Finally, there is a decree from Ephesus dating to about 325–320 BC that awards citizenship of Ephesus to two Athenians, Kittos and Bakchios, sons of Bakchios, and their descendants, since they undertook to provide 'the black pottery for the city and the *hydria* for the goddess, at the price established by law'. It is possible, therefore, that these two sons of Bakchios, having been involved in the production of black-glaze vessels, very probably monumental examples with gilding, in the workshop of their father and uncle, later migrated to Ephesus in the 320s BC and continued their craft to great success in their new home.

Pottery wine bowl

Greek, made in Athens, Hellenistic, *c.* 340–320 BC

From Capua, Campania

Ht 68.5 cm

GR 1871,0722.3

75 THE KNIDIAN LION

Marble funerary sculpture

Greek, made at Knidos,
Hellenistic, 330–300 BC

From Knidos

Found by Richard Pullan

Length 3 m; ht 2 m

GR 1859,1226.24 (*Sculpture* 1350)

High on a headland near the Classical city of Knidos once stood this colossal marble lion, looking out to sea. It sat on top of a tall podium-tomb, eighteen metres high, the funerary monument for a wealthy family no doubt of particular importance in the ancient city. The two and a half times life-sized lion is carved from a single huge block of Pentelic marble quarried from Mount Penteli near Athens. The underside was hollowed out to save weight, but it still weighs around seven tons. The eyes were once filled with bronze, coloured stone or glass, or perhaps a combination of all three.

This great lion was discovered in May 1858 by Richard Pullan, architect to Charles Newton's excavation team on the peninsula of Knidos. It had fallen on its face and nearby were scattered the remains of the tomb's superstructure and core. Pullan reconstructed the tomb monument as a temple-like structure resting on a platform some twelve metres square and set within its own enclosure. Inside the structure there was a tall cylindrical chamber topped by a corbelled dome. At the base of this huge chamber radiated twelve passages for individual burials. The exterior was decorated with four Doric half-columns on each side and, above a metope and triglyph frieze, rose a stepped pyramid, which was surmounted by the lion, set on a high rectangular plinth.

The lion is now badly weathered from being so long exposed to the salt winds driving off the sea and, of course, damaged from its fall off the top of the tomb (the lower jaw is lost). Nevertheless, it still has great majesty. The treatment of its thick mane continues to evoke a sense of movement, suggesting perhaps the restless power both of this royal beast and the family that chose it as their monument for eternity.

76 ASKLEPIOS FROM MELOS

Head from a marble cult statue

Greek, probably made on Melos, Hellenistic, late fourth century BC

Found on Melos, Cyclades

Formerly in the collection of the Duc de Blacas

Ht 61 cm

GR 1867,0508.115 (*Sculpture* 550)

This head came from a colossal cult-statue of Asklepios, the god of medicine and healing. It was found in 1828 in the sanctuary of Asklepios on Melos, along with two votive inscriptions to Asklepios and Hygieia (the goddess of good health). In addition, a contemporary account relates that 'not far from the spot where the head was found there was the upper part of the torso … lying above ground, but in a very neglected and mutilated state'.

The head was originally pieced together from three sections of Parian marble (that forming the back of the head is lost). There was once a bronze wreath in the hair (presumably gilded), the leaves originally held in place by means of some 150 bronze stems, set in three rows. When discovered there were still traces of paint in the left eye, marking the iris and pupil.

According to myth, Asklepios was the son of Apollo, educated in the arts of medicine and healing by the wise Centaur Cheiron, part man, part horse. The type of Asklepios head represented by the Melos head is derived from images of Zeus, which in turn ultimately stem from Pheidias' great ivory and gold Zeus at Olympia. Here the face is given greater pathos and sensitivity, thus suggesting perhaps a greater concern for human ills. Stylistically it stands on the boundary between Classical and Hellenistic, pointing on to the baroque expressionism of the Pergamene style, of which the Great Altar of Zeus at Pergamon is the archetype (p. 159).

The head probably came from a standing figure, draped in a thick *himation* (cloak) and with Apollo's sacred snake coiled around the stick on which he leant. The cult of Asklepios was very popular in the Late Classical and Hellenistic periods, with particularly important centres at Epidauros, Knidos, Kos and Athens.

77 THE SANTA EUFEMIA DIADEM

After a night of heavy rain, on 7/8 April 1865, some gold objects were washed clean at the bottom of a two-metre-deep trench dug in an olive grove at the foot of a hill known as Elemosina, near Santa Eufemia in Calabria, South Italy. An inhabitant of Santa Eufemia was the first to spot these glittering things as he was out collecting brushwood. He took them back to two of his fellow villagers, who persuaded him to show them the spot: there they found still more treasures, as well as fragments of bone and pottery. These spoils were then taken to the Estate Keeper employed by Pasquale Francica, the landowner. He knew the value of gold, but not of the objects themselves, and after a further, productive visit to the site, he crushed many of the objects and sold them to the local goldsmith. Some two months later, Francica, the landowner, eventually came to hear of the find and sought to retrieve as much as he could. Sadly most had been melted down and only this splendid diadem and a few other items were saved.

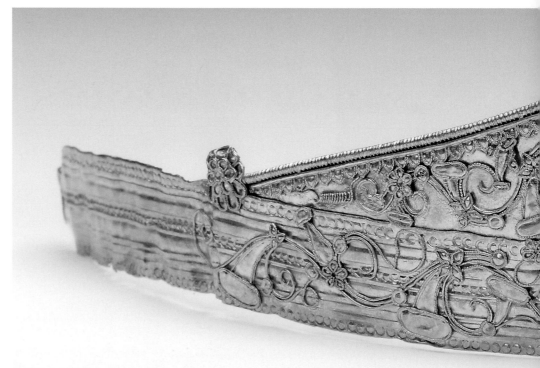

Gold diadem

Greek, perhaps made in Taranto, Hellenistic, *c.* 330–300 BC

Found at Santa Eufemia Lamezia, Calabria

Unbent length 15.0 cm; wt 45.8 g

GR 1896,0616.1 (*Jewellery* 2113)

This beautiful sheet-gold diadem consists of a long band to which has been soldered a central triangular pediment. This pediment and the central part of the strap below it are decorated with symmetrical floral tendrils done with decorative wires, together with trumpet-shaped flowers and small rosettes. In the apex of the pediment is an embossed frontal head, perhaps a deity associated with the abundance of nature. The tiny corkscrew spirals in the two lower corners of the pediment can be matched with similar spirals on other objects from the find, and from elsewhere, to identify a particularly important jeweller's workshop in Taranto in the last decades of the fourth century BC, which is called the Santa Eufemia Workshop after this diadem.

The thickness of the sheet gold and the sturdiness of the whole, together with traces of ancient repairs to a break in the strap, indicate that this exquisite diadem was actually worn in antiquity. The whole group probably came from the tomb of a wealthy woman.

78 THE ABERDEEN HEAD

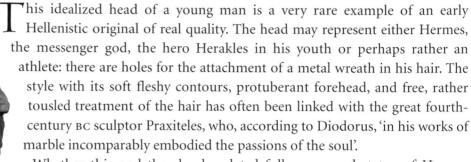

This idealized head of a young man is a very rare example of an early Hellenistic original of real quality. The head may represent either Hermes, the messenger god, the hero Herakles in his youth or perhaps rather an athlete: there are holes for the attachment of a metal wreath in his hair. The style with its soft fleshy contours, protuberant forehead, and free, rather tousled treatment of the hair has often been linked with the great fourth-century BC sculptor Praxiteles, who, according to Diodorus, 'in his works of marble incomparably embodied the passions of the soul'.

Whether this and the closely related fully preserved statue of Hermes holding the infant Dionysos from the temple of Hera at Olympia are original works by Praxiteles himself or perhaps rather by a follower we may never know, but they may certainly stand for his style and his genius. Praxiteles, the son of the sculptor Kephisodotos, was active between about 375 and 335 BC. He was one of the best known of all Classical sculptors, along with Pheidias, Polykleitos and Lysippos. He achieved fame for his marble sculptures and was most celebrated for his female nudes, especially the Aphrodite that was acquired by the citizens of Knidos. His male statues were elegantly, almost languorously posed; his heads psychologically charged.

The Fourth Earl of Aberdeen travelled widely in Greece in 1803 and rivalled Lord Elgin in his interest in Classical antiquity, even excavating for himself in Athens on the Hill of the Nymphs where he discovered the ancient Pnyx, the meeting place of the democratic Athenian assembly. There does not, however, seem to be any certain record of where or when Lord Aberdeen acquired this superb head, but it is tempting to think that it came from Messene, where he also carried out excavations and removed 'a head, well preserved, which was over the gate'.

Marble head

Greek, probably made in the Peloponnese, Hellenistic, *c.* 330–280 BC

Perhaps from Messene

Formerly in the collection of the Earls of Aberdeen

Presented by the Fifth Earl of Aberdeen

Ht 29.9 cm

GR 1862,0817.1 (*Sculpture* 1600)

79 BRONZE PORTRAIT OF A YOUNG LIBYAN

Bronze portrait

Greek, perhaps made at Cyrene or in South Italy, Hellenistic, *c.* 300 BC

From the Temple of Apollo at Cyrene, Libya

Excavated by Captain R. Murdoch Smith and Commander E.A. Porcher

Ht 30.5 cm

GR 1861,1127.13 (*Bronze* 268)

A wonderful bronze head from Cyrene is that of a young man with high prominent cheekbones, short curly hair, a sketchily incised moustache and a thin beard. The modelling is exquisite, both of the cheekbones and of the brow, and even the texture of the skin is somehow suggested. The sculptor has imbued the head with a strong sense of personality that indicates that the head is indeed a portrait. Although it is strongly Hellenized and idealized, there is something African about the fullness of the mouth and the set of the eyes, suggesting that the youth may well have been descended from the Berbers, the native people of Cyrenaica.

The youth's lips were made separately and put in place from the inside. The original reddish tint of the copper would have contrasted with the once gleaming golden bronze colour of the rest of the head. The lips are slightly parted to reveal teeth made from bone. His eyelids and eyelashes were also made separately: the eye sockets were filled with white enamel paste (magnesium carbonate); the inserted pupils are now lost.

This bronze head was found on the marble paving of a Hellenistic temple, nearly four metres below the mosaic floor of the Roman reconstruction of the building, which housed the colossal cult-statue of Apollo (**152**). With it were found charred fragments of a bronze horse's legs, and the remains of gold leaf, indicating perhaps that the sculptures were once partially gilded. It is quite likely that this handsome young man was a victor in an equestrian event, whether chariot-racing or horseback riding. He would thus most probably have been part of the ruling elite.

80 SILVER *PHIALE* FROM ÈZE

Around the interior of this shallow silver libation bowl or *phiale* race a succession of galloping four-horse chariots. Each of the five chariots is driven by a winged Nike, the goddess of victory. They carry a series of deities: Athena wearing a crested helmet and thin *chiton* and holding a shield; Herakles, bearded and with his club; Ares, bearded and with a shield; Hermes with his *kerykeion* (messenger's staff); and Dionysos with his *thyrsos* (ivy-topped fennel staff). In the centre of the bowl is a raised dome or *omphalos*, which helped the user hold the vessel when tipping it to pour a libation to the gods.

The procession of deities in the chariots suggests a narrative idea centred on the apotheosis of the hero Herakles, that is his elevation to Olympos to join the gods. The vessel might, therefore, have been intended as a specific funerary gift or more generally as a wish for the future. Vessels like this were copied by potters in Campania.

We know that silver *phialai* were stored in some sanctuaries, as part of the wealth of the deity and the city. Records of the treasures held in the Parthenon and the Erechtheion on the Athenian Acropolis mention numerous silver *phialai*: indeed it seems that *phialai* weighing 100 drachmas (*c.* 430 g) were regularly kept as reserve bullion, some in the Parthenon being melted down at the end of the Peloponnesian War perhaps to cover the cost entailed by such a crushing defeat.

Silver bowl

Greek, probably made in southern Italy (perhaps Taranto), Hellenistic, *c.* 300 BC

Said to be from Èze (southern France)

Formerly Seillière collection

Diam. 20.6 cm; wt 393.6 g

GR 1891,0627.3 (*Silver* 8)

This bowl was found together with two other fragmentary silver *phialai* at Èze in southern France in about 1870. One of these has a similar chariot scene, the other only floral decoration, but it is clearly of the same date and very probably from the same workshop. It is likely that all three formed part of a hoard buried in a time of crisis. They had perhaps been a diplomatic gift to one of the chieftains in the hinterland beyond the Greek colonial zone of Marseilles.

81 GOLD RIBBON DIADEM FROM MELOS

Some of the greatest masterpieces of Greek jewellery were made for the adornment of the heads of wealthy women. The arms of this delicate and most unusual diadem consist of three long narrow sheets of gold loosely twisted to form ribbons – textile turned to gold.

The central ribbon of the trio is decorated with a rosette on each frontal plane, and each rosette petal was once decorated with coloured glass enamel, alternately green and blue. In the centre of the diadem is a so-called Herakles knot, the bands of the knot decorated with twisted wire ropes and the centre highlighted with a circular garnet. The collars linking the knot and the ribbons are decorated with three rows of scales alternately filled with blue and green enamel.

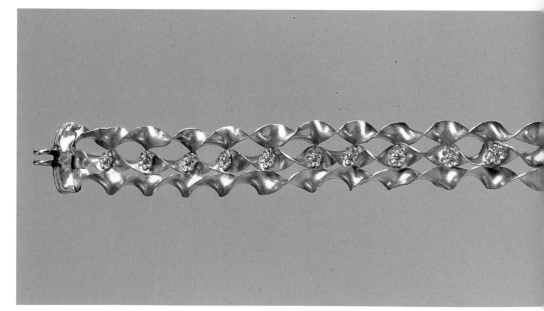

Gold diadem

Greek, perhaps made in northern Greece or South Italy, Hellenistic, c. 300–280 BC

Said to be from Melos

Length 27.9 cm; wt 32.7 g

GR 1872,0604.815 (*Jewellery* 1607)

The idea of a twisted ribbon was also employed, singly, on a small number of bracelets from both Sicily and northern Greece. Other, simpler diadems are known that use plain, flat gold ribbons. The motif of the Herakles knot is frequent in Greek jewellery. The name is derived from the way that the legs of Herakles' lion-skin were tied at his neck, but its precise meaning or significance is unknown, although it is no doubt connected with ideas of joining and uniting, both magically and in marriage. We sometimes find a figure's hair itself tied up in a Herakles knot, as on the Chatsworth head (**51**).

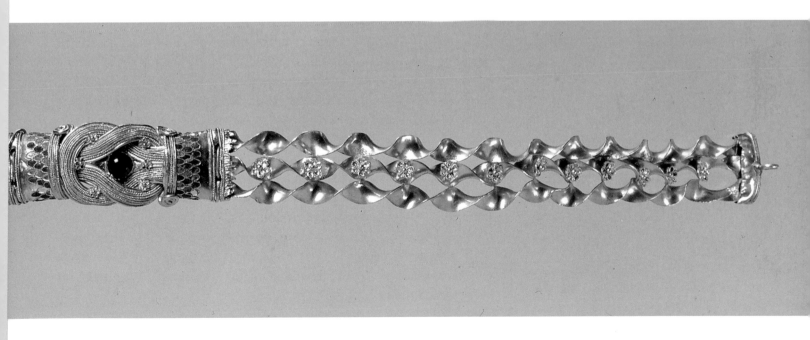

83 PORTRAIT OF PHILETAIROS

(*right*) Engraved sealstone

Greek, probably made at
Pergamon, Hellenistic, perhaps
c. 270–250 BC

Length 2.8 cm; width 2.3 cm

GR 1872,0604.1333 (*Gem* 1184)

(*above*) Photograph of a cast of an
impression from the sealstone

Here the portrait of Philetairos, ruler of Pergamon (*c.* 302–263 BC), has been carved into a chalcedony stone that is mottled with yellow jasper inclusions.

The identity of the man may be recognized by comparison with coins struck by his successor and nephew, Eumenes I (263–241 BC). His strong face and powerful neck combine a lack of classical beauty with a vivid sense of strength and determination. The overall heaviness of the face is no doubt connected with the reality of Philetairos' physical condition – he was a eunuch.

Philetairos was the founder of the Attalid dynasty at Pergamon and turned the city into a great cultural and political centre. Historical poems were written about him and his defeat of the Gauls. In the Hellenistic period it became common for rulers of the separate and fiercely independent Hellenistic kingdoms to have their own images, whether realistic or idealized, engraved on sealstones, as well as struck on coins. The fashion for such portraits seems to have started with Alexander the Great, who is said to have granted the engraver Pyrgoteles a monopoly in portraying the royal image in this medium.

Such gemstones were probably set into rings or pendants and owned by members of the elite, perhaps those within Philetairos' own circle. In the case of this piece, the coloration and complexity of the stone not only give it a real decorative quality, but they also render the image essentially secret, perhaps deliberately so, until it was used as a seal (above left).

84 FAIENCE EROS ON A GOOSE

Faience ritual vessel

Greek, probably made in Alexandria, Egypt, Hellenistic, 275–250 BC

Said to be from Tanagra, Boeotia

Ht 17.8 cm

GR 1875,1110.2 (*Vase* K 1)

This extraordinary object in the form of a plump goose with the little figure of Eros, the winged god of love, riding on its back is the finest faience (glazed frit) vessel to survive from the Hellenistic world.

The chubby-bodied young Eros, a garland in his hair, leans back slightly as he tugs at the cord that passes round the bird's neck in an attempt to get it to move. But the bird turns only its head, perhaps in annoyance at being so abused: its legs are tucked underneath and so it should be thought of as being on dry land.

The details of the goose's feathers are modelled and picked out in brown against the cream background. The neck and head are in an attractive shade of bluish-green that has been given a dappled effect by scraping off some of the glaze. At the bottom of its neck is a decorative circlet, coloured brownish black and yellow to suggest two cords wound together. Eros' damaged wings were once white, brown and yellow. He wears a short brown *chlamys* (cloak) over his shoulders. The cord round the goose's neck is also brown – a section of it once ran between the bird's neck and Eros' left hand.

In addition to a large spout on the back of the goose, the vessel has a small pouring spout under the bird's chest and is, therefore, a *rhyton* for pouring liquid into another vessel, or on to an altar or the ground in some ritual act. Eros was the companion of Aphrodite and the goose was beloved of Aphrodite (see **48**), so the vessel may have been intended for a festival of Aphrodite.

The Greek manufacture of faience, essentially an Egyptian technique, gained in popularity in the Hellenistic period under the Greek Ptolemies. In about 275 BC Ptolemy II Philadelphus (285–246 BC) married his sister Arsinoe II, who was identified with Aphrodite. As a result, it is possible that this vessel was intended for rituals associated with her and Aphrodite. It is said to have been found with a faience *kantharos* at Tanagra in Boeotia. This must have been the tomb of a wealthy person to have had two such unusual pieces. Faience was also exported to the Black Sea, Asia Minor and Italy at this period, but it remained very rare.

85 THE BRAGANZA GOLD BROOCH

The figure of a naked warrior dominates this extraordinary gold brooch. He is equipped with Celtic weapons: helmet, sword and shield are all of Celtic type of the third century BC.

Behind the back of the warrior, the arched bow of the brooch has side panels decorated with spirals and loops that were once surrounded by blue glass enamel; on the top are large curls. Each end of the curved bow takes the form of a dog's head. The hinge or spring at the furthest end of the bow, together with pin, are lost, but when worn the pin would have been held in place by the sliding catch-plate in the form of a boar's head. The long, projecting part of the brooch is formed from two thick wires twisted together that end in the jaws of a dog with raised ears. Beyond a bead with spiral decoration is the forepart of a rearing dog, its front paws resting on the bottom of the warrior's large oval shield.

A group of Iberian fibulae of the same form are of gilded silver and are decorated on the bow and projecting element with figures of warriors on horseback, hunting dogs, and a boar. They have all been found in the Andalucia region of southern Spain. Both style and technology, however, suggest that the Braganza Brooch is not a purely native Iberian piece but rather a hybrid work of a craftsman influenced by or trained in the Hellenistic Greek tradition. In this unique gold version the jeweller has simplified the narrative to a warrior and his hunting dog, which leaps up enthusiastically at his master, while the rest of the hunt motif is merely hinted at by the other dogs' heads and the boar's head.

The Greeks had traded with the Iberians for centuries, even founding colonies. They called the Iberians 'the richest of men'. The warrior brooch, however, is the only witness to a Greek jeweller's journey to the Pillars of Herakles (Straits of Gibraltar) in search of such rich, far western clients and the only such commission by a member of the princely Iberian elite. Since the pin and spring appear to have been deliberately torn off the brooch, it is possible that it was buried as part of a special ritual offering to a deity, rather than in a tomb or as part of a hoard hidden at a time of unrest.

Gold brooch

Greek, probably made in Iberia, Hellenistic, 300–200 BC

Formerly in the collection of the Royal House of Braganza and
Thomas F. Flannery Jr

Purchased with the aid of the Heritage Lottery Fund, the Art Fund,
the Duthie Fund, the British Museum Friends, the Caryatid Fund
and Dr Roy Lennox and Ms Joan Webermann

Length 14 cm; wt 113.76 g

GR 2001,0501.1

86 GOLD-GLASS BOWL FROM CANOSA

This beautiful colourless glass bowl with gold foil decoration inside is both an artistic and a technical masterpiece. It was found together with a number of other remarkable glass vessels, including a second piece made in the same technique, in a tomb at Canosa in northern Apulia.

In order to make the vessel, inner and outer glass bowls had to be produced that fitted inside each other perfectly. The two parts were made by a process which involved slumping the molten glass into or over a mould or form. After cooling, the surfaces were then cold-worked. The cut-out thin gold-sheet decoration was stuck to the inner bowl, using a simple adhesive. The inner bowl was then carefully lowered into place and the whole then gently heated so that the bowls just began to fuse together. The gold leaf decoration trapped between the two glass bowls consists of an eight-petalled rosette at the centre of the base from which rise four large white lotus leaves, alternating with four acanthus leaves and scrolls. A double wave pattern encircles the cup rim above.

A number of these remarkable 'sandwich' gold glass bowls have been found. In addition to the two from this Canosan tomb, others are known from Rhodes, Gordion in Phrygia and Olbia on the coast of the Black Sea. One example is decorated with scenes that suggest a setting on the river Nile, but such Egyptian themes were popular in many parts of the Hellenistic world. It does seem likely, however, that, at least before the Roman period, the great centres of glass production were in the east, whether in Alexandria in Egypt or in some other metropolitan centre on the eastern seaboard of the Mediterranean.

In the description of the Grand Procession of Ptolemy Philadelphus (preserved in the writings of Athenaeus), perhaps of the 270s BC, we hear of two glass vessels described by the adjective *diachrysa* (with gold in it) – these are most probably sandwich glasses like the examples from Canosa. There are many connections between such vessels and those in precious metal (see **89**), but the form and decoration were also imitated by potters and makers of faience.

Glass bowl

Greek, perhaps made in Alexandria or an eastern Mediterranean city, Hellenistic, 210–160 BC

Found in a tomb at Canosa, Apulia (South Italy)

Bequeathed by Felix Slade

Diam. 19.3 cm; ht 11.4 cm

GR 1871,0518.2

87 STATUETTE OF SOKRATES

Sokrates (469–399 BC) is considered to be the intellectual father of modern Western thought. His method of enquiry was to enter into a penetrating discussion with his companions, relentlessly probing the nature of knowledge itself in pursuit of absolute truths. According to both Plato and Xenophon, his pupils, Sokrates' physical appearance was portly, pug-nosed and fleshy-lipped – far from the physical ideal of his day. This satyr-like appearance, however, hid an inner nobility and beauty of spirit. The portraits that survive must all have been made after his death. This Hellenistic marble statuette presents a somewhat idealized, but nevertheless recognizable, vision of the philosopher's face and form, with his large, balding head, his broad nose and heavy lips, and his paunch swelling beneath his mantle or *himation.*

Sokrates' pursuit of true knowledge brought him into direct conflict with the contemporary laws of his native Athens. Accused of *asebia* (impiety), failing to worship the state gods, introducing new religious practices and corrupting the youth, he was brought to trial, convicted and forced to commit suicide by drinking hemlock.

Since this fine statuette is said to have been found at Alexandria, it is not too fanciful to imagine that it once stood on the desk of some scholar in the Great Library of Alexandria, founded by Ptolemy I, the first research institute that allowed scholars of all branches of learning to devote themselves totally to their study. The fashion for such small-scale statuettes in marble, bronze and terracotta is typical of the Hellenistic period and must reflect the spread of culture among the new cosmopolitan bourgeoisie.

Marble statuette
Greek, perhaps made in Alexandria, Hellenistic, 200–100 BC
Said to be from Alexandria, Egypt
Purchased with the aid of the Art Fund
Ht 27.5 cm
GR 1925,1118.1

88 BRONZE PORTRAIT

Bronze portrait

Greek, perhaps made at Pergamon, Hellenistic, second century BC

Said to be from Smyrna

Formerly in the collections of the Earl of Arundel and Dr Richard Mead

Presented by the Earl of Exeter

Ht 29.5 cm

GR 1760,0919.1 (*Bronze* 847)

This very striking bronze portrait was first identified as Homer, but is now more often considered to be the Greek poet and dramatist Sophokles (*c.* 496–406 BC).

It represents a man of middle age, with a thick beard, slightly thinning hair and a keenly severe expression, engendered by a deeply wrinkled brow, taut eyebrows and powerfully modelled eyes and cheeks, and a fine straight nose. His hair is bound by a rolled band. The eyes have been made separately and inserted into the head. The lips were also separately made of copper. One would expect the complete statue to have been partially draped, with the body also probably showing signs of ageing.

This bronze head differs somewhat from the idealized portraits believed to represent the tragedian Sophokles. It has a real sense of a strong intellect, but also of authority. This, together with the fact that the type of diadem worn is more like that seen on the heads of Hellenistic rulers rather than poets or playwrights, makes one consider whether it might really be a Hellenistic creation, perhaps for the Attalid dynasty at Pergamon, and an imaginary portrait of one of the Great Sages – Greek thinkers and politicians. He might even be Thales of Miletos (*c.* 624–546 BC), the famous pre-Socratic philosopher who is often referred to as the father of science but whose political skills and awareness were also very important.

The head was acquired in Smyrna in 1625 by William Petty, the extremely energetic agent sent out by the Earl of Arundel (1585–1646), the first great British collector of antiquities. It was said to have been found in a well there. The reported provenance may well have encouraged the early identification of the head as Homer, who was regularly associated with Smyrna, but would not be out of place either for a figure like Thales.

89 THE BERSU SILVER BOWL

Silver bowl

Greek, perhaps made in Egypt, Hellenistic, 150–100 BC

Said to have been found near the Macedonia/Bulgaria border in 1936

Bequeathed by Dr Anna Maria Bersu, in 'grateful recognition of the help shown to her and her husband in England during the war'

Ht 8.4 cm; diam. 15 cm; wt 415 g

GR 1989,0724.1

The low relief decoration of this extremely fine gilded silver bowl consists of carefully delineated, waving acanthus leaves and large stiff white lotus leaves. These leaves all grow from a double rosette complex under the base. Above is a border of double cable pattern, framed between dots. On the plain rim is a dotted inscription – a complex monogram, perhaps recording the maker's name rather than the owner's. There is also a scratched letter epsilon, probably the numeral 5, perhaps suggesting that this bowl may at some time have been part of a larger group.

The bowl was cast together with much of the design and then worked by chasing and, in the case of the cable pattern, also with punching. The gilding was done with gold leaf, which was heated to improve the bonding. From the same workshop clearly came two bowls now in Munich that are said to have been found in the Egyptian Fayoum; a third bowl, now in Cleveland, should also be a product of this workshop.

There are many interconnections between such bowls in precious metal and those of pottery. The sandwich-glass bowls (see **86**) are also clearly connected. The silver bowls may well have been used in cult events, such as the grand Ptolemaic processions, as well as at the banquets of the rich Hellenistic elite. The weight of the bowl can only be estimated, as it is damaged, but it was probably about 430 g, which is the equivalent of ten *drachmai*.

90 BRONZE HUNTSMAN

Bronze statuette

Greek, perhaps made in northern Greece or Egypt, Hellenistic, 100 BC

Formerly in the collections of Count Collalto (Vienna), G. Fejérváry and F. Pulszky

Ht 47.5 cm

GR 1868,0520.65 (*Bronze* 1453)

This unusually large and splendid bronze statuette represents a youthful hunter, clad only in a short cloak or *chlamys*. He once held a spear with which he thrust downwards at an animal near his feet. His face, hair and heroic torso suggest that he might be Alexander the Great.

The royal hunt, especially the lion hunt, was a way for ancient dynasts to demonstrate their power and heroic courage. It was a common subject in the art of Pharaonic Egypt and of Mesopotamia. From Mesopotamia the motif, perhaps best known to us from the palace of the Assyrian King Assurbanipal at Nimrud, spread to other areas of the Near East, including Achaemenid Persia. Such hunts, however, were often staged for the ruler's benefit.

As with Alexander the Great's portrait sculpture, Lysippos was a key figure in the development of another sculptural genre, the royal hunt. Pliny notes a group by Lysippos, 'Alexander's Hunt, dedicated at Delphi', and a second by his son, Euthykartes, 'Alexander hunting, at Thespiae'. The Delphi group reflected a real hunt in which Alexander deliberately risked his own life, not only to test his courage but also to convince his officers that they should not allow themselves to grow soft following their victory over the Persians. His life was saved by Krateros, who later 'set up a memorial of this hunt at Delphi and had bronze statues made of the lion and the dogs, and also the King locked in combat with the lion, and himself coming to the King's aid. Some of these figures were made by Lysippos, others by Leochares' (Plutarch).

This superb bronze, made up from several separately cast pieces (head, legs, arms, feet), may have come from a reduced-size copy of such a group and originally shown the reckless Alexander on foot struggling with the lion before he was rescued. The scarring and lead drips on the hunter's back make one wonder if the group might have ended up gracing a Roman house only to be buried by the eruption of Mount Vesuvius.

Fired clay group

Greek, probably made at Myrina,
Hellenistic, *c.* 100 BC

Ht 20.5 cm; length 25 cm

GR 1885,0316.1 (*Terracotta* 2274)

91 TERRACOTTA GROUP OF TWO WOMEN

The two women lean closely together as they sit on a couch with finely turned legs, heavy rugs and plump cushions. The intimacy is remarkable and the execution of this terracotta group particularly delicate.

The seemingly younger woman on the left has her legs crossed and rests her feet on low footstool; the taller, and probably older, woman on the right has her feet in their thick-soled sandals on the ground. This older woman, who rests her right hand on the couch, holds her right breast in her left hand. She wears a long, thin *chiton*, dropped on one side to reveal her breast, and a *himation* or mantle that is pulled up over her head and the bun of hair at the back. The younger woman leans forward and toward her companion, her right arm bent across her body, her left resting in her lap – it once held a fan. She also wears a ring with a circular bezel on the fourth finger of her left hand. Resting on the couch between them is what seems to be a folded garment.

The intimacy shown by these two women would have been typical of citizen women at home in the secluded women's quarters (*gynaikeion*), but the fact that the group must have been placed in a tomb suggests that the two women were really intended to be the Underworld deities, Demeter and her daughter Persephone. Demeter would, then, be holding her breast as a sign of her role as a nurturing divinity.

Terracottas were regularly painted with bright colours. On this example they are unusually well preserved. Over a white slip, we find vivid pinks, blues and red, all added after firing. The deep pink, found on the younger woman's *himation*, the older woman's *chiton* and the cushions on the couch, is rose madder, obtained from the root of the plant *rubia tinctorum*. The lighter pink, on the flesh of the women, is a mixture of red ochre and chalk; the blue on the rug is Egyptian blue; and the red on the soles of the older woman's sandals and on the younger woman's *chiton* is red ochre.

92 GREEN STONE HEAD OF A YOUTH

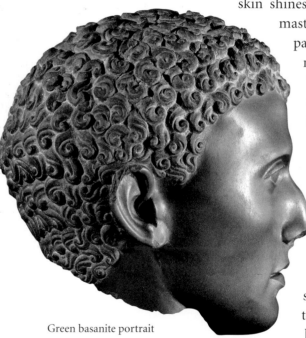

This extraordinary portrait of a youth, probably of southern Egyptian origin and high social rank, comes from a statue that once stood at Alexandria in Egypt. There is no vertical support at the back of the head, something that is typical of Egyptian figures, and it is clear, therefore, that the statue was freestanding and of Greek design.

The face is gently modelled, but the strength of the bone structure beneath the skin shines through. Temples, brow and cheekbones are all prominent and masterfully realized. The nose is hooked and the full lips only slightly parted; the jaw line and chin strong. The hair has been rendered as a mass of tight curls that frame the forehead in a slightly irregular line. The high polish of the face contrasts wonderfully with the matte chiselling of the curls. One feels that any more detail in the carving of the face would have broken the beauty of the finish that reflects every nuance of light and shadow with perfect clarity.

The technique of the sculpture is essentially Egyptian, as the carving and grinding of such a hard stone as basanite was not something Greek artists normally attempted, yet the conception of the whole statue and the realization of the portrait are purely Greek. This combination suggests that the sculptor was either a Hellenized Egyptian or a Greek who learned his craft in an Egyptian workshop. The two artistic traditions, the Greek and the Egyptian, seem normally to have remained separate. The fusion of material, technique and style to be seen in the case of this youth is exceptional both in itself and in its success.

Green basanite portrait

Greek, probably made in Alexandria, Hellenistic, 100–75 BC

From Alexandria

Formerly in the collection of A.C. Harris

Ht 24.5 cm

EA 55253 (AES 1875,0810.13)

93 GODDESS FROM SATALA

In about 1872 a man digging his field at Sadak (ancient Satala) in Turkey struck with his pickaxe this remarkable bronze head as it lay buried under the ground. Nearby he also found a bronze hand. They were all that remained of a colossal statue of a goddess.

The goddess's hair is waved on each side and gathered under a thick fillet in which ornaments were once inserted. The mouth is slightly open and the eyes were once inlaid with stones and glass. The hand found with the head is a left hand holding a swag of drapery. The style, condition and alloy of the bronze indicate that it belonged to the same statue. On the basis of this hand the figure is usually restored on the lines of the famous Aphrodite at Knidos, the left hand holding her drapery at her side. The broad planes and powerful conception of the head, with its somewhat passionless feel, continue the baroque style developed at Pergamon into the first century BC.

There is, of course, no real certainty that the figure was actually Aphrodite. Indeed, the find-spot has led to the suggestion that she might have been revered rather as the Armenian or Iranian goddess Anahita, who was later assimilated with the Greek goddesses Aphrodite and Athena. Her maker, however, was clearly a very talented Greek artist.

Bronze head and hand from a cult statue

Greek, probably made in a Greek city in Turkey, Hellenistic, first century BC

Found at Satala (modern Sadak, northeastern Turkey, once Armenia Minor)

Hand presented by Alessandro Castellani

Ht of head 38.1 cm

GR 1873,0820.1 (*Bronze* 266) and GR 1875,1201.1

5 ANCIENT CYPRUS *c.* 3000–100 BC

Although Cyprus is usually regarded as part of the Greek world, its location in the eastern Mediterranean has always meant that it has as much in common with the Near East and Egypt, if not more. The island lies at the intersection of several Mediterranean trade routes, from Asia Minor to Egypt and North Africa and from Italy and Greece to the Levant, Assyria and Persia. As a result it was a multicultural environment, eclectic and polyglot.

The earliest human habitation dates back at least to 9000 BC (Final Palaeolithic). During the Early Neolithic period there were close connections with the Levant, while levels of settlement increased throughout the succeeding Chalcolithic period, especially in the western part of the island. Copper metallurgy began to be adopted and carved stone ornaments became popular (**94**). The island combined fertile soil with rich sources of copper, which was already being smelted by the Early Bronze Age (*c.* 2300–1900 BC).

A village-based economy had been firmly established by the Middle Bronze Age, and in the Late Bronze Age (*c.* 1650–1050 BC) this led to the rise of several prosperous towns on the south and east coasts. At this time an energetic trade developed with the Near East, Egypt and the Greek world. Indeed, contemporary inscribed clay tablets from el-Amarna in Egypt mention the island of Alashiya, rich in copper. This may be Cyprus, although the identification is not certain. Clearly, however, there were real connections with the east, as technological innovations in the working of bronze (**98**), ivory (**99**) and glass (**97**) reveal.

In the twelfth century BC Cyprus enjoyed renewed prosperity, partly as a result of settlers displaced by upheavals in the Aegean but also because of continued contact with the Near East. Following further waves of destruction in about 1100 BC, there were massive refugee immigrations from the Greek world. In due course, such new settlements turned into the capital cities of the kingdoms of historic Cyprus.

The early first millennium BC was not, as elsewhere, an isolated or impoverished time, since the island maintained external contacts. The arrival of the Phoenicians at Kition in the middle of the ninth century BC perhaps accelerated development. Pottery was imported from Greece and imitated locally, but the traffic was not just one way, for Cyprus was probably instrumental in the revival of iron-working in Greece.

The succeeding centuries saw Cyprus come under various foreign influences, each adding to the range and nature of the island's diversity and commercial reach. In 709 BC Sargon II of Assyria claimed to have brought the island and its city-kingdoms to submission, although this was perhaps achieved by diplomacy rather than military

action. By the middle of the seventh century BC, however, Assyrian power was crumbling and Cyprus regained its independence. During this period the art of large-scale sculpture flourished in both limestone and terracotta, while smaller works in various materials were also produced, often in mixed styles that echoed the ever-changing cultural mix of the island. Pottery similarly reveals a wide range of influences from the East Greek world and from the Levant.

In 545 BC the island was absorbed into the Persian empire. Paradoxically, this brought closer ties with the Greek cities of Asia Minor and through them with Athens. From this period, indeed, we find both Cypriot imitations of Athenian pottery and Athenian imitations of Cypriot shapes for the Cypriot market, while East Greek influences are seen in limestone statues and terracottas. In 499 BC, however, the Greek city-kingdoms joined a short-lived revolt by the East Greek cities. This was brutally suppressed and Cyprus remained under Persian control (see **101**). Although Athens did attempt to free Cyprus (see **51**) and continued cultural contact throughout the fifth century BC, the island remained under Persian rule until early in the fourth century BC, when Evagoras I of Salamis, with the help of Athens, gained control of most of the island. This independence, however, did not last long.

Only when Alexander the Great defeated the Persian empire in 333 BC was Cyprus finally released. After his death, however, the island eventually became a dependency of the Ptolemaic kings of Egypt. This spelled the end of the city-kingdoms of Cyprus, and its distinctive local writing system was rapidly replaced by the Greek alphabet. Now, too, a non-Cypriot *strategos* (governor-general) held sway, aided by a new Greek elite (see **102**). The Ptolemies ruled Cyprus until 58 BC, when it became a Roman province.

94 THE LEVENTIS LADY

This figurine of a heavily stylized naked female was probably carved in the western part of Cyprus in about 3000 BC. The type is usually made of blue-green picrolite, a soft stone found in only one river bed on the entire island of Cyprus, near Erimi in the west of the island, which weathers to black when worn for even a short period against the skin. This relatively large example, however, has been made from dark limestone.

The details of the head are schematically rendered. The hairline, large round eyes, straight nose and projecting ears are clear, but the mouth and chin have been omitted. The neck is very long, the arms outstretched, the breasts rendered as flat circles and the pubic triangle clearly marked. The arrangement of the legs, with thick thighs, narrower lower legs and out-turned stubs for the feet, has been thought to indicate that the figure was seated in a birthing position – the outstretched arms would have been held by helpers at the birth.

The earliest figurines of this type have simple cylindrical bodies with stubby arms and resemble phallic amulets. There seems to have been a development from male figurines to female ones. A certain duality of meaning may well have been retained in the later figurines through the long neck and rounded head, which continue to recall *phalloi*. Such figurines, indeed, seem to have been worn as amulets by both men and women, as is suggested by the discovery of examples in both male and female burials. That they were worn round the neck is indicated by a small number that show just such a figurine attached to a cord. The apparent duality of their form no doubt made them suitable as fertility charms for both sexes.

The natural springs around the famous sanctuary at Palaiopaphos (old Paphos, near Kouklia) in southwestern Cyprus may have been the focus for a fertility cult from the very earliest times, and figurines such as this one may well have been connected with it. Much later the poet Homer recorded that 'smile-loving Aphrodite went to Cyprus, to Paphos, where are her temple and sacrificial altar'. Perhaps the connection between Aphrodite and the area looked back to a much older cult.

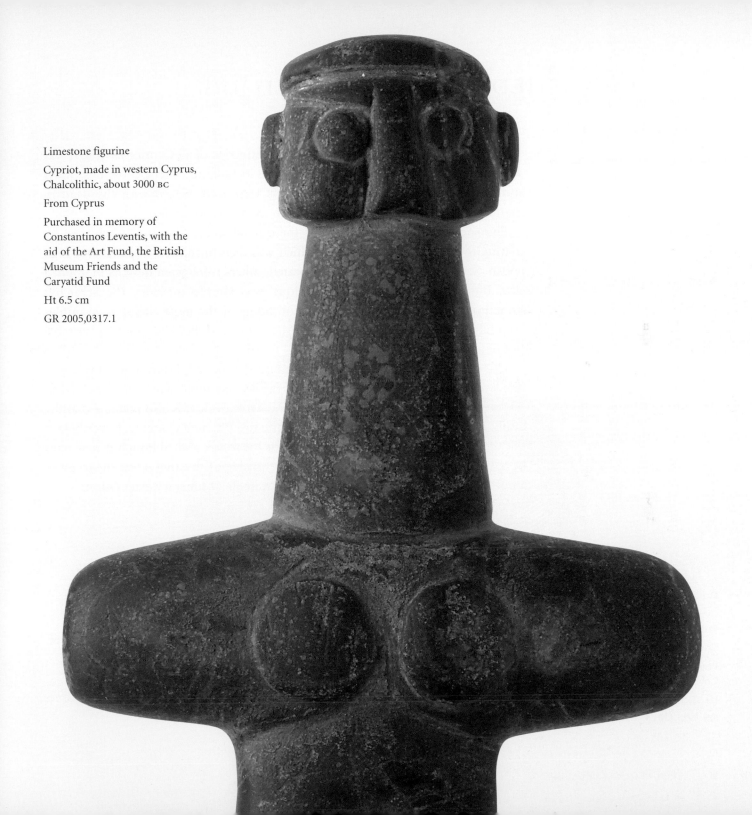

Limestone figurine

Cypriot, made in western Cyprus,
Chalcolithic, about 3000 BC

From Cyprus

Purchased in memory of
Constantinos Leventis, with the
aid of the Art Fund, the British
Museum Friends and the
Caryatid Fund

Ht 6.5 cm

GR 2005,0317.1

White Slip ware juglet

Cypriot, made on Cyprus, Late
Cypriot Bronze Age I, 1650–1450 BC

From Cyprus

Formerly in the Cesnola collection

Ht 16 cm

GR 1876,0909.21 (*Vase* C 255)

Unpainted White Slip I juglet

Cypriot, made on Cyprus, Late
Cypriot Bronze Age IA, 1650–1500 BC

From Cyprus

Formerly in the Cesnola collection

Ht 14.2 cm

GR 1876,0909.22 (*Vase* C 175)

Base Ring ware I juglet

Cypriot, made on Cyprus,
Late Cypriot Bronze Age IA,
1650–1500 BC

Probably from Cyprus

Ht 13.6 cm

GR 1999,0802.1

96 POPPY-SHAPED OPIUM JUGLETS

Alabaster juglet

Cypriot, made on Cyprus, Late Cypriot Bronze Age IA2–B, 1600–1450 BC

From a tomb near Klavdia, Larnaka, Cyprus

Ht 12 cm

GR 1899,1229.93

Sometimes the shape of a vessel imitates its contents – a simple but effective form of self-advertisement. This seems to be the case with a particular form of juglet that was very popular on Late Bronze Age Cyprus.

The alabaster example of such a juglet (far right), so delicately carved that it is translucent, is a masterpiece of line and form, its fine twin-ridged handle echoing the line of the swelling body, its spreading mouth inverting it. The pottery versions of the shape range from the common handmade, brown-slipped and burnished Base Ring juglet with its trumpet-like foot and mouth (second from right), to the rarer White Slip ware example (far left), decorated with lattice-lozenges and lines. The final example shown here (second from left) is, however, exceptionally rare: it is an unpainted white-slipped version made from a very delicate white fabric, and is perhaps itself an imitation of the alabaster version.

The form of these jugs has often been compared with the opium poppy capsule. This has led to the investigation of their possible contents. In the case of the Base Ring version here, the mouth is still sealed and by drilling into the base it has been determined that the contents indeed included suspended opium. The effects of the opium extracted from the *papaver somniferum* were well known in antiquity for it was used as both a sedative and a narcotic, whether taken internally or applied externally. On Minoan Crete it was clearly used to induce a state of ecstasy essential for the performance of some sacred rites, and this was most probably the case on Cyprus too. In addition, however, since many examples of the Cypriot poppy-shaped juglets have been found all round the Mediterranean, it seems possible that the Cypriots were a major exporter of opium.

97 GLASS POMEGRANATE

This glass vessel takes the shape of a pomegranate, with a realistic row of six pointed calyx-tips on top. It is made from clear dark blue glass decorated with trails of light blue, orange and opaque white glass that have been laid on the surface and worked while still soft into festoon patterns.

A number of other vessels of this type have been found on Cyprus, including several from the same rich tomb at Enkomi as that in which this example was found. They belong to a series of core-formed vessels that were probably made on Cyprus as counterparts to the products of Egyptian glasshouses, which were common in the Late Bronze Age. The technology of glass-making was no doubt brought to Cyprus by immigrant craftsmen from Egypt or the Levant. In Greece itself, it would seem craftsmen did no more than reheat ready-made glass ingots and pour the molten glass into small moulds to produce necklace ornaments; they were not introduced to the technology necessary for producing core-formed vessels.

Pomegranates with their multitude of seeds were popular symbols of fertility in many Mediterranean cultures. On Cyprus, as elsewhere, they appear throughout the centuries as pendants on jewellery worn by women. In later Greek cult they were particularly associated with Persephone, daughter of the goddess Demeter, who was carried off by Hades, god of the Underworld. There she ate pomegranate seeds and was as a result confined below the earth for three months of the year. Her return to the world above brought joy to her mother, as spring brought renewed fertility to the land.

Pomegranates began to be cultivated in Mediterranean countries from the middle of the second millennium BC. Their medicinal value in treating stomach ailments, wounds and inflammation was recognized in antiquity.

Tomb 66 at Enkomi, in which this vessel was found, was an underground vault built in finely cut masonry. A large array of luxury grave goods, including gold jewellery, faience vases from Egypt and tableware from the Mycenaean world, was deposited alongside the deceased.

Glass pomegranate vessel

Cypriot, made on Cyprus, Late Cypriot Bronze Age IIC, 1340–1200 BC

From Enkomi, tomb 66 (Miss E.T. Turner Bequest excavations)

Ht 8.5 cm

GR 1897,0401.1052 (*Glass* 14)

98 BRONZE WHEELED VESSEL-STAND

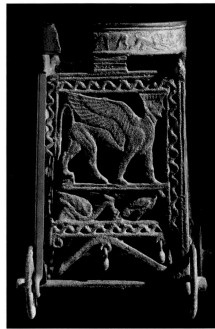

Bronze stand
Cypriot, made on Cyprus, Late
Bronze Age III, 1225–1100 BC
Formerly in the collection of the
Duke of Buccleuch
Bequeathed by Miss H.R. Levy
Ht 31 cm
GR 1946,1017.1

Cypriot bronze box-like stands are masterpieces of metallurgy and this is one of the very few virtually complete examples.

The main decoration is in openwork technique and consists of two registers on each of the four sides. At front and back, as determined by the wheels, are subjects familiar from Greece and Crete. One panel shows a large sphinx wearing a flat cap, the other a lion that grips a long-necked waterbird by the neck. The other two panels have figured scenes that concentrate on aspects of the king's life. On one side he is shown in his chariot, off to a hunt or battle, in Near Eastern manner. On the other side a seated woman, perhaps the king's consort, plays a stringed instrument. She is approached by two figures: the first is another woman playing a similar instrument; the second a serving boy carrying a jug in his right hand and a stemmed cup high in his left. The lower registers on all four sides of the box depict a variety of birds and fishes. The cast ring on the top of the stand bears a frieze of animals in low relief. Similar scenes are to be found on contemporary ivory objects, such as the gaming box from Enkomi (**99**).

The technical skills of casting, hard soldering, hammering, and openwork that were required to construct this elaborate stand were adopted by Cypriot bronze-workers under influence from Greece, Egypt and the Near East. There are a number of such four-sided stands (the variety with wheels is rarer) and they have been found throughout the Mediterranean, even as far west as Italy and Sardinia, where they seem to have been much prized and even imitated.

The stand, which would have supported a cauldron or similar object, was probably used in an elite ceremony, whether in honour of the gods or some visiting dignitaries. The musicians suggest the existence of a bardic tradition similar to that found in the Near Eastern and Greek worlds. Indeed, the legendary Cypriot king Kinyras, 'beloved of Aphrodite', was said to have been a bard, while Homer's son-in-law Stasinos was reputed to have come from Cyprus.

99 IVORY GAMING BOX

Ivory carving flourished on Cyprus in the twelfth century BC, drawing on a rich mixture of influences from Mycenaean Greece, Egypt and the Near East. The ivory itself must have been imported from Egypt or Syria.

This gaming box has its top laid out for a board game: the playing pieces were probably kept inside. The layout is for the 'game of twenty squares', which had a long history: similar gaming boxes were used in Ur in the third millennium BC, and in Egypt of the New Kingdom (*c.* 1550–1070 BC), as well as contemporary Canaan.

The box is beautifully carved on its four sides and must have been a rare and very valuable object. The decoration consists of images of animals and scenes of hunting. On the best preserved of the two long sides a figure, perhaps a king, stands in a chariot aiming his bow. His charioteer controls the pair of horses pulling the light, two-wheeled chariot, while behind him a man on foot wearing a feathered headdress carries an axe, presumably to dispatch any wounded prey. The latter's costume resembles some of the 'Sea Peoples' depicted on Egyptian monuments of this period. A large bird is shown over the horses' backs, while a hunting dog runs beside the horses. At the left end of the panel, a hunter on foot thrusts at a lion with his spear, as a host of other animals flee. One large bull, however, pierced by an arrow, has turned with his head down to charge the oncoming chariot.

The style of this hunting scene, and the similar, though less well preserved scene on the other side, reveals strong influence from the Near East. In contrast, however, the ends of the box are very Mycenaean in style: one shows a pair of bulls sitting quietly in front of a tree, the other two have goats flanking a central tree. The mix of styles, however, is typically Cypriot and no doubt reflects the diverse makeup of the wealthy trading centre of Enkomi.

Ivory box
Cypriot, probably made in Enkomi, Late Bronze Age III, 1200–1100 BC
Excavated at Enkomi, tomb 58 (Miss E.T. Turner Bequest excavations)
Length 29.1 cm
GR 1897,0401.996

100 BICHROME BOWL WITH EROTIC SCENES

Pottery bowl

Cypriot, made on Cyprus,
600–500 BC

Said to be from Achna

Diam. 34.3 cm

GR 1905,0712.1 (*Vase* C 838)

From Achna in eastern Cyprus comes this extraordinary vessel. It is decorated in the Bichrome technique, using red and black, which, along with the White Painted technique, was the main fabric for the pictorial style that became common on Cyprus from the eighth century BC onwards. The scene depicted is unique, as indeed is the shape.

Four pairs of women in long robes sniff flowers, surrounded by trees or tall plants, but in one section there is a riotous love-making scene. On the right a woman, seemingly in a short thin *chiton*, is dancing, one leg kicked up behind her, while in front a diminutive bearded man reaches out as if to lift her skirt. To the left, a bearded man enters a woman from behind; she is bent over resting her hands on the ground. Above these lovers are two further small figures, a bearded man and a naked woman – she is masturbating him.

The shape, with its handles on the side and slightly squashed form, is unparalleled. It perhaps suggests a basket, or even a shell. The frieze of pairs of facing sphinxes on the exterior of the vessel is inverted, indicating perhaps that the vessel was intended to rest on its rim or rather be hung up on a hook, thus keeping the scenes on the interior hidden when not in use.

We know of a sanctuary of Artemis at Achna and another at Kition to the south on the coast, but, although Artemis was a goddess of the countryside and nature, such erotic scenes might be more easily associated with a cult of Aphrodite, whom the Greeks believed to have been of Cypriot origin. Religious orgies and sacred prostitution may have been part of her worship, especially if on Cyprus she was assimilated with the Near Eastern goddesses Astarte and Ishtar, whose worship did involve bawdy songs and even bawdier rituals. The unusual scene on this vase may depict such an exotic religious ceremony, whether in honour of Astarte or Aphrodite.

101 COLOSSAL LIMESTONE STATUE

Colossal limestone statue

Cypriot, made at Idalion, 475–450 BC

From the sanctuary of Apollo, Idalion (excavated by Sir Robert Hamilton Lang)

Ht 1.04 m

GR 1917,0701.233 (*Sculpture* C 154)

This impressive figure of a bearded man wears a long *chiton* with crinkly folds and a plain mantle or *himation* over his left shoulder and round his waist: the contrast between the two materials is beautifully worked out. His right arm is bent forward slightly; his left is within his *himation* but clearly held a laurel spray vertically. On his head he has a wreath of laurel and rosettes. His elaborate corkscrew curls and the square cut to his beard seem to link him with Achaemenid art – Cyprus had been under Persian control since 545 BC – but his dress and facial structure suggest the artistic styles of the Greek world.

The figure was placed in the centre of a series of statues in the front of the main court of a sanctuary, probably dedicated by one of the rulers or chief nobles of Idalion, one of the major city-kingdoms of Cyprus. The sanctuary was dedicated to a male deity who seems to have been identified, at least by the fifth century BC, as both Reshef Mikal, the Canaanite smiting god, and Apollo Amyklos. Early dedications in the sanctuary depict a male figure in a lion-skin, brandishing a club in one hand and a lion in the other. These are reminiscent of both the Phoenician Melqart and the Greek Herakles (and are often described as the 'Cypriot Herakles'), but the figure was probably also identified with Reshef. Apollo Amyklos is no doubt equivalent to Apollo Amyklaios, who in his original cult in Lakonia in Greece clearly had a warlike character. The assimilation of Apollo and Reshef also seems to have occurred at Tamassos by the early fifth century BC (see **51**). In general it was not until the fourth century BC that Greek cults became widespread on the island. The religious mix of Cyprus clearly reflected its complicated cultural history.

The precise identity of this colossal figure is problematic. The laurel wreath and spray, of course, connect him with Apollo, but he is usually supposed to be an important priest or one of the city's elite, rather than the deity himself.

102 PEARL PIN

An exceptional gold-plated bronze pin is topped by the largest pearl to have survived from the ancient world. It was found in the sanctuary of Aphrodite at Paphos. Below the large pearl, itself topped by a smaller one, there are four goat's heads, separated by lotus flowers, springing from acanthus foliage; above are four doves with outspread wings bending forward to drink from the cup of a lotus flower.

The large, egg-like pearl might be associated with the doves below, for according to one version of the birth of Aphrodite doves helped to hatch the miraculous egg that fell from the sky into the river Euphrates. Of course, the pearl could also simply be a reference to the shell in which Aphrodite was believed to have been carried ashore on western Cyprus – and it is a marine pearl.

The sanctuary of Aphrodite was situated at the site of the old city of Paphos, near the modern village of Kouklia (Palaiopaphos). It was the chief religious centre of the island of Cyprus in antiquity, and the cult was famous throughout the ancient Mediterranean world. The earliest remains date from about 1200 BC, but the sanctuary continued uninterrupted throughout the following millennium. In the Roman period, by which time the sanctuary had been remodelled, it was joined by a Sacred Way with the new city of Paphos (Nea Paphos) to the west.

The gold-plated shaft of the pin bears the inscription: 'To the Paphian Aphrodite, Eubola vowed this, the wife of Aratas the kinsman, and Tamisa.' 'Kinsman' is a term for a member of the Ptolemaic court and makes it clear that the two women, perhaps sisters, who dedicated this pin with its exceptionally large pearl to Aphrodite, were members of the rich and aristocratic elite of Hellenistic Paphos, the administrative capital of Cyprus in this period.

Gold-plated pin

Cypriot, probably made at Paphos, Hellenistic, 200–100 BC

Found in the Sanctuary of Aphrodite at Palaiopaphos

Length 17.8 cm

GR 1888,1115.2 (*Jewellery* 1999)

6 EARLY ITALY *c. 3000–100 BC*

Around 5000 BC the first wave of immigrants reached the Italian peninsula. They came from the east and brought with them new skills that enabled the development of agriculture and the creation of more stable communities. The Chalcolithic period (*c.* 3000–2000 BC) saw the beginning of metalworking in the more dynamic north, but a growing isolation in the south (compare **103**). From the middle of the second millennium BC, however, there are signs of both growth and an equalizing of cultural development throughout the peninsula. In the south, on Sicily and the Aeolian Islands, as well as on Sardinia to the west, there was also much contact with the Mycenaeans of Late Bronze Age Greece and, indeed, some Greek traders may well have established enclaves amidst the native Italians.

With the collapse of the Mycenaean world at the end of the Bronze Age, connections were severed. Italy now looked northwards and across the Adriatic Sea. By the ninth century BC, however, eastern contacts were restored, especially through the Greeks and the Phoenicians. The Greek Euboeans landed first on Pithekoussai (Ischia) early in the eighth century BC and established a trading post, presumably with the aim of accessing central Italy's mineral wealth. Their interests soon spread to Cumae on the coast opposite. The Euboeans also settled at Naxos on Sicily in 734 BC and in the following year the most important Greek site, Syracuse, was founded by Corinthians. Other Greek colonies followed, while the Phoenicians also established themselves in western Sicily and on Sardinia.

Both peoples had considerable impact on the native cultures of Italy. On Sicily an intriguing seventh-century gold bowl seems to be a native work with Greek and Phoenician elements (**106**). On Sardinia the so-called Nuragic culture produced a remarkable series of bronze figurines (**104**). The most important people of the Italian peninsula for most of the first half of the first millennium BC, however, artistically and culturally, were the Etruscans. Their lands stretched from the river Arno in the north to the Tiber in the south, but they also sent out colonies south into Campania, north-east into the Po valley and west to Corsica. Their wealth was based on agriculture and rich mineral resources, which were particularly sought after by the Greeks and Phoenicians.

The origin of the Etruscans remains uncertain. The fifth-century BC Greek historian Herodotos claimed that they came from Lydia. Recent DNA analysis seems to support an eastern origin, while the Etruscan language is not Indo-European and resembles a dialect found on the island of Lemnos in the eastern Aegean. Dionysios of Halikarnassos (first

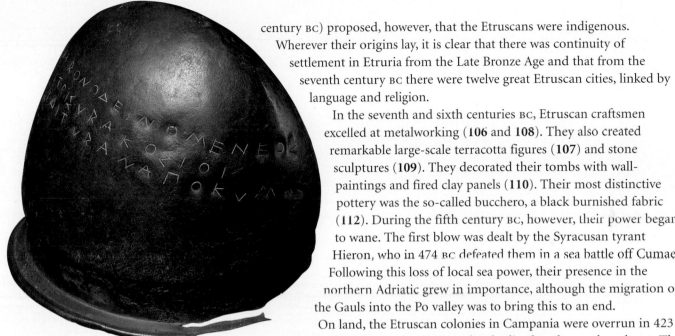

century BC) proposed, however, that the Etruscans were indigenous. Wherever their origins lay, it is clear that there was continuity of settlement in Etruria from the Late Bronze Age and that from the seventh century BC there were twelve great Etruscan cities, linked by language and religion.

In the seventh and sixth centuries BC, Etruscan craftsmen excelled at metalworking (**106** and **108**). They also created remarkable large-scale terracotta figures (**107**) and stone sculptures (**109**). They decorated their tombs with wall-paintings and fired clay panels (**110**). Their most distinctive pottery was the so-called bucchero, a black burnished fabric (**112**). During the fifth century BC, however, their power began to wane. The first blow was dealt by the Syracusan tyrant Hieron, who in 474 BC defeated them in a sea battle off Cumae. Following this loss of local sea power, their presence in the northern Adriatic grew in importance, although the migration of the Gauls into the Po valley was to bring this to an end.

On land, the Etruscan colonies in Campania were overrun in 423 BC by the Samnites, a warrior people who lived to the south and east. The rise of Rome also began to affect the Etruscans: Rome had already absorbed the Latins, who had occupied a large territory to the south of Etruria. In the early fourth century BC Rome expanded further and even encroached on Etruria's southern boundary. Rome also began to press on the Faliscans to the north and east of Rome.

By the end of the fourth century BC it was clear that no single people alone could oppose the Romans, and by about 280 BC Etruria had been subjugated. During the final centuries of the first millennium BC, the Etruscans (**119** and **120**) and the Latins (**121**) continued to be influenced by the Hellenistic Greek world, preserving a degree of artistic independence from Rome, and indeed themselves influenced Roman artistic production. By the beginning of the first century AD, however, all had been submerged in the art of imperial Rome.

Etruscan bronze helmet dedicated by Hieron at Olympia after the battle of Cumae in 474 BC, ht 19 cm (GR 1823,0610.1; *Bronze* 250)

103 GAUDO CULTURE *ASKOS*

A remarkably well preserved and particularly large, burnished pottery *askos* (vessel in the shape of a wineskin) is decorated with incised decoration in the form of lines and herringbone patterns. These probably imitate the stitching on such containers when made from animal skins and organs. It seems that the incised decoration was regularly filled with white, either paint or chalk, to make it more visible (compare **95**).

The vessel is said to have been found with a long flint knife in a tomb at Paestum. Both pieces belong to the Gaudo Culture of the Chalcolithic phase (3000–2000 BC) of Italian prehistory: Gaudo is the name of the cemetery area on the northern outskirts of Paestum in the south of Italy. A Gaudo tomb took the form of a rock-cut chamber with a vertical shaft that was closed by a stone slab. The bodies of the deceased were arranged on the floor or even propped against the walls. Their grave-goods regularly included flint weapons and highly burnished brown vessels, including cups, *askoi* and multiple vessels, but only a few copper objects.

In the Chalcolithic period Italy was very much divided north from south. In the north were rich, varied settlements and much evidence for bronze-working that reveals connections with central Europe. The south, by contrast, was much more pastoral, with less evidence of metalworking.

Pottery vessel

Italic, made in the region of Paestum, 2800–2400 BC

From Paestum, South Italy

Formerly in the collection of Sir William Hamilton

Ht 27 cm

GR 1772,0320.351 (*Vase* H 69)

104 SARDINIAN BRONZE ARCHER

Bronze figurine
Sardinian, made on Sardinia,
perhaps about 800 BC
Ht 17.4 cm
GR 1974,1201.2 (*Bronze* 337)

This bronze figurine, as spare in its modelling as a sculpture by Giacometti, shows an archer in the act of firing his bow. It is a product of a remarkable people native to the island of Sardinia between about 1800 BC and 500 BC.

The archer has a long simple bow with leaf-like terminals. On his left wrist is a guard to protect his skin when loosing the arrow. He has a cylindrical quiver on his back holding a sheaf of arrows; to the right is a short sword with a double pommel, while on the left is a small conical object usually interpreted as a container for the oil necessary to grease the bow. There are also two projecting rings probably to attach the bow when not in use.

He wears a close-fitting knee-length tunic: this may have been the fur *mastruca* recorded by Cicero. Over this, at the front, is a rectangular breastplate that has a fringed border at the neck and, below it, suspended from a bandolier (visible on his back), is a dagger with a gamma-shaped hilt. The archer also wears a pair of leggings or greaves and a helmet with a pair of horns that point forward. The actual breastplates and greaves of these warriors may have been of leather rather than bronze.

This archer belongs to a group of votive figurines of various types: musicians, shepherds, warriors and so-called chieftains. The warriors include archers, spearmen and slingers, but this figurine is unusual in that it shows the warrior in action, rather than just standing holding his weapons. He leans back and seems about to loose his arrow on a high trajectory, typical of the way the long bow was used over the centuries. Other examples of shooting archers are known both from sanctuary and tomb deposits. The identity of such figures, whether gods or mortals, is as uncertain as is their chronology.

The culture responsible for their production has been called Nuragic, after the Sardinian word for the thousands of ruined stone towers that characterize the ancient landscape of the island, the *nuraghi*. The island had important mineral wealth that led many foreign traders there. By the end of the sixth century BC the Carthaginians had taken over most of the island; later it fell to the Romans.

105 ETRUSCAN GOLD BROOCH

Gold brooch

Etruscan, probably made at
Cerveteri, 675–650 BC

From Vulci (perhaps the Ponte
Sodo necropolis, found in 1812),
Etruria

Formerly in the collection of
Thomas Blayds

Length 18.6 cm; wt 712 g

GR 1862,0512.16 (*Jewellery* 1376)

The lions go in two-by-two. On the extended 'foot' of this extraordinary gold brooch or safety pin for holding together clothing is a procession of eight pairs of lions, each with its head turned back over its shoulder; at the tip are the heads of two lions. The bow, made of three curved tubes, is packed with further lions and sphinxes, as well as the heads of lions and horses. Each element is intricately worked in minute detail from gold sheet and further adorned with lines of tiny granulation (minute drops of gold).

Such wonderful jewellery was no doubt made at several Etruscan and other Italic centres. This example, however, may be connected with a number of other

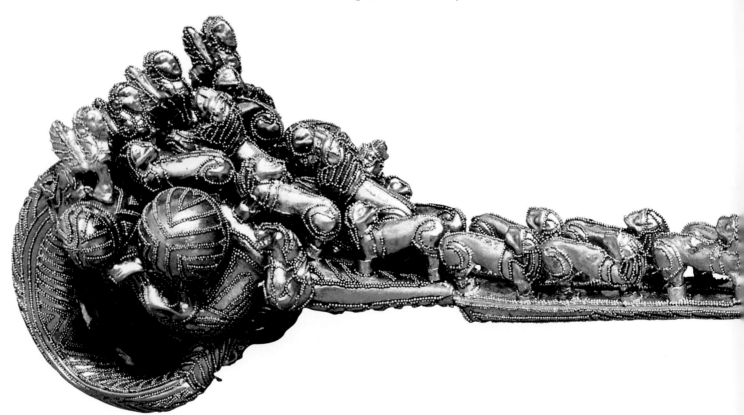

pieces of elaborate jewellery from southern Etruria and was probably the product of a south Etruscan workshop based in Cerveteri. Etruscan goldsmiths took the decorative technique of granulation to greater heights than any other people at any other period – the droplets of gold seem as small as grains of sand.

The brooch had a continuous history in Italy from the Late Bronze Age into Etruscan times, with the Etruscans taking over the forms developed in the ninth to eighth centuries BC. The Etruscans, however, produced luxury versions in gold, like this example, which not only translates the form into precious metal, instead of bronze, but also enlarges and exaggerates it into something quite exceptional.

106 SICILIAN GOLD BOWL

This bowl is said to have been found in a tomb in the village of Sant' Angelo Muxaro, north of Agrigento on Sicily. In 1769 it was reported that there were four bowls, two plain and two decorated with bulls, in the Episcopal Library in Agrigento: they were presumably all found together. Thereafter, however, a church official apparently sold two to an Englishman, as though they were private property. No later sighting has ever been made of the second decorated bowl, or the two plain ones.

The Hamilton bowl is decorated with horned cattle which are rendered in relief by hammering from the outside, using a single stamp, but have had their contours engraved from the inside. Within the circle formed by the hooves of the cattle, there is a broad depressed disk and in the centre of that a low circular wall of sheet gold. This central setting may have held a domed disk of rock crystal or amber. Attached to the setting wall are rings, alternately of plain wire and granulation (tiny droplets of gold). In the plain field between the cattle and the central element a crescent moon has been represented with punched dotting from underneath. The rim of the bowl is ornamented with a twisted, hammered strip.

The decorative scheme of a piece of rock crystal or amber in a setting surrounded by granulation and filigree wire may be paralleled on a number of late eighth-century BC pieces of Greek jewellery from Athens, Crete and even Cumae in Italy. The style is rather stiff: the bulls have straight lines for the ribs, the horns are pointed forward, the hooves are large and there are dots near the major joints. The closest parallels are a pair of rings from the twin-chambered rock-cut tomb, the so-called Prince's Tomb at Sant' Angelo Muxaro. These heavy gold rings are probably from the same workshop as the bowl and, indeed, one might wonder whether the Prince's Tomb was the original find-spot of the bowls. The style of all these pieces suggests the second half of the seventh century BC. They are all prestige objects, no doubt made for a member of the native Sicilian elite by a goldsmith of great skill, whether local or foreign-trained.

Gold bowl

Sicilian or Greek, probably made on Sicily, 650–600 BC

From Sant' Angelo Muxaro, Sicily

Formerly in the Hamilton collection

Diam. 14.6 cm; wt 2893 g

GR 1772,0314.70 (*Jewellery* 1574)

107 ETRUSCAN TERRACOTTA FIGURE

Five remarkable terracotta figures were discovered in the Tomb of the Five Chairs at Cerveteri in 1865. These seated figures were originally enthroned on chairs cut from the rock in a side chamber to an elaborate rock-carved tomb of the second half of the seventh century BC. They are perhaps to be thought of as ancestors who were occasionally visited inside the tomb for the consumption of a ritual meal. There were two tables in front of the chairs and against another wall two empty chairs, presumably for the two deceased occupants of the main chamber, who had their own couches there.

The figures were not found complete, and only three, those of one man and two women, could be restored (one is in the Capitoline Museum, Rome). The women have large hoop earrings, the men flaring hair cut short over the nape of the neck. All of the figures wear a chequered tunic with a red painted border and a red mantle fastened at the shoulder with a large comb-shaped brooch. All have broad bracelets rendered in paint and are barefoot. Each figure's left hand lies flat on his or her lap; the right hands are extended, palm upwards, to receive an offering or food at the ritual banquet they are attending.

The figures with their rounded, overly large heads have considerable vitality despite their rather dumpy, formless bodies. They resemble North Syrian and other eastern prototypes, but the details of the clothing and jewellery are distinctly Etruscan. So too is the way that in such a ritual banquet men and women could participate on equal terms.

Terracotta statue

Etruscan, made in Cerveteri, 625–600 BC

Found in the Tomb of the Five Chairs, Cerveteri, Etruria

Ht 58 cm

GR 1873,0820.638 (*Terracotta* D 219)

108 ETRUSCAN BRONZE BUST

Bronze bust

Etruscan, probably made in Vulci,
600–575 BC

Said to be from the Polledrara
Tomb, Vulci, Etruria

Formerly in the Canino collection

Ht 34 cm

GR 1850,0227.15 (*Bronze* 434)

This remarkable bronze bust of a woman is one of the earliest large-scale Etruscan bronze figures to survive. It was found in the so-called Isis Tomb in the Polledrara cemetery at Vulci (compare **109**). The tomb was rich in imported luxury goods from Egypt and the eastern Mediterranean. These included faience flasks with hieroglyphic inscriptions, painted ostrich eggs, carved tridachna shells and ivory and alabaster objects.

The bust is made of bronze sheet, hammered to shape (the *sphyrelaton* technique) and then riveted together, like some early Greek bronze figures of the seventh century BC. The right hand and the bird, however, were cast and added separately, the bird being covered with gold leaf.

The woman's face is dominated by her wide mouth, large nose and almond-shaped eyes which were once inlaid, perhaps with amber and ivory. Her hair hangs down over her back, while two rather ungainly tubular tresses fall forward beside her breasts. She appears to be naked above the waist, except for an elaborate three-tiered pendant necklace. At her waist is a wide belt, which is decorated with a meander pattern. The top of her skirt, over her hips, carries a low, repoussé relief frieze of monsters derived from Corinthian art. Originally a skirt was attached below this, made of horizontal strips of bronze sheet, nailed to a wooden core and decorated with animals, but only fragments of the skirt survive.

The horned bird in her right hand was originally thought to identify the figure as the Egyptian goddess Isis, which is why the tomb was given its name. However, it is more likely that the figure represents a native Italic deity, perhaps a fertility goddess, as she holds one hand to her breast, like earlier figures from Syria and Asia Minor. A horned bird was sometimes depicted by the early peoples of Italy, and north of the Alps: it presumably had some particular significance, and here served to identify the goddess as a mistress of the animals.

109 ETRUSCAN GYPSUM FIGURE

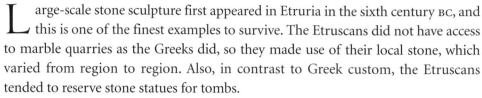

Large-scale stone sculpture first appeared in Etruria in the sixth century BC, and this is one of the finest examples to survive. The Etruscans did not have access to marble quarries as the Greeks did, so they made use of their local stone, which varied from region to region. Also, in contrast to Greek custom, the Etruscans tended to reserve stone statues for tombs.

This half life-sized statue, carved from gypsum, the masterwork of a local craftsman, was probably influenced by Greek prototypes, particularly from Crete and the Peloponnese, but there also seems to be some Phoenician and Near Eastern influence. It is said to have been found in one of the most important tombs of the Etruscan Archaic period, the Polledrara Tomb, sometimes called the Isis Tomb, which was opened in 1839 by Lucien Bonaparte, Prince of Canino, but the contents of which were dispersed after his death (compare **108**).

It is uncertain whether this stiff figure with her large staring eyes, the pupils once perhaps inlaid, represented a deity or the deceased. The object that she once held in her extended left hand may have been a torch, for there are traces of burning down the front of the figure: it would have been lit as part of some ritual associated with the dead. Her right hand is held out with the palm upwards in a gesture of offering.

She wears a long, belted *chiton* with a lower border that was once brightly decorated with a chain of lotus flowers: there are still traces of blue and yellow paint, while her belt preserves some gilding. A long mantle covers her back and hangs down from either shoulder. She wears sandals that were once red.

Gypsum statue
Etruscan, made in Vulci, 570–560 BC
Said to be from the Polledrara Tomb, Vulci, Etruria
Formerly in the Canino collection
Ht 89 cm
GR 1850,0227.1 (*Sculpture* D 1)

110 THE ETRUSCAN BOCCANERA PANELS

Five large painted terracotta panels were found in a tomb in the Banditaccia cemetery of Cerveteri in 1874. The tomb was named the Boccanera Tomb after the two brothers who found it. The three central panels were mounted on the wall at the back of the tomb, and two more panels, showing sphinxes, flanked the inside of the doorway – in Etruria sphinxes were often associated with death and served as guardians of the tomb.

The three central panels seem to represent a Greek myth, the Judgement of Paris. From left to right are shown Hermes, messenger of the gods, approaching Paris with the news of the task he must perform. Next come the three goddesses, Athena, Hera and Aphrodite, from among whom he had to choose the most beautiful. Paris was to select Aphrodite, as she had promised him the most beautiful woman in the world for a wife. Aphrodite is shown here at the rear of the group, her *chiton* already removed and draped over her arm in order to better reveal her shapely legs.

The four women facing to the right, away from the Judgement scene, seem to be from a later moment in the same story. Three carry offerings in the form of vessels (*pyxis* and *alabastra*) while the fourth, on the extreme right, stands with arms akimbo in a very provocative and self-confident pose. She has very long, luxuriant hair and seems to be winding, or provocatively unwinding, a long belt. She is surely Helen, Paris' prize, the gift from Aphrodite that was due to set off a chain of events that began with the Trojan War.

Such terracotta panels were probably also used to decorate the interior walls of temples and even aristocratic residences in Cerveteri, as numerous fragments have been found on the city plateau. There the subjects were taken not only from mythology but also from daily life.

Terracotta panels
Etruscan, made in Cerveteri, 560–550 BC
From the Boccanera Tomb, Cerveteri, Etruria
Ht 98 cm
GR 1889,0410.1 (*Painting* 5c–e)

111 THE EYRE *HYDRIA*

Pottery water jar

Etruscan, made in Cerveteri or Vulci, about 550 BC

Name-piece of the Eyre Painter

Formerly in the collection of Charles Eyre

Purchased with the aid of the Art Fund and the Caryatid Fund

Ht 26 cm

GR 1998,0114.1

This small *hydria* (water jar) is a particularly fine work by a Greek vase-painter, most probably Athenian, who moved to Italy in the middle of the sixth century BC and established a local school of Etruscan pottery there.

The figured scene is dominated by a boy on horseback, who holds a spear, a second horse by his side. He is flanked by two spear-carrying stately, long-haired draped youths who wear richly decorated long *chitons* and mantles, one of whom holds a wreath, the other seems to loose a bird. The scene is completed by a lithe hunting dog, a so-called Laconian hound with white, ivy-leaf shaped markings, that disturbs the two horses, perhaps barking at them, and causes them to restlessly paw the ground. It is the absence of the second rider that perhaps suggests a narrative behind what is otherwise a very conventional representation of the young, wealthy elite of the ancient Greek world. We might imagine that a warrior has been taken to the battlefield by his squire, but the squire has had to return without him. The other youths, his companions, are there to mourn his death. Under each handle is a sphinx: a mythical creature often connected with death. This invisible, but highly charged core marks the vase out as exceptional.

This vase is one of the earliest products of a workshop based in Etruria, either at Cerveteri or at Vulci, that has been misleadingly called Pontic by scholars. Other Greek workshops producing black-figure pottery in the second half of the sixth century BC can be isolated elsewhere in Italy, including a very important one at Reggio (Chalcidian, **31**) and several more minor ones at Taranto, as well as some in Campania and on Sicily.

112 ETRUSCAN BUCCHERO *AMPHORA*

Pottery wine jars

(*right*) Etruscan, made in
Cerveteri, 560–530 BC

Ht 33.6 cm

GR 1984,1023.1

(*left*) Greek, made in Athens,
530–520 BC

Signed by the potter Nikosthenes

From Italy

Ht 33.4 cm

GR 1842,0407.22 (*Vase* B 296)

Early in the seventh century BC a particularly distinctive type of pottery developed in Etruria. Its surface was polished and it was fired in such a way as to make the clay turn greyish black; today this fabric is called 'bucchero'. Early pieces were sometimes very finely potted and thin-walled; later, the fabric became heavier.

A typical but finely made *amphora* (wine jar), probably produced in the Etruscan city of Cerveteri around the middle of the sixth century BC, has panels of impressed relief decoration on the strap handles (right): they show parading felines (below). Elsewhere, on the body of the vessel, there are groups of three lightly dotted lines, sprays that derive from the earlier dotted fans that frequently decorated seventh-century bucchero pottery.

In the second half of the sixth century BC, as the Etruscan market for Athenian pottery was at its height, we find that some Athenian potters tailored their products deliberately to attract Etruscan customers. Such a potter was Nikosthenes and one of his signed works is here shown (left) alongside the Etruscan 'original'. The Athenian potter has decorated his piece with figures and animals in the black-figure technique typical of his city, but the shape is purely Etruscan. It is clear that Nikosthenes was a real entrepreneur of the Athenian Kerameikos and we can see him and his workshop imitate other Etruscan shapes. His success with his Athenian versions of the Etruscan *amphorae* was so great that some Etruscan potters, in turn, began to try to imitate the Athenian works by livening up their own black vessels with added decoration in the form of simple motifs such as stripes, zigzags and rows of circles painted in red, white, blue, green and yellow, after firing.

113 ETRUSCAN SILVER PANELS

Silver panels

Etruscan, made in Etruria,
540–520 BC

From Castel San Mariano, Perugia,
Etruria

Bequeathed by Richard Payne
Knight

Ht 21.5 cm

GR 1824,0420*.1 (*Silver* 3)

Fragments of splendid silver reliefs that once decorated one or two richly ornamented objects were discovered in April 1812 near Castel San Mariano, southwest of Perugia, together with a group of bronze statuettes and reliefs. The breaking or cutting up of some of the finds and the destruction of others make any understanding of the find context very difficult, but it seems likely that they all came from the rich chamber tomb of a leading aristocrat.

The scene on the main panel shows two riders leaping over a fallen figure. It is most probably an excerpt from a horse race, with a fallen competitor. The silver has been overlaid with gilded silver sheets in order to bring out various details. The long-haired figures wear short tunics and long boots. The furthermost rider holds a goad to encourage his horse. The reins of the nearer horse must have been added in silver or gold wire: they were held in the rider's left hand – his right perhaps once held his goad. Both horses have elaborate harnesses and saddle-cloths.

The two other fragments that were found together with this relief show lions attacking a boar. They seem to have decorated a prism-shaped, trough-like object with sloping ends as well as sides. All the fragments were attached by means of gilded silver nails to a wooden backing. One might imagine that they once decorated some elaborate pieces of furniture.

The style of the reliefs suggests influence from East Greek artists, as is often the case with Etruscan art, whether terracotta roof ornaments, terracotta wall panels (**110**) or pottery. Migrant craftsmen, as well as traders, from all over the Greek world had an impact on Etruria, especially through the Greek trading posts on the coast, such as Pyrgi and Gravisca.

114 CAMPANIAN AMBER PENDANT

Amber pendant

Campanian, probably made in
Capua, 500–480 BC

Said to be from Armento, Lucania,
or from Ruvo, Apulia

Formerly in the Pourtalès-Gorgier
collection

Ht 17.3 cm

GR 1865,0103.46 (*Amber* 35)

A large, irregularly shaped piece of red translucent amber has been skilfully and elaborately carved in low relief to reveal a group of a satyr and a maenad, while on the other side there is a bearded snake. The piece was drilled for suspension as an amuletic ornament.

On the right of the main group the satyr seems to kneel, his leg with its horse's hoof bent under him. On the left the maenad, who wears a voluminous *himation* (mantle), has her right leg off the ground and her left drawn up as if for an energetic jump or as part of a dance. She has her right hand on her knee and her left behind the satyr's head. His left arm is raised above his head, the hand perhaps holding the maenad's head; his right arm is outstretched behind her and his hand is just visible behind the furthest edge of her drapery. Between the two figures is a hind, standing on its rear legs, its head turned towards the satyr. This extremely complex group may have been intended to show a satyr molesting a maenad, but the action is not entirely clear, perhaps because of the irregularity of the original piece of amber. Snakes were sometimes held by maenads and used almost as weapons against attacking satyrs.

This is one of the finest Italic ambers to survive. A number of other pieces may be grouped with it and it is likely that all were carved in South Italy, probably in Campania, as there are clear stylistic similarities with the cast figures on pieces like the great bronze *dinos* from the Barone collection (**115**).

Amber, mostly imported from the Baltic Sea to the far north, was particularly prized by the ancients (compare **142**), as it smelled pleasantly of pine, was cool to the touch and exhibited magnetic properties if rubbed. For these reasons it gained a reputation for magical and amuletic powers. It was also believed to have great medicinal value.

Bronze wine bowl

Campanian, probably made in Capua, about 480 BC

From Capua, Campania

Formerly in the Barone collection

Ht 67 cm

GR 1855,0816.1 (*Bronze* 560)

During the period of Etruscan control of Campania, the craft of bronze-working seems to have particularly flourished. From this moment comes a splendid *dinos* (mixing bowl for wine and water) with figured decoration. It was found in the tomb of one of the members of the Capuan aristocracy, together with a fine Athenian red-figured drinking cup.

To the thin hammered lid of this vessel has been attached a lively group of a man and a woman dancing – unless he is actually attempting to abduct her in a ritual enactment of marriage. The image recalls that found on a contemporary amber pendant (see **114**). To the rim of the *dinos* are attached four figures of mounted archers with pointed caps, presumably Amazons, who turn and shoot from the saddles of their proudly prancing horses.

These superb figures are all cast, but around the body of the *dinos* is engraved a long frieze of figures. The subject is Herakles herding cattle, while a figure hangs suspended by his feet from the branch of a tree. This figure has been interpreted as the mythical monster Cacus who lived on one of the hills on the future site of Rome, a very Italian story. Indeed, the Etruscans adopted some Greek heroes, such as Herakles and Odysseus, embellished their stories and embedded them into their own beliefs. Cacus stole some of Herakles' cattle (which he himself had actually taken from the triple-bodied monster Geryon), but Herakles caught and killed him. The remainder of the incised frieze shows funeral games, appropriate for a vessel that held the ashes of the deceased. To match the ornamental rim of the *dinos*, which was cast, there is a cast ring support with three clawed feet.

In addition to fine bronzes and ambers, craftsmen in Campania also produced pottery, in both the black-figure and red-figure techniques, imitating Athenian works.

116 ETRUSCAN BRONZE MIRROR

The back of this bronze mirror is decorated in low relief with the scene of a man grasping a woman round the waist and lifting her up, a motif representing abduction. The quality of the cast relief is wonderful, and the minute cold-worked details are done with great delicacy and precision.

The man wears a lion-skin tied at his neck and covering his back; he grasps a club in his right hand, while a bow and quiver are to be seen in the field. An incised inscription names him as Herecele, the Etruscan for Herakles, the Greek hero. The woman wears a thin *chiton* and a mantle: she is named Mlacuch. We know nothing from our ancient literary sources of Herecele (or Herakles) abducting such a woman; nor is the name Mlacuch otherwise recorded. Herakles, like many Greek heroes, was certainly noted for having carried off women on occasion. In this case one might think that it was a local myth about Herecele, who had several sanctuaries in Etruria (a very rich one in the cemetery area of Cerveteri), carrying off a local woman (compare **115**). There remains the suggestion that Mlacuch was actually the name of the owner of the mirror, and so of the deceased in whose tomb it was found. Abduction symbolized not only marriage but also death.

The palmette border has inlaid silver linking details; there is also a silver band round the rim. The other side of the mirror was smooth and highly polished to enable the owner's reflection to be seen, although it would have had a somewhat yellowish hue. The tang at the bottom of the mirror was for insertion into a bone or ivory handle.

Most Etruscan mirrors bear incised decoration. Subjects range from the domestic to the mythological; many carry the name of their owner, suggesting they were given as presents, perhaps on marriage. There are only some half a dozen examples known with the design cast in low relief and with silver inlays. All these heavy and elaborately decorated pieces were probably produced in the Etruscan city of Vulci.

This mirror was said to have been found with a group of fine gold jewellery (earrings, necklace and ring) at 'Atri in the Abruzzi', but this may have been a mistake for Adria in the Po Valley, where there was a strong Etruscan presence.

Etruscan, probably made in Vulci, 500–475 BC

Said to be from Atri, but perhaps from Adria

Formerly in the collection of Sir William Hamilton

Diam. 18 cm

GR 1772,0304.4 (*Bronze* 542)

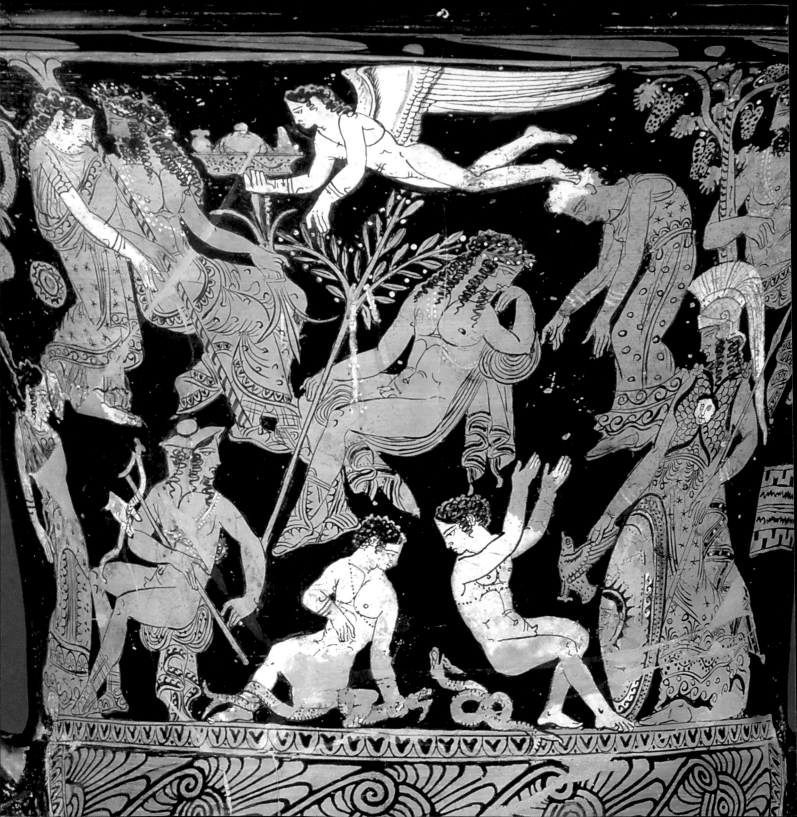

117 FALISCAN RED-FIGURED *KRATER*

Pottery vessel

Faliscan, made in Falerii,
390–370 BC

Attributed to the Nazzano Painter

Ht 50 cm

GR 1888,1015.13 (*Vase* F 479)

Itself an impressive feat of potting, this monumental calyx-*krater* (bowl for mixing wine and water) is elaborately decorated in the red-figure technique. It is quite likely that the workshop which created this and a number of other monumental pieces, very much in Athenian style as well as technique, was established by one or more Athenian migrant potters to Falerii in central Italy.

The scene on the front of the vase is particularly elaborate and the figures are arranged up and down the field in the manner that we hear from our literary sources was used by the painters of panels and walls from shortly before the middle of the fifth century BC. Apollo is seated in the centre, left hand to his chin in a contemplative pose, and with a laurel staff in his right. Below him the infant Herakles strangles one of the snakes sent by Hera (in revenge for Zeus' infidelity with Alkmene, compare **68**), while his mortal half-brother, Iphikles, appeals to a white-haired nurse above for help. To the right stands armed Athena, Herakles' protectress, with her owl. Above her sits Dionysos, god of wine, with his vine staff and large *kantharos*, accompanied by a maenad. Zeus sits up on the left of the scene holding a striped sceptre, with perhaps Alkmene by his side, as two Erotes hover about the pair. On the lower left sits Hermes with his traveller's hat and messenger's staff (*kerykeion*), accompanied by Artemis with her bow.

Athenian red-figured pottery had proved a massive export success to Etruria and Campania in the fifth century BC and so, at the end of the century, when perhaps life in Athens had become difficult following the humiliating defeat in the Peloponnesian War and the consequent deprivations, emigration westwards seemed an attractive prospect to some potters. The move to Falerii, the capital of the Faliscans, probably happened in about 400 BC. The workshop established there was clearly a considerable success, exporting its wares throughout most of Etruria, as well as to Rome. It lasted for most of the fourth century BC, although, after the first generation or so, the technique declined and stylistic links with the home city gradually lapsed.

118 ETRUSCAN LION VASE

This exquisite terracotta vessel in the form of a crouching lion is some sort of a *rhyton*, the liquid being poured in through the flaring spout beside the handle, and out through the hole in the animal's mouth. It was probably made at Chiusi, an important city in northern Etruria, where animal-shaped vessels and those in the form of human heads were popular in the fourth and early third centuries BC.

The body and legs are painted with a stipple effect that well suggests the texture of the lion's skin. The face, mane and paws have been given an added coating of white slip, over which further colours were perhaps painted, although only a yellow can now be made out on the face and paws. The lion's tail, which is tightly wrapped round its haunch, bears the remains of a bright red colour, probably cinnabar. The unnatural dog-like pose of the lion may be compared with the fine early Corinthian bronze lioness from Corfu (**25**) or indeed the lions that stood guard around the Nereid Monument (compare **61**).

The function of this extraordinary vessel is uncertain. It may, like the vessel in the form of an actor on an altar (**82**), have served to pour oil or some spicy sauce on food at the banquet, whether in life or after death. It was found in the famous François Tomb, named after its excavator Alessandro François, at Vulci in 1857. This was a large chamber-tomb complex, with some thirteen chambers in all, and was decorated with remarkable scenes from the history of Etruria and Rome. The lion was probably found in either Chamber IV or VI.

Pottery vessel

Etruscan, probably made at Chiusi, 340–300 BC

Attributed to the Deer Workshop, near the Clusium Group

Found in the François Tomb, Vulci, Etruria

Ht 15.3 cm; length 17.7 cm

GR 1873,0820.269 (*Vase* E 803)

119 ETRUSCAN DRINKING BOWL

The design on the interior of this pottery bowl is painted entirely in added colour. A naked youth sits on a rock, over which is draped his cloak. He holds two spears in his right hand, while supporting his head on the palm of his left hand, as he stares up into space, either deep in thought or full of sorrow and despair. His faithful dog is at his side and seems to look up at him in sympathy.

The extraordinary use of shading and highlights on the limbs and body is particularly successful. It shows what fourth-century wall- and panel-painting may have been like. Human figures are rarely painted on vases after the end of the fourth century BC: this example may, therefore, depend directly on some famous wall-painting. There is actually nothing essentially Etruscan in the style so the painter of this vase, and the small group of vases that go with it, could actually have been trained in South Italy.

The figure is most probably an excerpt from a larger composition, but there is not enough information to decide who the youth might be. He could be the young Paris struggling to decide who is the fairest goddess among Hera, Athena and Aphrodite (compare **110**), or Perithoos trapped in the Underworld, or simply some love-struck hunter. Equally, however, it could have been intended to have a funerary meaning – the dead young hunter mourning the loss of his life.

Pottery bowl

Etruscan, perhaps made in Volterra, 300–280 BC

Attributed to the Hesse Group

Formerly in the collections of Pizzati and Thomas Blayds

Presented by Chambers Hall

Diam. 18.5 cm

GR 1855,0306.16 (*Vase* F 542)

This monumental, brightly painted terracotta sarcophagus consists of the life-size statue of a woman reclining on a chest-like couch decorated with an architectural frieze of triglyphs and rosettes and equipped with a mattress and a pillow. Into the edge of the mattress was cut, before firing, her name, Seianti Hanunia Tlesnasa.

Seianti wears a high-belted, sleeveless white *chiton* and a purple-bordered mantle, which she has lifted away from the side of her head in a bridal gesture. As she examines her reflection in a circular, lidded mirror held in her left hand, her attention seems to be caught by someone entering the room (or tomb). She is decked out in all her finery – diadem, snake bracelets, armlets, elaborate strap-necklace with pointed pendants, earrings and finger rings.

The lid of the sarcophagus and the figure of Seianti herself were constructed in two halves, presumably to aid removal from the kiln and placement in the tomb. The figure and chest were once brightly painted over a white slip. There are remains of a bluish green for the bronze mirror, yellow for the gold jewellery and the triglyphs; pink for her flesh, reddish purple for her hair, the cushion and the decoration of the mattress, and bright pink for the borders on her drapery and for the large rosettes on the side of the chest.

Seianti's sarcophagus was found in 1886, by itself in a small rock-cut chamber tomb at Poggio Cantarello, near Chiusi in Etruria. From iron nails on the interior of the walls of the chamber had hung five silver objects, one of which was still hanging from its nail when the tomb was discovered. The silver objects (mirror, scent-bottle, jewellery box and scraper), now lost, all seem to have been specially made for the tomb, not for regular use. Inside Seianti's sarcophagus were the well-preserved skeletal remains of a woman about 1.52 m tall. Her teeth indicate that she was probably about fifty to fifty-five years old when she died. Her rather more youthful portrait in terracotta is typical of the idealized representation of the dead in later Etruscan art, when it was heavily influenced by the Hellenistic

Terracotta sarcophagus

Etruscan, made in Chiusi, 200–180 BC

From Poggio Cantarello, near Chiusi, Etruria

Length 1.83 m

GR 1887,0402.1 (*Terracotta* D 786)

world. Her bones reveal also that she had in life been something of a horsewoman and had suffered an accident, perhaps being crushed under her horse. Her given name was Hanunia, her family name Seianti, and the family name of her husband Tlesna.

The sarcophagus of a woman of the same clan as Seianti Hanunia, one Larthia Seianti, has also been found. It was clearly made in the same workshop, although probably slightly later in date. It contained a coin, the ritual offering to Charon, the ferryman of the dead, dated between 189 and 180 BC.

121 LATIAN BRONZE FIGURE

Bronze figure

Latian, perhaps made in Praeneste, c. 200–100 BC

Said to be from the Sanctuary of Diana, Lake Nemi, Latium

Bequeathed by William Waldorf Astor, First Viscount Astor

Ht 97 cm

GR 1920,0612.1

Near the sanctuary of Diana on the shore of Lake Nemi in the Alban Hills, southeast of Rome, is said to have been found this half life-sized bronze figure together with seven smaller statuettes of draped women and youths, each holding a libation bowl and a small incense box.

The sanctuary of Diana Nemorensis was famous in antiquity and the remains of a temple and offerings dating from around 700 BC down to the Roman Imperial period have been found there. The figures from this sanctuary are thought to be representations of priests and priestesses of Diana. They are typical of the votive statuettes found in Etruria and Latium between the third and first centuries BC.

The larger young woman, however, is rather different and not simply because of the fact that her size has led the craftsman to assemble her from nine separately cast pieces. She wears a long Hellenistic *chiton* with a high belt and a mantle draped around her lower body. She has a torque around her neck and a bracelet on either wrist. Her small head and slim, willowy build, and her strong *contrapposto* pose, with weight on one leg and hip thrust out, are typical of figures of the later Hellenistic period. Unlike the smaller figures, however, she has none of the usual attributes. Her pose and the way that her arms are arranged suggest that she might actually have been shown spinning wool. There is a small hole at her left elbow that might have been where a separately made distaff could have been inserted, tucked between elbow and hip. She would then have been holding its wool-covered end lightly in her fingers. A thin bronze wire representing the thread could have passed across to her right hand from which it would have continued down to a weighted spindle (compare **45**).

She might, thus, have been intended to represent the ideal of Roman matronhood, perhaps even Diana herself in such a guise, but the possibility that she represents Clotho, the Fate who spun the thread of all life, should not be excluded.

7 ROME AND ITS EMPIRE

c. 100 BC–AD 300

Occupation of the hills of Rome goes back to about 1000 BC, although tradition records the city as having been founded only in 753 BC. In 509 BC a monarchy was replaced by a republic. By the middle of the third century BC Rome had absorbed all immediate neighbours, as well as Greek Taranto in the south, and had thus become the dominant power on the Italian peninsula. In the second half of the century the Romans twice fought their deadly enemy, Carthage, and won Sicily, Corsica, Sardinia and even Spain. The second century BC saw them turn eastwards, annexing all of Greece by 146 BC, the same year in which Carthage was finally destroyed. Rome had become master of the Mediterranean.

Rome's governing magistracies were the subject of annual competition between a limited number of wealthy families. The resultant rivalries flared in the first century BC into a series of civil wars between the great men of the age – Sulla, Pompey, Crassus, Julius Caesar, Mark Antony and Octavian. These generals, however, also added lands: in 63 BC Pompey defeated the Seleucids, thus completing the absorption of the Hellenistic east, while in 56–51 BC Caesar took Roman culture north as far as Britain. These incessant power struggles were finally ended when Octavian defeated Mark Antony at Actium in 31 BC, a defeat which brought with it the province of Egypt.

With Octavian's victory and his assumption of a new title, Augustus, came a propagandist programme for the rebuilding and adornment of Rome. He also created a new public image of himself (**127**). Augustus' successors (AD 14–68), the Julio-Claudians Tiberius, Caligula, Claudius and Nero, recognized the need for a sense of continuity which included artistic style; indeed, it is often very difficult to determine whether a particular piece is of Augustan date or later.

After the civil war of AD 68/9, Vespasian brought peace and stability, inaugurating the Flavian dynasty (AD 69–96). He erected the Forum Pacis (of peace), which contained loot from the sack of Jerusalem and Nero's own collection (including a fluorite cup once gnawed by a consul, see **137**). He also completed the Colosseum. The short reign of his successor, Titus (AD 79–81), saw the catastrophic eruption of Vesuvius. After the despotism of his younger brother, Domitian, the senate selected Nerva. In his short reign he attempted a return to Augustan ideals, but more important for the future was his choice of a successor, Trajan.

Marble throne from the Panathenaic stadium at Athens, built by Herodes Atticus for the festival of AD 143/4, ht 70 cm (GR 2001,0508.1; purchased with the aid of the Olympic Museum, Lausanne)

Trajan (AD 98–117) carried the Roman eagles as far as Romania and the Persian Gulf, and his successor Hadrian (AD 117–38) built his wall in northern England to secure final peace (**143**). These were great years for the Roman world: commerce linked east and west, north and south; populations increased enormously; and new cities and civic buildings were erected across the known world. Trajan's masterpiece was his Forum with its richly decorated column. Hadrian had an ambition to be his own architect: he designed much of his great villa at Tivoli and probably brought to completion the rebuilding of the remarkable Pantheon in Rome, a project begun by Trajan. Hadrian travelled extensively, visiting Greece several times. Indeed, his reign was marked by a Greek revival in thought, art and customs – the emperor even grew a Greek-style beard and took a lover, the young Antinous.

In AD 138 Antoninus Pius (**148**) succeeded Hadrian, giving his name to the Antonine dynasty. Greece was still a focus of cultural attention. In Athens, indeed, the local wealthy magnate, Herodes Atticus, rebuilt the Panathenaic stadium in marble. In the west, too, there was great wealth, and the silver figurine from Mâcon (**151**) and extraordinary gilded statuette of Hercules from Hadrian's Wall (**154**) are both probably Gallo-Roman works.

The Antonine age, however, ended in violence, brought on by its last scion, Commodus (AD 180–92), who in his derangement identified himself with Hercules. From a series of wars of succession emerged Septimius Severus (**155**). He attempted to establish a dynasty based on the support of the army, but his sons were not able to secure stability and the Roman world descended into anarchy after the first decades of the third century AD. There were some twenty emperors in the next fifty years, but at the end of the third century Diocletian (AD 284–305) attempted to restore the empire with a new governing structure, the rule of four, the Tetrarchy. Constantine the Great (AD 306–37) built on this and achieved a lasting order, ending violence and persecution, and so opened the doors on a new world.

122 BRONZE HEAD OF A SALIAN PRIEST

The identity of this superb bronze head has been much disputed. After having been first thought to represent a Roman priest, it was later considered the head of an athlete in a close-fitting leather cap of a sort worn by wrestlers and *pancratiasts* (no-holds-barred fighters), and to be Etruscan or Faliscan of the third century BC, reflecting Greek work of the fourth century BC. There is, however, a flatness and control about the features that is very different from the Hellenistic tradition with its richer, rounder modelling. Indeed, the head has recently been persuasively re-identified as that of a Salian priest and a Roman work of the first century BC.

The Salii were twelve young men of patrician birth, with both parents living, who performed ritual dances in honour of the god Mars. They carried a sword, a shield and a spear or staff. They wore the dress of an Archaic Italian foot soldier: tunic, breastplate and cloak. On their heads they wore the *apex*, a leather skull cap made from the hides of sacrificed animals and fastened under the chin with straps passing either side of the ears. Most examples of these ritual caps have a spike attached to the top, but there are some that do not have such an adornment and this bronze head is surely one of them.

As the Salii leapt and danced, they beat their shields and sang the *Carmen Saliare*. The mouth of this bronze youth is slightly open, suggesting perhaps that he was to be thought of as singing. The lips were probably once covered with copper sheets. The eye sockets were originally filled with separate inserts, presumably consisting of bronze eyelids that held coloured materials for eyeball, iris and pupil.

Bronze head

Roman, made in Rome, first century BC

Said to be from near Rome (acquired 1785)

Bequeathed by Richard Payne Knight

Ht 21.5 cm

GR 1824,0427.1 (*Bronze* 1614)

123 PORTRAIT OF AN OLD MAN

(*right*) Marble head
Roman, made in Rome, 60–40 BC
Ht 45.7 cm
GR 1973,0330.7 (*Sculpture* 1966)

(*below*) Terracotta votive head
Etruscan, made in Etruria,
300–200 BC
Ht 30.5 cm
GR 1839,0214.9

This marble head shows an old man, clean shaven and with closely cropped hair, indicated with rows of simple, shallow gouges on the head (right). The details of the face are closely observed, especially the rather small eyes and the jowels and cheeks, which are heavy and sagging. This realistic, 'warts and all' type of portrait was popular during the late Republic and early empire (first century BC to first century AD). It was initially the preserve of the upper echelons of society such as senators, generals and other high-ranking officials. The idea, however, was already part of the mid-Italian tradition, as a remarkable, over life-size Etruscan terracotta votive head demonstrates (left).

In the case of the Roman examples, there seems to be a connection with the patrician practice, already recorded in the second century BC, of carrying wax likenesses of one's ancestors in a funeral procession and at public sacrifices. Such images were kept in the home where they were a reminder of the person's good name and deeds and acted as a legitimization of the family's high status and lineage.

The Roman portraitist approached the sitter objectively, concentrating on the accurate transmission of external features. By contrast the Hellenistic artist aimed at the reconstruction of a personality, using the accidents of nature as superficial adjuncts to a generally idealized structure. From early in the first century BC Roman patrons came into contact with Greek sculptors who were creating marble portraits of non-royal patrons. This fusing of the Hellenistic use of marble and the Roman tradition resulted in the remarkable series of portraits that document for us the public and private figures of the Roman world.

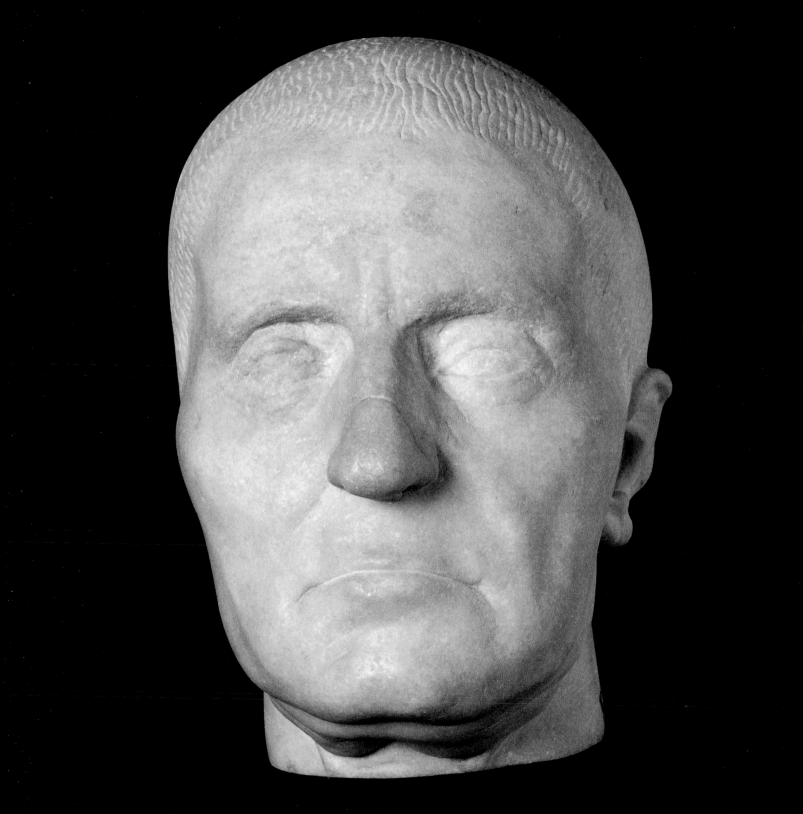

L·ANTISTIVS·CN·L·HOR·SARCVLO · ANTIS
SALIVS·ALBANVS · IDEM·Ñ·MAG·SALIORVM   L·L·PLVT
RVFVS·ANTHVS·IMACINES·DE·SVO·FECERVNT·PATRON· C·ET·PATRON·AE·EN
EORVM

124 FUNERARY RELIEF

Originally part of their funerary monument, this marble relief shows Lucius Antistius Sarculo, a free-born Roman priest of the Salian order (compare **122**), and his wife and former slave Antistia Plutia. It was set up after their death by two of their freedmen. The two portrait busts are set within scallop shells, upon which the soul was thought to float to the other world, and surrounded with wreaths symbolizing the triumph over death; between them is a Salian staff.

The lines around the eyes and the mouth, the slightly hollowed cheeks and the prominent ears and the scrawny neck of Antistius, together with the thin-lipped countenance of his wife, continue the realistic style of the late Republic into the early Principate of Augustus. Their hairstyles indicate a date towards the end of the first century BC. Antistius' hair is cut close to his head, realistically emphasizing his retreating hairline. Antistia's is drawn back into a small bun, with some curls brought forward and a small topknot at the front of the head, following the hairstyle of Livia, wife of Augustus. In the Roman manner, both heads are set fully frontal.

During the Republic, large numbers of slaves were brought to Rome following the conquests of countries like Spain and Greece. Many worked the land or on building projects, while others were teachers or craftsmen, or served as cooks or domestic workers. Augustus gave freedmen and freedwomen many rights and privileges, including the right to marry Roman citizens. Antistia's rise from humble slave to wife of a Salian priest reveals the extent of Augustus' social revolution. The roads around Rome and other cities in the empire were lined with monuments from which similar reliefs of freedmen (*libertini*) and their families looked out proudly proclaiming their full membership of Roman society.

Marble funerary relief

Roman, made in Rome, 30–10 BC

From Rome, Italy

Bruto della Valle and Bessborough collections

Length 95 cm

GR 1858,0819.2 (*Sculpture* 2275)

125 MOSAIC *EMBLEMA*

Mosaic panel
Roman, perhaps made in Rome or an eastern Mediterranean city, 70–10 BC
From Naples, South Italy
Formerly in the Barone collection
Length 37.7 cm
GR 1856,1213.5 (*Mosaic* 1)

A tawny yellow lion with a brown mane is taunted by four Cupids. In the foreground one pulls a rope attached to the lion's hindmost leg, while the one in the top right corner waves a pink and grey cloth like a bullfighter. Behind the lion a cupid bends forward as he clashes a pair of cymbals, while on the left the fourth member of the troupe holds a *beitel* (aniconic cult figure). In the foreground is an overturned metal bucket, while on the hillside in the background is a rural sanctuary of Bacchus with a statue of the god holding a *thyrsus* (ivy-topped staff) and a *cantharus* (special cup) and a dark green tree.

This delicate mosaic panel is an *emblema*, a decorative feature designed to be the central element of an otherwise plain floor or wall. Such *emblemata* were usually much more finely worked than ordinary mosaics, achieving a degree of detail, perspective and shading more akin to the subtleties of painting. This was attained through the use of very small *tesserae* (cubes of stone or glass from which mosaics were made) in a technique called *opus vermiculatum*. Such *emblemata* were made up on wooden or clay backings and were sometimes imported from eastern Mediterranean cities such as Pergamon, Ephesus or Alexandria, although they were also made in metropolitan Rome.

As with sculpture and paintings in the Roman period, several copies were regularly made of the same composition, and other examples of this *emblema* can be found in Rome as well as Naples. Furthermore, the sculptor Arkesilaos is said by the ancient writer Pliny to have made a group of a lioness bound by Cupids. The allegory of strength tamed by love was a common one in art and literature.

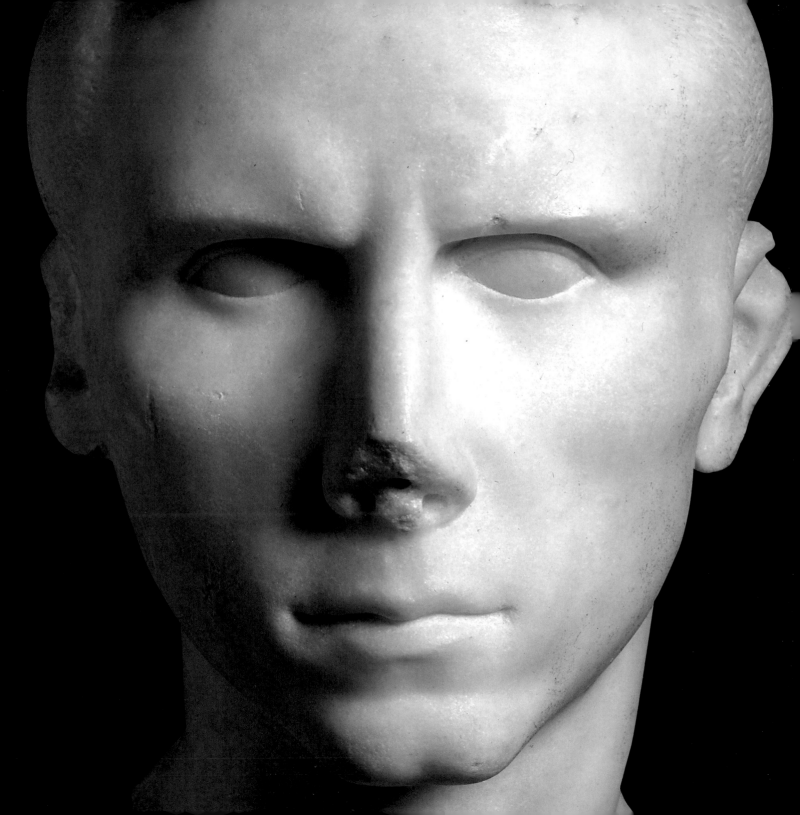

126 PORTRAIT OF A ROMAN, FROM CYPRUS

Marble portrait

Roman, perhaps made in Greece
or on Cyprus, 50–40 BC

From Cyprus

Ht 31 cm

GR 1902,1011.1 (*Sculpture* 1879*)

This portrait in Parian marble is of exceptional quality. The man's close-cropped hair stands up in a little peak over the brow; it recedes at the temples. The brow is furrowed at the bridge of the nose, the deep-set almond-shaped eyes are long and hooded, the long nose hooked, the lips thin and unsmiling, the cheek bones angular, the chin bony and the Adam's apple prominent in the sinewy neck. The head was originally pieced, with an L-shaped block (now lost) forming the crown and back of the head.

There is a strong degree of realism in this bony clean-shaven face, the skull only thinly covered by its envelope of skin. Its verism, however, has been modified by the Hellenistic tradition, for, instead of the strict frontality of the Roman tradition, we find the slight turn of the head that is Hellenistic motion. Furthermore, there is a wonderful assurance to the modelling and a fine sense of its suggestiveness as an index of character. It is most probably the work of a Greek artist trained in the Hellenistic tradition seeking to match contemporary Roman taste and style.

This portrait has occasionally been identified as Octavian (before he took the title of Augustus), but the face lacks Octavian's broader cheek bones and jaw, while such hooded eyes are not to be found in his portraits. The person must, instead, have been a senior official of considerable authority and force of personality. The head's reported find-spot of Cyprus might make one wonder if it could be the portrait of a young Marcus Porcius Cato, who was sent to Cyprus to administer the annexation of the island in 58 BC.

127 THE MEROË AUGUSTUS

Bronze portrait

Roman, made in Rome, 27–25 BC

From Meroë, Sudan (excavated by Professor J. Garstang)

Gift of the Sudan Excavation Committee, with the aid of the Art Fund

Ht 47.7 cm

GR 1911,0901.1

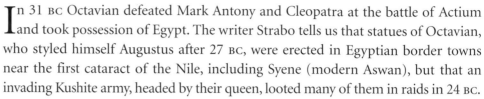

In 31 BC Octavian defeated Mark Antony and Cleopatra at the battle of Actium and took possession of Egypt. The writer Strabo tells us that statues of Octavian, who styled himself Augustus after 27 BC, were erected in Egyptian border towns near the first cataract of the Nile, including Syene (modern Aswan), but that an invading Kushite army, headed by their queen, looted many of them in raids in 24 BC.

Although Roman counterattacks reclaimed some of the statues, they did not reach as far as Meroë in the Sudan, the ancient capital of the kingdom of Kush, where this head was later buried beneath the steps of a temple of the Kushite god of victory. It seems likely that the head was deliberately set so the feet of its Kushite captors would walk over it in a ritual act of triumph. The theme of triumph was continued on a painting inside the temple which showed the king and queen sacrificing to the god Amun. His feet rested on a stool decorated with bound and kneeling prisoners – one of them seems to be wearing a Roman legionary helmet.

Early images of Octavian portrayed him bearded, in mourning for his murdered adoptive father, Julius Caesar; later portraits took on a more animated, almost Alexander-like appearance, clean shaven, with windswept hair and upturned head, as a result perhaps of his activities in the Greek east. Following the battle of Actium and the adoption of his new persona as first citizen and restorer of the Republic, Augustus had a new image designed. This showed him in the manner of a Classical Greek hero with perfect, idealized features and a serene, somewhat aloof expression.

The Meroë head has eyes inlaid with white marble, green coloured glass for the iris, dark glass for the pupils, and red glass for the tear ducts. The figure most probably wore a cuirass and was shown addressing the troops. The Meroë statue was clearly an important metropolitan work of the first rank, not a provincial piece like the Hadrian from London (**143**), and it must have been created and set up in the furthest extremity of the Roman world very soon after the new image of Augustus was created.

129 THE GUILFORD PUTEAL

This cylindrical marble drum is decorated in very low relief with ten figures of deities and heroes. It was greatly admired by nineteenth-century travellers, who saw it at Corinth, because they judged it a very rare example of early Greek art. It is rather an important Roman work of the last quarter of the first century BC with interesting links to Augustus' victory at the battle of Actium in 31 BC, when he defeated Antony and Cleopatra to become sole leader of the Roman world.

The top of the drum was worked to receive a moulded element to match the one at the bottom. Originally, the whole was probably set on a square base in or near the Roman *agora* of Corinth and served either as a ceremonial altar or as the base for a pillar monument. In the medieval period it was hollowed out and reused as a well-head or puteal, hence its name.

The figures, now sadly very heavily weathered, form three groups. At the front, two short processions of three figures meet: from the left comes Apollo with his lyre, leading Diana (with bow and stag) and another woman (probably their mother); from the right approach Minerva leading Hercules and a veiled woman (perhaps Juno). At the back, from left to right, Mercury with winged feet leads three dancing women, perhaps Nymphs or Graces.

An exact parallel has been excavated at Nikopolis in northwestern Greece on the site of Octavian's military camp before the battle of Actium. There a monumental structure, decorated with the prows of captured ships and enclosing a large rectangular altar, as well as a pair of small semicircular altars, was set up to celebrate the victory. One of the semi-circular altars is preserved intact and is carved with the very same sequence of figures and by the same workshop of sculptors as the Guilford Puteal.

The theme of the Actium altar and the Guilford Puteal seems to be the reconciliation of Apollo and Hercules and in this it alludes to the conflict between Augustus (Apollo) and Antony (Hercules) and the need to reconcile the parties after such a damaging civil war.

Marble sculptured base

Roman, made in Greece, 25–15 BC

From Corinth

Formerly in the collections of Frederick North (Fifth Earl of Guilford) and Thomas Wentworth Beaumont MP

Purchased with the aid of the Art Fund, the Caryatid Fund, the British Museum Friends, the Henry Moore Foundation and the Dilettanti Society

Diam. 1.06 m; ht 50 cm

GR 2003,0507.1

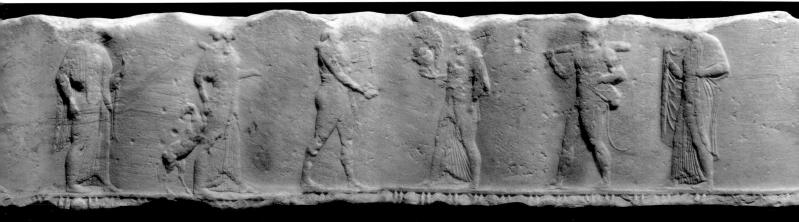

130 THE ACTIUM VASE

Pottery jar

Roman, probably made in
Campania, 30 BC–AD 10

Said to be from Capua

Formerly in the collection of
Napoleon III

Ht 35.2 cm

GR 1873,0208.3 (*Vase* G 28)

Pottery in the Roman period was most often mass-produced in moulds, but this large and exceptional piece could nevertheless be considered a masterpiece – it was certainly a very special and important vessel in its day, richly coloured and proudly signed by its potter, Bassus.

It takes the form of a lidded jar and has two large vertical handles adorned with female masks. The lid is decorated in relief with olive leaves forming a wreath. The body of the vase is also covered with relief decoration created by pressing stamps into the mould. There are two main friezes: the upper one has olive trees linked by heavy festoons, above which a Cupid plays the *syrinx* (multiple pipes). Above one of the Cupids is the maker's name, Bassu[s]. The lower zone contains the same scene repeated five times: a bearded figure, presumably Neptune, sits on a rock, his lower body draped, facing to the right with his head turned back over his shoulder. In his left hand he holds a long arching palm branch, while below him is an altar. To the left, a winged Victory riding on the back of a sea creature offers the sea god the prow of a ship, decorated with the head of a sea monster. Above the figures a small four-columned temple is repeated several times.

In addition to gilding on the lid, the wings of the Victories and the palm branches held by Neptune were also gilded. Pink was used to decorate the bodies of Victory and Neptune and blue for all the border patterns. These colours have been analysed and found to be pink madder and lapis lazuli.

The vase, although sometimes referred to as 'black Arretine', was more probably made in Campania as part of the final phase of black-glaze pottery produced there. The scene of Neptune being offered the prow of a ship has been interpreted as an allegory on Octavian's victory over the naval forces of Antony and Cleopatra at the battle of Actium in 31 BC. The expensive gilding and added colours suggest that, although only made of clay, the vessel was an object of particular significance and may even have been made as a funerary urn to accompany a veteran of that great battle.

131 THE CHRYSES SILVER CUP

Although this magnificent Roman silver *cantharus* (drinking cup of special shape) is missing both its foot and its two high-arching handles, its relief work is a masterpiece of Roman toreutics, the craft of metalworking. It must have been commissioned by a wealthy Roman for use at one of the banquets (*convivia*) at which he gathered his friends and dependants. Part of the entertainment at such gatherings seems to have been conversations and discussions that developed from the guests' surroundings. Such a silver cup with its complex scenes would clearly have provoked much discussion.

The relief shows a scene from the myth of Orestes and Iphigenia, the children of Agamemnon of Mycenae. They have stolen the statue of Artemis from the Tauri, a fierce people on the northern shores of the Black Sea, who practised human sacrifice, and are seeking sanctuary at the rural shrine of Apollo at Sminthe. Next to the diminutive image of the god sit Pylades, Orestes' closest friend, and Iphigenia, close-wrapped and holding the statue of Artemis. Orestes stands further forward, still clutching the branch of the sacred tree to ensure his safety. In front of him is Chryseis, daughter of Chryses, priest of Apollo. She is whispering to her son, also called Chryses (after his grandfather), that he too is the son of Agamemnon. As a result, Chryses refuses to give up his half-brother and sister and their companion to King Thoas of the Tauri, who is seen coming up from the right, accompanied by an attendant, both dressed in outlandish garments.

The host of the *convivium* at which this cup was used might well have hoped that his guests would not be able to recognize the scene. But, even if one of them did recall a recent production of Pacuvius' tragedy *Chryses*, he could perhaps have trumped this with the knowledge that Sophokles had written an earlier version.

Beneath this rich scene, there is a frieze of flowers and birds in much lower relief. The design recalls the florals on the marble reliefs that decorated the Ara Pacis in Rome (Altar to Peace, dedicated 9 BC). The frieze also links the vessel with two other cups from the same find that are decorated only with floral scrolls.

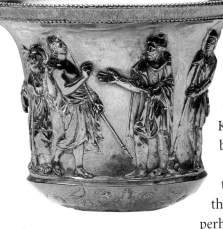

Silver cup

Roman, probably made in Rome, 10 BC–AD 20

Said to be from Asia Minor

Ht 9.8 cm

GR 1960,0201.1

132 THE WARREN CUP

Silver cup

Roman, made in Rome, AD 1–15

Said to be from Bittir, Israel

Formerly in the collection of E.P. Warren

Purchased with the aid of the Heritage Lottery Fund, the Art Fund and the Caryatid Fund and Group, including Dr Roy W. Lennox, Ms Joan E. Webermann and Mr and Mrs Richard W.C. Kan

Ht 11 cm

GR 1999,0426.1

The Warren Cup is an exceptional masterpiece of Roman art. It combines extraordinary skill in the very low-relief decoration with unique and challenging scenes of male homosexual lovemaking.

Two pairs of male lovers are represented on the cup. On the front a youth gently lowers himself on to the lap of a bearded man, while at the far right of the scene a slave boy peers round a door. On the other side, a youth and a boy are making love. Details of the hairstyles, the cloaks and the musical instruments allude to a Greek setting and suggest that the participants are, in fact, all Greek citizens. It may, therefore, be a Roman view of the Greek concept of pederasty that saw the older lover (*erastes*) take on an educative and protective role in respect of the younger partner (*eromenos*). The slave boy in his ungirt tunic serves as an image of the Roman viewer or voyeur, and, of course, as ourselves.

The cup, or rather *cantharus*, was probably made in Rome in the first decades of the first century AD by a Greek craftsman. It is constructed from five silver elements: a pair of simple, vertical cast handles, now missing; a cast and elaborately turned foot; a thin hammered wall with its low relief scenes; and a sturdier liner with a thick rim to which were soldered both outer wall and handles, a liner that also facilitated the cleaning of the interior. Details of the figured scenes would have been highlighted with gilding, but this has all now worn away.

The cup was designed to be used as part of an elaborate silver drinking and eating service at banquets (*convivia*) when the high-ranking host and his guests might well have talked about the elaborate scenes that decorated it (compare **131**). It is said to have been found at Bittir, some nine kilometres south of Jerusalem, together with coins of the emperor Claudius (AD 41–54). This suggests that its last owner took it out to Judaea for use during his period of official service there. It was probably in the face of the severe unrest that culminated in the Jewish revolt of AD 66 and the complete takeover of the city by Jewish rebels that its owner hid it for safekeeping at Bittir.

133 THE PORTLAND VASE

The Portland Vase is one of the most famous cameo-glass vessels in the world. Sadly, it is not known for certain when or where the vase was found. It is first recorded, in the winter of 1600/1, as being in Rome in the collection of Cardinal del Monte, the prosecutor of Galileo and patron of the young Caravaggio.

In 1626 it passed into the collection of the powerful Barberini family, when a connection was made with a marble sarcophagus found just outside Rome in 1581/2. This sarcophagus was believed to have contained the ashes of Severus Alexander and his mother and regent, Julia Mammaea, a connection that was based on the misidentification of its scenes.

The Barberini vase, as it was then called, was purchased in about 1780 by the great connoisseur and collector Sir William Hamilton. He in turn sold it to the Dowager Duchess of Portland. At the sale following her death, the vase was bought back by her son, the Third Duke, and thus won its modern name. After a domestic accident it was placed on loan in the British Museum in 1810, only to be shattered by a young Irishman in 1845. The vase was swiftly and expertly restored by John Doubleday and it remained on loan in the Museum until 1945, when it was purchased from the Seventh Duke.

The bottom of the vase seems to have been broken in antiquity – originally it was probably pointed in form. The repair that was carried out included the addition of a new base in the form of a disc (overleaf). This was itself cut from a superb flat cameo-glass plaque, which shows the head of Paris – originally the scene on the plaque probably represented the young Trojan's judgement among the three goddesses, Aphrodite, Athena and Hera.

The scenes on the vase itself have received many different interpretations over the last four hundred years. The first was made in 1633, when it was suggested that they illustrated the dream of Olympias, the mother of Alexander the Great. Thus the young man emerging from the shrine would be Alexander, the reclining lady on both sides Olympias, his mother, and the snake Jupiter, his father. This interpretation was soon developed into Julia Mammaea and her son Severus Alexander, of whom a similar tale of reptilian paternity was told. Most

Glass vessel and plaque

Roman, made in Rome, AD 5–25

Probably from Rome

Formerly in the Barberini, Hamilton and Portland collections

Ht of vase 24 cm; diam. of disc 12.2 cm

GR 1945,0927.1–2 (*Gem* 4036)

other later interpretations offer either a mythological or a historical key, the most recent seeing Antony and Cleopatra on one side, with the deserted Octavia consoled by Augustus under the gaze of Venus on the other. The most enduring mythological interpretation, however, identifies the subject as the marriage of Peleus and Thetis.

Cameo-glass vessels, that is vessels simulating the appearance of carved layered gemstones (cameos: e.g. **135**) were probably all made within the space of two

generations, as prestige experiments. Recent research has suggested that the Portland Vase was probably made by the so-called dip-overlay method, whereby an elongated bubble of glass was partially dipped into a crucible of opaque white glass, before the two were blown together. After cooling, the white layer was cut away to form the design. The cutting must have been performed by an extremely skilled gem-cutter, perhaps someone like Dioscurides, mentioned by Pliny, who worked with gemstones and glass.

134 FRESCO PAINTING OF PHAEDRA

Fresco painting

Roman, probably painted in
Pompeii, Third Style,
c. 20 BC–AD 40

Probably from Pompeii

Formerly in the collection of G.
Fejérváry and F. Pulszky

Width 28.5 cm

GR 1856,0625.5 (*Painting* 29)

This beautiful fragment of fresco wall-painting probably formed part of the decoration of a room in one of the wealthy houses at Pompeii. It shows a woman seated on the end of a couch, her pose and wide-open eyes revealing her inner turmoil and despair, a servant or nurse by her side.

The lady is richly adorned with gold jewellery and elaborately dressed. Over the back of her head is a white stole with a greenish tinge – it falls down on her left side to end in a bunch of folds on the couch, while on her right it crosses over her knees to fall between her legs and the end of the couch, where its long fringe is visible. She wears a similarly coloured garment over her right shoulder and legs. Beneath this outer garment is a transparent, long-sleeved garment, the hems of which can be seen at neck and wrist. Below this delicate shift there is a dark red area, which may be part of her breast band. She also appears to have a pinkish red garment wrapped round her waist. A yellow slipper peeps out from under her drapery (there is restoration here, as a footstool should support her foot). Her right elbow rests on her left hand, on top of her slightly raised knee, as her hand almost touches her chin. The couch on the side of which she sits is shown in three-quarter view. One elaborately faceted leg and part of the horizontal side beam are revealed, but the end and the rising back are covered with a red blanket dotted with yellow flowers. The painter has shown the light coming from the right of the scene, shining on the woman's left cheek and shoulder.

On the left stands a servant holding a thin stick-like object with a bulbous end: it is a writing *stylus*. On the extreme left are traces of a third figure, probably standing and male. Behind the women an architectural setting is suggested. The scene is Phaedra contemplating her passion for her stepson, Hippolytus. The nurse whispers to her that she might write a message to Hippolytus to explain how she feels, hence the *stylus*. A terrible chain of events ensues: Phaedra writes the note; Hippolytus rejects her; she commits suicide, but not before blaming Hippolytus; and finally her husband, Theseus of Athens, curses his son to death.

135 THE BLACAS CAMEO

The great Blacas Cameo was carved from a four-layered sardonyx (brown and white). It shows the head and shoulders of the first emperor of Rome, Augustus (27 BC–AD 14). He faces to the left but is seen from the back. He wears a belt over one shoulder, to hold a sword at his waist, and carries a sceptre or spear at a slope, beyond his body. He also has the *aegis* (magical protective goatskin) of Jupiter over his left shoulder. This has been hastily thrown over the shoulder like a shield: the hole for the head reveals the point of the shoulder. The aegis, somewhat unexpectedly, is decorated with two heads. For, in addition to the severed head of the gorgon Medusa, whose gaze was said to turn people to stone, on his back, there is also flapping up in front of him a bearded head with wings, which is perhaps to be identified as Phobos (the personification of Fear), who was mentioned in Homer's description of the aegis.

The diadem around the head of Augustus is not ancient. When the cameo was in the collection of Bishop Leo Strozzi, at the beginning of the eighteenth century, the gold diadem set with gems was apparently much decayed. As a result he had it repaired, reusing the setting but adding other gemstones, including cameos, emeralds and diamonds. The setting itself appears to be medieval, suggesting that the cameo may at some time in the Middle Ages have formed part of a reliquary. The original diadem may well have been just a simple fillet.

The pose of Augustus would seem to be Hellenistic in conception, for the same back view and the wearing of the *aegis* is found on Hellenistic coins and on a small Hellenistic cameo, depicting perhaps Philip V of Macedon (220–179 BC). As a result we should think of Augustus on the Blacas Cameo as a fighting ruler, in the tradition of Alexander the Great. The presence of the aegis indicates that Augustus' rule had been sanctioned by Jupiter. This powerful image must have been created after Augustus' death as a reminder of the power and continuing influence of the first Roman emperor. Such an overt profession of divinity could only be contemplated at this time within the closest court circle, but just how such a large cameo was kept or displayed is unknown.

Sardonyx cameo
Roman, made in Rome, AD 20–50
Formerly in the Strozzi and Blacas collections
Ht 12.8 cm
GR 1867,0507.484 (*Gem* 3577)

136 SILVER AND BLUE GLASS BEAKER

The beautiful combination of silver casing with blown blue glass lining in this vessel is completely unparalleled. The casing is of a very simple ovoid shape, with a slight ridge to form the base and one at the lip. Eight rows of oval openings have been cut in the wall, their size decreasing towards the base. There is a further row of oblong ovals cut near the rim, and six more openings under the base itself. Blue glass has been blown into this casing so that it swells slightly out of every opening like rows of dark blue sapphires.

The ovoid shape of the beaker is typical of the middle of the first century AD. By this time the Roman elite were facing something of a dilemma in connection with their tableware. This was voiced by Trimalchio at his famous fictional dinner party described by Petronius in his *Satyricon*: 'You may forgive me if I say that personally I prefer glass; glass at least does not smell. If it were not so breakable I should prefer it to gold, as it is so cheap.' He goes on, however, to reveal that, although the smell of metal vessels was an issue, he was very proud of his silver vessels.

Indeed, this remarkable vessel would have been ideal for Trimalchio. The glass liner meant the vessel did not smell or taste, but the use of silver would have ensured that a proper impression was made on the guests. The silver casing might not have rendered it unbreakable, but it might have saved one of his slaves from being ordered to 'get out and hang yourself'.

Blown glass vessels were to become extremely common throughout the Roman world from early in the first century AD, for the technology made them cheap and easy to make. From the later first century AD onwards colourless glass was preferred and Pliny was to comment that 'the most highly valued glass is colourless and transparent, resembling rock-crystal as closely as possible'.

Silver and glass beaker
Roman, made in Italy, AD 25–50
Probably from Brindisi
Ht 9.3 cm
GR 1870,0901.2

The Crawford Fluorspar Cup

Roman, perhaps made in Parthia or in Rome, first century AD

Said to be from Turkey or Syria

Presented by the Art Fund, in honour of Lord Crawford (Chairman of the Art Fund, 1945–70)

Ht 9.7 cm

GR 1971,0419.1

Both these cups, one a *cantharus* (special drinking cup), the other a mug, have been carved from the mineral known as fluorite (fluorspar) that is richly veined with purple, green, yellow and white, and the two were found together Fluorite has been identified with the Latin word *murra*. It is a very rare mineral that, according to Pliny, was known in the Roman period as coming from the Persian Gulf. Vessels made from it, murrhine vessels (*vasae murrinae*), are first mentioned in connection with a very wealthy Roman, Opinius, consul in 121 BC. Pompey the Great brought some back from his victories in the east in 62/1 BC and dedicated them in the temple on the Capitoline Hill. Augustus, too, kept a murrhine vessel for himself from the capture of Alexandria, while the Emperor Nero paid the fabulous sum of 1,000,000 sesterces for a cup (enough for a thousand slaves or 25,000 *amphorae* of the best wine).

We also hear of a former consul who was so fond of his cup that he gnawed its rim, a report that we can probably connect with the poet Martial's assertion that the flavour of wine was improved if drunk from a *vasa murrina*. We may explain this by considering the likely method of manufacture. Fluorite, which rarely occurs in pieces large enough from which to create vessels, has a very loose crystalline structure which makes carving hazardous. The risks can be reduced by smearing on resin and heating it, a technique still used in the modern production of Derbyshire fluorite, known as 'Blue John'. Wine, of course, would have gradually dissolved the resin and if the gum resin was of myrrh, then it would certainly have given off both a pleasant smell and distinctive flavour. This would also explain the word *murrina*.

The Crawford *cantharus* (left) is undecorated, but the Barber mug (right) has a low-relief panel of vine leaves, grapes and tendrils, and a bearded head, presumably Bacchus, the god of wine, under its handle. The decoration is very carefully cut and can be paralleled in both Roman silver ware and glass. Both pieces are said to have been found together during the First World War, near the then border between Turkey and Syria. We hear of a marble cist in which there was a lead casket containing the two vessels, which both held ashes.

The Barber Fluorspar Cup

Roman, perhaps made in Parthia or in Rome, first century AD

Said to be from Turkey or Syria

Formerly in the collection of Baron Adolphe Stóclet

Purchased in honour of Nicholas Barber (Chairman of the British Museum Friends, 1993–2003) with the aid of the British Museum Friends, the Art Fund, the Caryatid Fund and Mr and Mrs Frank A. Ladd

Ht 13.5 cm

GR 2003,1202.1

138 CHALCEDONY PORTRAIT OF DRUSILLA

This superb head of a young woman, carved from a large piece of green chalcedony, has been identified as the portrait of Julia Drusilla (born about AD 16), second daughter of Germanicus and Agrippina, and favourite sister of the emperor Caligula (AD 37–41).

Her head is turned very slightly to the right and there are holes in her earlobes, suggesting that she was originally adorned with miniature gold earrings. Her hair is centrally parted and brushed to either side of the head in a series of tight waves; around the face is a row of small snail-shaped curls. She has a full face with a squarish jaw, small mouth and somewhat sullen expression. The highly polished skin contrasts well with the matte effect of the hair with its engraved detail. Part of her tunic is preserved at the bottom right of the piece, but the whole is likely to have taken the form of a draped bust, rather than a complete figure.

This remarkable sculpted portrait, together with a fragment of a similar one (in Cambridge) and a series of cameos, was probably carved after Drusilla's untimely death in AD 38 and presented to a member of the imperial court in her memory. She had been very close to her brother Caligula – indeed, there were rumours that their relationship was incestuous, even though she was twice married. She was named as Caligula's heir when he was ill in late AD 37. When she herself died the following year, public mourning was enforced throughout the empire and, although there was no precedent for the deification of a woman, Caligula had her consecrated as Diva Drusilla Panthea (universal goddess), probably on the occasion of the centenary of Augustus' birth.

Chalcedony portrait
Roman, probably made in Rome,
AD 38–41
Presented by J. Pierpont Morgan
Ht 9 cm
GR 1907,0415.1 (*Gem* 3946)

Bronze statuette

Roman, probably made in Gaul,
mid first century AD

Perhaps from Creeting, near
Coddenham

Given by the Earl of Ashburnham

Ht 57.5 cm

PE 1813,0213.1

139 BRONZE STATUETTE OF A RULER

An extremely rare find for Britain is this superb bronze statuette. It represents a beardless man, standing in a heroic pose, gazing slightly upwards, with left foot raised and his right hand held up high, presumably once grasping a spear which is now lost. His left arm is also missing.

He wears a richly ornamented cuirass with inlaid patterns including florals in silver and black bronze (so-called Corinthian bronze, the equivalent of Japanese *shakudo* or Chinese *wu tong*). The lower edge of the cuirass has two rows of scale-shaped lappets, similarly inlaid. Beneath is a short tunic that falls in narrow folds to just above his knees and has a fringe of tassels. Over the cuirass is a *cingulum*, a soldier's sword belt. On his feet he wears leather boots with open toes. The bottom of his raised left foot has a strongly curved contour suggesting that it rested on some rounded form, perhaps the back of a defeated enemy.

The man's upswept hair and upward gaze recall portraits of Alexander the Great (**71**). Although the figure has on occasion been identified as the emperor Nero, there are no precise iconographic parallels. The absence of the Roman military *paludamentum* over the figure's shoulder and of figural decoration on the cuirass itself mark it off from normal imperial cuirassed images. Nor is the plain diadem or fillet in his hair, decorated with a dogtooth pattern of silver and black bronze, the sort of thing worn by Roman emperors, who preferred wreaths. Indeed, it seems better suited to a Greek ruler from the time of Alexander the Great onwards. Since there is no clear similarity with the portraits of any of Alexander's successors, however, we might perhaps best see the figure as a representation of Alexander himself.

It is a very fine work, hollow-cast, and was probably not made in Britain, but rather in southern Gaul where artists worked in a strongly Hellenistic tradition. It seems that it was found in 1795 at Creeting near Coddenham, just to the north of Ipswich. Excavations nearby indicate the presence of a large temple complex; there was also a first-century fort at Coddenham. The superb condition of the statuette suggests that it might well have been hidden for safety in the face of an attack by the native Iceni, never to be recovered until modern times.

Marble sculpture of a dog

Roman, probably made in Rome, first or second century AD

Formerly in the collection of H.C. Jennings (acquired in Rome in the late 1750s)

Purchased with the aid of the Heritage Lottery Fund, the Art Fund, the British Museum Friends, the Caryatid Fund, Mr and Mrs Frank Ladd and members of the public

Ht 1.18 m

GR 2001,1010.1

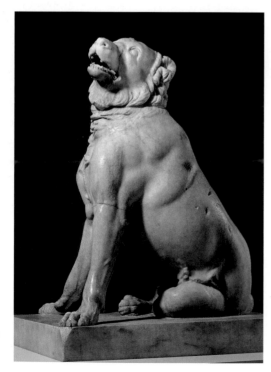

The momentary pose of this huge dog is particularly effective. He rises, with forelegs spread apart and body turning, as his head tilts up in a responsive fashion to some movement, perhaps by his master (there is a cutting round the neck for a bronze collar). The treatment of his relaxed lower haunch, with the folds of loose skin and slack muscles, contrasts well with the tensed upper body and forelegs. The representation of the ridges of hair and the ruff, together with the veins and muscles, are masterfully realized.

The Jennings Dog, named after its first owner who acquired it in the late 1750s, is regularly identified as a Molossian hound, the ancestor of the modern mastiffs. The Molossian was an Epirot breed and was suited not only for guard duty, both of home and herd, but also for hunting fierce animals, such as wild boar.

We know five other ancient versions of this sculpture. This makes it one of the very few examples of a Greek animal sculpture that was copied in the Roman period. The model was probably an important Hellenistic bronze sculpture of about 220–150 BC. Such an over life-size bronze must have been a major dedication in a sanctuary or in a civic context. The trace of a collar and the way that the mastiff turns as he rises, attracted by a movement, would seem to indicate the presence of his owner at his side. The Epirot origin of the Molossian breed might suggest a monument to Pyrrhos, king of Epirus, whose faithful hound is said to have leapt on to the king's funerary pyre when he died in 272 BC. Epirus was sacked by the Roman Consul Aemilius Paullus in 168 BC and much booty brought back to Rome.

In Rome, divorced from any Hellenistic context and without its master, the mastiff took on a new and independent role. Since such mastiffs were frequently used as killers in the boar hunt and as fierce guard dogs, large-scale sculptures of them no doubt became popular in the gardens of wealthy villas (as indeed were nineteenth-century replicas in England). Indeed, it is possible that it came from a villa near Lanuvio (see **149**).

141 GOLD ARMLET FROM RHAYADER

This elaborate armlet from Rhayader in Wales, though broken and flattened, is a remarkable masterpiece of Roman goldwork that seems to combine Hellenistic and Roman traditions with some Celtic elements.

The armlet is made from two sheets of gold – the front one hammered to give it grooves, the back one plain. In the grooves of the front sheet have been set various decorative wires, in particular two rows of cable pattern. These cables or plaits are made up of two sets of three plain wires passing under and over each other. On either side are elaborate wires – three are thick plain beaded wires and four are formed from two plain wires twisted together to form a rope. The end-plates (only three of the original four are preserved) have been decorated with spiral-beaded wires that have been set in an unusual swirling floral motif with areas filled with green and blue glass paste enamel.

The wire-work and the enamel are in the Hellenistic tradition, and the latter is very rare indeed in Roman jewellery. Coloured enamels, including red, green and blue, are also to be found in a Celtic milieu. It is, however, the pattern on the end-plates that is most remarkable, for the motif and syntax find their best parallels in contemporary or earlier Celtic art. The exceptional jeweller who created this armlet was probably trained in a Hellenized workshop in Italy but moved north where he came into contact with Celtic work.

This armlet was found in May 1899 together with a ring of the second century AD and a gaudy gem-set ornament that might have served either as a diadem or a belt. No coins were found in the group, which might suggest that it was not a hoard hidden in time of danger, but the find circumstances are not clear, and the bracelet has been broken and cut up, perhaps already in antiquity.

Gold armlet

Roman, probably early second century AD

Found at Rhayader, Powys, Wales

Length *c.* 18.7 cm

PE 1900,1122.1 (*Jewellery* 2798–9)

142 AMBER PERFUME VESSEL

Amber vessel

Roman, made in Aquileia, early second century AD

Said to be from Aquileia, North Italy

Ht 5.2 cm

GR 1866,0412.3 (*Amber* 114)

This remarkable little vessel has been carved from a single piece of orange red amber of roughly oval shape. The lively relief on the outside shows two Cupids picking grapes, while a panther tries to interrupt them.

The Cupids have been carved in high relief, the vines and bunches of grapes in low relief. One Cupid is shown picking a bunch of grapes from a tree with his right hand, while holding another bunch in his left hand. Beneath the tree is a large basket for transporting the grapes. The other chubby Cupid seems to be lazily sitting on a branch of the vine, holding in his right hand a *rhyton* and in his left a small bunch of grapes. A panther on the ground below tries to snatch at the grapes. In front of this animal of Bacchus, the god of wine, is his *cantharus*, a two-handled wine vessel with ribbed body and neck.

In the Roman period amber was imported from the far-off coasts of the Baltic Sea to Aquileia in the extreme northeast of Italy, where it was carved by specialist craftsmen. Indeed, the first-century Roman author Pliny tells us in his encyclopaedic work on natural history of one enterprising and intrepid trader who travelled all the way to the Baltic to establish a direct trade link with the natives himself. Although Roman amber objects occur from the first century BC, most were imported between about AD 130 and 180; by the third century AD the import of amber had ceased.

Amber was a highly prized material (compare **114**) and we hear of a portrait of Augustus carved from amber at Olympia. Pliny also tells us that the cost of a little amber figure of a man 'exceeds that of a healthy slave'. In the second century AD the trade was clearly controlled through Aquileia, where fine carvers created objects of high quality, especially small toilet vessels and rings for women.

143 BRONZE HEAD OF HADRIAN

(*right*) Bronze head
Roman, made in Britain, about AD 122
Head found by London Bridge (third arch)
Ht 43 cm
PE 1848,1103.1

This over life-size bronze head of the emperor Hadrian (AD 117–38) was found near London Bridge in 1834 (right). It came from a full figure of the emperor, probably wearing a cuirass and a military cloak (*paludamentum*). A bronze hand that was found a few years later in Lower Thames Street has a similar alloy, is on a similar scale and may come from the same statue (left). The right hand makes the gesture known as *adlocutio*, used when addressing the troops. This bronze statue was clearly a very important piece and was most probably set up in London's forum or perhaps on the bridge over the Thames itself.

(*above*) Bronze hand
Found in Lower Thames Street, and probably from the same statue
Formerly collection of Charles Roach Smith
Length 33 cm
PE 1856,0701.18

The technique is rather rough and individual, and it seems most likely that it was created by a local craftsman. The front and the back of the head seem very different. The back is very roughly formed; the front is rather summary in its treatment, but nevertheless careful. Mouth and nostrils are closed and no cold-work was done on the eyebrows. It has been suggested that the artist only had the face of Hadrian to work from, and created the back of the head for himself. Even in the face, however, there are anomalies compared to other known portraits of Hadrian and it is possible that the artist actually worked from a coin or a medallion showing the emperor only in profile. Indeed, the general contour of the face, the width of the forehead and details of the eyes, nose and mouth are at variance with the standard metropolitan portraits of Hadrian. Furthermore, the hair on top of the head and at the back recall images of Hadrian's predecessor, Trajan. It would seem that the artist was intent on creating as recognizable an image of the new emperor as he could, but lacked details of Rome's latest fashions.

The London head probably belongs early in the series of Hadrian portraits. It may date to about AD 122, the year of Hadrian's brief visit to Britain, and the delivery of his instructions for the building of his great northern wall.

144 THE TOWNLEY DISCOBOLUS

Marble statue

Roman, made in Italy, second century AD

From Hadrian's Villa at Tivoli, near Rome (found in 1781)

Formerly in the collection of Charles Townley

Ht 1.7 m

GR 1805,0703.43 (*Sculpture* 250)

The discobolus, a youth in the act of throwing a discus, is one of several Roman copies known of a lost bronze of the middle of the fifth century BC. The original sculpture was created by the sculptor Myron, as we learn from the ancient writer Lucian who described the statue as 'stooping in the pose of one preparing to throw, turning towards the hand with the discus and gently bending the other knee, as ready to rise and cast'.

There is a superb line that passes from the right hand through the arms and the left hand, lying loosely against the right knee, on to the figure's pointed left foot. It seems to make the figure echo a strung bow, with the powerful torso, dominated by the figure's strong median line, as the arrow ready to be loosed. In general the sculpture still retains a rather two dimensional appearance: it was for later generations to master the confident placement of the figure in three dimensions so that it can be viewed from many different angles.

The popularity of Myron's discobolus in the Roman period was no doubt due to its representation of the Greek athletic ideal. This example comes from the huge villa at Tivoli designed by the philhellenic emperor Hadrian (AD 117–38). Its head is set at the wrong angle and, indeed, must come from a different statue from among the many Classical sculptures that have been discovered in the great villa complex. Hadrian's choice of sculptures, both copies of Greek originals and classicizing pastiches, was deliberate. It reflected his cultural and intellectual interests and the extent of his travels. Several areas were set out with sculptures, arranged in pairs or groups, often creating spaces rich in allegorical as well as political significance. Sadly we do not know precisely where this discobolus was found.

145 BRONZE BUST OF A YOUNG MAN

This very fine bronze bust has inlaid silver eyes with pupils of black, deliberately patinated bronze, known as Corinthian bronze (see **139**), and inlaid copper nipples. There are the remains of a pin in a different metal for a brooch on the left shoulder.

The tousled locks of hair are carefully detailed. The hair of the beard follows the jaw line and begins as cold-worked incisions, continuing then as three-dimensional curls; there is an additional tuft below the lower lip. The moustache is formed of a relief ridge marked with incised curls, while the eyebrows are done with diagonal incisions. The long face has finely modelled cheek bones and a long, bony nose. The torso is naked except for a cloak fastened at the left shoulder.

The dress and pose, with the head turned to one side, recall those of Hellenistic philosopher portraits. The hairstyle suggests a date in the AD 130s, a period of a great resurgence of interest in Greek culture, encouraged by the personal commitment of the emperor Hadrian (AD 117–38). The man represented in the bust was most probably a member of Hadrian's inner circle. Indeed, he has been identified as Aelius Verus, who was named by Hadrian as is successor, but died too soon to become emperor. However, comparisons with other known portraits of Aelius Verus reveal too many differences and as a result, for the time being at least, this wonderful image of a young man must remain anonymous. As a private portrait, it was probably made for private contemplation by the man's family and descendants.

Bronze portrait
Roman, made in Italy, AD 130–40
Possibly from Rome
Ht 19 cm
GR 1873,0820.40 (*Bronze* 834)

146 MARBLE PORTRAIT OF A YOUNG MAN

The finest portraits of the second century AD show a technical brilliance and a psychological insight that were never surpassed in antiquity. This bust, which seems to abound in intellectual as well as physical vitality, may have been of an Athenian of the circle of Herodes Atticus (AD 101–77), the great benefactor of Athens. The emperor Hadrian (AD 117–38) had given a new importance and pride to Greece, and this imperial support and interest was also continued by his successor Antoninus Pius (**148**).

This superb portrait shows a young man with a short beard, a thick moustache curving down around his mouth and a head of curly hair rendered with very richly modelled locks. His garment, a *himation* (mantle) thrown around his shoulders, marks him out as an intellectual and probably an orator of some distinction. His head is strongly turned to his right, a trick often seen in Hellenistic sculpture, and one that imparts much life and power to such a bust.

The sculptor shows that he knew and understood everything that could be expressed by the raising of an eyebrow, the curl of a lip or the faintest possible inclination of the head on the neck. He must have been one of the leading artists in the Athens of his day.

Percy Smythe, Sixth Earl of Strangford (1780–1855), had a distinguished diplomatic career and became Ambassador at Constantinoople in 1820. He acquired a number of important Classical sculptures (eg. **40**). His second son, the Eighth Viscount, had a remarkable gift for languages and also served in the Embassy in Constantinople. Sadly, neither recorded the orign of this exceptional portrait.

Marble portrait

Roman, probably made in Greece, AD 130–50

Probably from Greece

Formerly in the Strangford collection

Ht 66 cm

GR 2007,5005.1 (*Sculpture* 1949)

147 PALMYRENE FUNERARY RELIEF

In a fertile oasis in the centre of the Syrian desert an Aramaean city, known as Tadmôr, flourished over many centuries, thanks to its location on an important east-west trade route. It was probably early in the first century AD that the city came under Roman control. Palmyra was the Latin name for the city – probably a translation into Latin of 'palm tree', using a false etymology of the city's Aramaic name, deriving Tadmôr from the Semitic word *tamar*.

From Palmyra comes a series of remarkable limestone funerary reliefs dating to the second century AD. The wealthier citizens built for their dead single-storey house-tombs and even tower-tombs. It is to such monuments that these funerary reliefs once belonged: they sealed the compartments that held the remains of the deceased and were set in the walls of the tombs.

The model is the Roman funerary bust of the early empire (compare **124**), but it is interpreted in an entirely eastern manner. The heads have individuality but they are not portraits in the way their western Roman counterparts seem to be and the details are conventional. The inscription on this relief names the woman as Tamma, daughter of Samsiqeram, son of Maliku, son of Nassum – a long aristocratic local ancestry. She wears a series of very rich garments and extremely elaborate jewellery, statements of her wealth and status. Her garments consist of a mantle that passes over her head and is wrapped round her shoulders and body, and a tunic that has an elaborately embroidered panel of rosettes and leaves passing down over her right breast. As for jewellery, she has a diadem with floral relief decoration, earrings, finger rings, a choker necklace with one central pendant, and a complex chain-like tripartite necklace combining beads and ovoid ornaments, from the centre of which hangs a medallion with three dangling strands ending in trefoils. On her left shoulder is a brooch with three similar pendant trefoils.

Combined with all this ostentatious display in native style is the spindle and distaff held in her left hand. Such domestic equipment appears in many other portraits of deceased women and is probably a symbol of their domestic virtue as Palmyran Roman matrons.

Limestone funerary relief
Roman, made at Palmyra,
AD 125–50
From Palmyra, Syria
Ht 50 cm
ANE 125204

148 PORTRAIT OF ANTONINUS PIUS

This over life-sized bust is a superb portrait of the emperor Antoninus Pius (AD 138–61), in military dress. Antoninus was adopted by the emperor Hadrian in February AD 138 and succeeded him in July of the same year. He persuaded the Senate to agree to the deification of his predecessor, and was in turn awarded the title of 'Pius'. His reign was generally one of peace and considerable prosperity, despite uprisings in Britain, Germany and Dacia. He also expanded the northern limit of the empire to the line of the Forth and Clyde estuaries, constructing a turf wall (the Antonine Wall).

His portrait has a confident, unwavering quality that seems to typify the untroubled calm of his reign. He is shown in a *paludamentum*, a military mantle with a fringed edge, which almost completely obscures the cuirass that he wears beneath – part of a shoulder strap shows on his right shoulder. Beneath the cuirass is, of course, a short-sleeved *chiton* or tunic. Antoninus is bearded, following Hadrian's lead.

The marble is polished in the flesh parts to a vitreous finish resembling porcelain, in marked contrast to the rough surface of the hair, which is chiselled and drilled with some elaboration. There is a real sense that the sculptor was aiming to achieve a special effect with the surfaces of his work. The present rusty colour of the hair may indicate that it was once painted, or even perhaps gilded, in order to produce, with the ivory-porcelain quality of the flesh, an effect of a chryselephantine (gold-and-ivory) statue. Perhaps on a portrait like this the flesh was actually left unpainted.

This bust was found, along with part of a dedicatory inscription to the emperor and several other sculptures (including portraits of Marcus Aurelius and Lucius Verus), in a large house at Cyrene, a Roman city in North Africa. The house, formerly called the Augusteum, but now referred to as the house of Jason Magnus (a rich priest of Apollo in the second century AD), has a group of formal rooms to the west that include a central court surrounded by mosaics and sculptures, and a richly paved *triclinium* (dining room). This is probably where the portraits once stood.

Marble portrait

Roman, made in Italy or at Cyrene, AD 140–60

From the House of Jason Magnus, Cyrene, Libya

Excavated by Captain R. Murdoch Smith and Commander E.A. Porcher

Ht 72.5 cm

GR 1861,1127.14 (*Sculpture* 1463)

149 THE TOWNLEY GREYHOUNDS

In contrast to the sculpture of the great Molossian hound, the Jennings Dog (**140**), this charming group of a greyhound bitch affectionately teasing a greyhound dog is a wholly Roman creation. She strokes him with her left paw, while nibbling his left ear. He turns round, ready to respond to her attentions, his erection clearly carved. Their lithe, almost delicate forms and the tight skin over their thin frames are very well captured by the sculptor.

This sculptural group, together with a second very similar but not identical pair of greyhounds, was found near Civita Lavinia (modern Lanuvio). The second group, which reverses the characters, the dog now teasing a shyer and more hesitant bitch, was acquired for the Vatican. These two pairs, and some other sculptures (including a pair of sculptures showing the mythical Greek hunter Actaeon attacked by his own dogs), were excavated in 1773 by Gavin Hamilton in one and the same room. This, he claimed, was part of a villa of the emperor Antoninus Pius (AD 138–61), but this cannot now be confirmed. Hamilton also judged the Vatican version to be the finer of the two groups, but the degree of sexual display may have played a role in his assessment, which was no doubt designed for the Catholic authorities, who consequently decided to retain one group and release the other for export.

The site of the villa had apparently been called Monte Cagnolo (Dog Hill) even before these sculptures were found. By the early nineteenth century it was being said that the Jennings Dog, known since the late 1750s, had been found there too. This might just be fanciful, but it is not impossible – after all, it would seem likely that the report of some antiquities being found there led Hamilton to the spot, and one of those antiquities could well have been a dog.

Marble group

Roman, made in Italy, probably second century AD

Found near Civita Lavinia, near Lanuvio

Formerly in the collection of Charles Townley

Ht 67 cm

GR 1805,0703.8 (*Sculpture* 2131)

150 THE WESTMACOTT ATHLETE

Several important fifth-century BC bronze statues are known to us only through Roman copies, generally in marble (compare **144**). The so-called Westmacott Athlete, named after its former owner, the sculptor Richard Westmacott, represents a young victor. He stands with his weight on his left leg, his right leg and left arm relaxed. His right arm was raised, probably to place a wreath on his own head, which is modestly bent downwards and inclined slightly to one side. It is a particularly beautiful statue.

It has been suggested that the figure is a copy of a bronze sculpture set up at Olympia, as its feet have been thought to match the depressions left in the statue base that is inscribed with the name of a youthful boxer, Kyniskos, attributed to Polykleitos by Pausanias, in his second-century AD description of the sanctuary. If this were the case, we should imagine a pair of boxer's thongs hanging loosely in the youth's left hand. The original of the Westmacott athlete, however, may rather be the work of a pupil of Polykleitos.

Polykleitos of Argos was a celebrated sculptor active between about 460 and 420 BC. He was also a noted theorist, developing a 'Canon' of the ideal proportions and measurements of the human body, on which he wrote a treatise. His work can be seen to embody perfectly the Classical Greek ideal of good and measured behaviour (*sophrosyne*), and of the striving for perfection in human body and mind (*kalos k'agathos*). Indeed, the careful but subtle contrast between muscles that are in play and those that are not seems to be a feature of the style of Polykleitos.

Polykleitan statues were much admired amongst wealthy Romans and were used to decorate their villas (unfortunately we do not know where this example was found, although it was probably Rome). In addition to copies of ancient statues, some Roman sculptors, especially Pasiteles and his school, combined them with other figures to make pastiche groups. Even portraits of Augustus, such as the famous Prima Porta statue in the Vatican, though draped in the Roman fashion, owe much to the structure and poses of Polykleitan figures.

Marble statue

Roman, made in Italy, mid second century AD

Probably from Rome

Formerly in the collection of Richard Westmacott

Ht 1.52 m

GR 1857,0807.1 (*Sculpture* 1754)

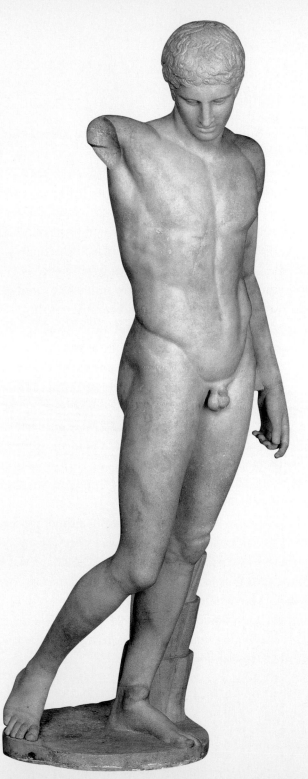

151 SILVER STATUETTE FROM MÂCON

Silver statuette

Roman, probably made in Gaul, middle of the second century AD

From Mâcon, southeastern France

Bequeathed by Richard Payne Knight

Ht 14 cm; wt 213.7 g

GR 1824,0424.1 (*Silver* 33)

This elaborate gilded silver statuette shows Fortuna (the goddess of good fortune), who in southern Gaul, where the statuette was found, may have been identified with Tutela (a local protective deity).

The goddess holds a *patera* (libation dish) in her right hand and an altar stands by her feet. In her left hand she holds a double cornucopia (horn of plenty), surmounted with the heads of Diana and Apollo. On her head she wears a walled crown, symbolizing the protection of a city, perhaps in this case Massilia (modern Marseilles). Attached to her long wings are the busts of the twin sons of Jupiter, Castor and Pollux (each with a star in his hair), and at their tips is set a yoke with seven further busts representing the deities of the days of the week – Saturn, Sol, Luna, Mars, Mercury, Jupiter and Venus. She stands on a twelve-ribbed base, perhaps suggesting the months of the year.

Fortuna was a Romanized version of the Greek deity Tyche, goddess of fortune, who originated in the Hellenistic period as the guardian deity of many new urban foundations, a function she advertised by wearing a crown in the form of a city wall. The gods of the days of the week were also a Hellenistic innovation, brought to the west from Babylon. They, and the busts of the Dioscuri, Castor and Pollux, are connected with the increase in interest in astrology in Gaul in the second century AD. The Mâcon silver figure thus combines many aspects into one powerfully complex protective deity.

The statuette was found with seven others representing various deities in a huge hoard that also included gold jewellery, five pieces of silver plate and some thirty thousand gold and silver coins. The hoard was found in 1764 at Mâcon in southeastern France, but apart from the eight statuettes only one large silver plate survives. The whole group is likely to have come from the domestic shrine (*lararium*) of a grand villa. We might note, however, that such silver statuettes of deities could also serve as table ornaments at lavish feasts, as is mentioned in Petronius' description of Trimalchio's feast. The hoard was probably hidden in about AD 260.

A colossal cult image of the god Apollo was excavated in the Temple of Apollo at Cyrene, near the large pedestal on which it had once stood: it had been smashed into 121 pieces.

Apollo is shown holding an elaborate *kithara* (complex lyre), thus highlighting his role as a god of music. Around the tree-stump that serves as a support for his heavy instrument and from which are suspended his quiver and bow coils a snake, the god's sacred creature, representing his connection with healing. The god and the snake seem to be looking at each other. Apollo stands in a very relaxed, almost effeminate pose despite his powerful musculature, his *himation* (mantle) precariously draped round his hips and thighs. His right arm was bent up over his head and originally held a plectrum. His hair is parted in the centre, with long locks falling over his shoulders and a fillet and a laurel wreath.

There are a number of other versions of this sculptural type, all probably copies of an original attributed to the second-century BC Athenian sculptor Timarchidas. He may have been amongst the first Athenian artists to work for the Romans.

The city of Cyrene in North Africa, originally a Greek colony, became a Roman province in 74 BC. After some destruction in the early second century AD it prospered again thanks to the influence and support of the emperors Trajan and Hadrian. Indeed, the city's patrons who commissioned the statue for Apollo's temple at Cyrene were expressing not only their wealth but also their Greekness, something that Hadrian must have encouraged. The result was a cult statue of great power and beauty, the work of a gifted sculptor, most probably of Greek origin.

Marble cult statue

Roman, made in Italy or at Cyrene, second century AD

From Cyrene, Libya

Excavated by Captain R. Murdoch Smith and Commander E.A. Porcher

Ht including plinth 2.29 m

GR 1861,0725.1 (*Sculpture* 1380)

153 MUMMY PORTRAIT OF A WOMAN

This lime-wood panel, painted in the encaustic technique (using hot wax as a paint medium), was once the head-piece of a mummy from Roman Egypt. Against a creamy grey background is painted the bust of a woman of exceptional refinement and delicate beauty.

The woman's face is dominated by large brown eyes, framed by individually painted lashes, and surmounted by strong straight eyebrows, dark like her wavy hair. She has a long straight nose and there is perhaps the hint of a self-confident smile on her fine lips. Her ivory complexion is tinted with pink and ochre. Her clothing is most unusual: a purple-blue tunic with gold *clavus* (vertical stripe) continued as a decorative band around the neck, where it is edged with gold leaf, and a creamy-white mantle draped over her left shoulder. She wears earrings of square emeralds set in gold with suspended pearls and around her neck is a heavy necklace with a variety of stones and settings – two large emeralds, a large oval carnelian and two rectangular gold plaques. On her head is a delicate gold wreath. All the settings and the wreath are done with gold leaf.

Mummification continued to be practised in the Roman period, even if the embalming techniques employed were inferior to those of earlier periods. Mummy portraits began to be used some eighty years after the Roman conquest of the country, from about the middle of the first century AD, and continued for some two hundred years. They were inserted over the face into an opening in the wrappings or shrouds that enveloped the body.

It is likely that such portraits represent members of a group of descendants of the Greek mercenaries who had fought for Alexander and the early Ptolemies and were granted land in the Fayum of Egypt after it had been drained for agricultural use in the early Ptolemaic period. These colonists would have settled and married local women, adopting Egyptian religious beliefs. This extremely elegant woman must have been from an elite, highly Romanized family, whether from er-Rubayat or Hawara.

Painted portrait

Roman, made in Egypt, AD 160–70

From the Fayum (perhaps er-Rubayat), Egypt

Formerly in the collection of Sir Robert Mond

Ht 44.3 cm

EA 65346 (AES 1939,0324.211)

From Hadrian's Wall comes this large gilded bronze statuette, a powerful yet enigmatic image of the Greek hero Hercules. He is shown wearing a short, close-fitting, sleeveless *chiton*, which does not quite cover his genitals and exposes his buttocks. A triple-clasped belt surrounds his waist and a lion-skin covers his head and left arm. His right arm is raised and clenched, presumably to hold his great club, now lost. His left hand is by his side, also clenched to hold some object.

The pose and dress recall images of the eastern incarnation of Hercules, known as Melqart. From such pieces one might imagine that he held the tail or leg of a small animal in his left hand. Nevertheless, there are elements of the dress that also seem to point in the direction of Roman gladiators and racing charioteers. The tunic is short and has a curved lower edge – this recalls some gladiatorial tunics as well as the tunics sometimes worn by charioteers. The way that the lion-skin is wrapped round the arm echoes the defensive arm-padding (*manica*) worn by gladiators, while a wide, elaborate belt is typical of gladiators, although a multi-strap version is best paralleled on racing charioteers.

This unusual combination of Herculean and possibly gladiatorial dress has prompted an identification of the figure as the emperor Commodus. For, towards the end of AD 191, this emperor began to equate himself with Hercules, calling himself *Hercules Romanus*, while for most of his reign he displayed a particular interest in performing as a gladiator and, no doubt, also as a charioteer. The absence of a beard is unexpected for Commodus, but it could be explained if in addition the artist wanted to suggest that he was a successor of Alexander.

Unexpectedly for such a large piece, it was cast solid. The highly reduced amount of lead in the alloy indicates that it was also always intended that the figure would be gilded. This means that the statuette must have been conceived as a particularly prestigious and expensive work. It is said to have been 'dug out of' Hadrian's Wall, near Birdoswald Fort. It may have been brought over to Britain by an army officer, recently appointed to the northern frontier. Once news reached Hadrian's Wall, however, of Commodus' death in AD 192, it would have been carefully buried, perhaps a revered, but dangerous, embarrassment.

Gilded bronze statuette

Roman, made perhaps in Italy or Gaul, perhaps in AD 191/2

Said to be from Hadrian's Wall, near Birdoswald Fort

Formerly in the collection of the Ninth Earl of Carlisle

Presented by Sir Arthur W. Franks

Ht 44.5 cm

PE 1895,0408.1

155 MEDALLION OF SEPTIMIUS SEVERUS

This copper-alloy medallion of the emperor Septimius Severus Pertinax (AD 193–211) was struck in Rome in AD 195 (as indicated by mention in the legend of his third tenure of tribunitian power and second tenure of the consulate). It combines a fine portrait on one side with an explicit scene of political propaganda on the other. Such scenes were common in Roman coinage, which often featured the emperor's head on one side and a building or event on the other. This contrasts strongly with the images on earlier Greek and Hellenistic coins, where although there may have been an important political message, it was regularly conveyed in symbolic terms.

Septimius, of mixed Punic and Italian origin, and from Lepcis Magna (now in Libya), was proclaimed emperor in AD 193. He soon set off for Syria to defeat a rival claimant and then to settle scores with the Parthians. In AD 195 he returned to Rome to consolidate his position and his dynastic connections. He made his elder son Caesar and renamed him M. Aurelius Antoninus.

Septimius also raised army pay and allowed soldiers to marry. The reverse of the medallion shows Septimius addressing a group of legionaries who hold their standards, his right arm raised in the *adlocutio* gesture, his left holding his spear or staff. Behind him stands his elder son, Caracalla, as we usually call him, now Caesar. The scene celebrates the relationship between the army and the emperor, the legend beneath acknowledging the trust of the soldiers (FIDEI MILIT), and one could imagine such medallions being issued to its officers.

The obverse of the medallion shows a powerful portrait of Septimius, his naked back towards the viewer, a shield on his left shoulder, and a wreath of laurel leaves in his hair. This image recalls that of Augustus on the Blacas cameo (**135**) and must have sought to echo representations of Alexander the Great and his eastern victories.

Copper-alloy medallion
Roman, minted in Rome, AD 195
Diam. 4.1 cm; wt 64.67 g
CM 1865,0606.3 (*RMBM* p. 32, 1)

156 SILVER PEPPER-SHAKER FROM CHAOURSE

Silver pepper shaker

Roman, made in Gaul or Italy, early third century AD

From Chaourse, France

Ht 9.0 cm; wt 52 g

GR 1889,1019.16 (*Silver* 145)

The gilded silver pepper-shaker (*vasum piperatorium*) from Chaourse takes the form of a sleeping African slave. He squats as he snoozes and has a small, footed lantern between his legs, a suspension chain for which reaches up to his left hand. He is closely wrapped against the night with a hooded cloak (*paenula*) over a sleeveless tunic. His features are rather coarse, his lips thick and his nose broad. His hair is crimped and he has a moustache and two tufts of hair on his chin. The exhausted slave, sleeping as he waits perhaps for his master to end his long night of debauchery, was a favourite motif in Roman art and probably in the theatre, too.

The figure is hollow and the base-plate (now lost) was removable so that the pot could be filled with pepper; the fiery condiment was shaken out through six holes pierced in the hair over his forehead.

Pepper began to be imported into the Roman world from India in the first century AD. This new spice was described by many ancient authors, including Pliny, who comments on the strangeness of the taste. It was widely used for flavouring both food and drink. Early Roman pepper-shakers were small and in shape imitated various vessels, but from later centuries comes a number of much more decorative pieces in the form of figures and animals. Contemporary with the Chaourse shaker is one in Boston (said to be from Sidon) in the form of a boy with a bunch of grapes (perhaps the young Bacchus) and one in Sofia (from Nikolayevo in Bulgaria), which takes the shape of an African boy holding a puppy. In the fifth-century AD treasure from Hoxne in Britain there were four remarkable pepper-shakers in human and animal form.

The Chaourse Treasure was discovered in 1883 in a field near Montcornet (Aisne) in France, wrapped in a piece of cloth. It consisted of thirty-nine items, thirty-three of silver, and six of silvered bronze, and also included six bronze coins dating between AD 90 and 267. The objects must have come from a domestic context, for they may be divided into a dining set (*ministerium*) and a toilet set.

157 BONE PORTRAIT OF A ROMAN SOLDIER

Bone portrait

Roman, made in Italy, mid third century AD

Formerly in the Morrison collection

Ht 6 cm

GR 1898,0715.2 (*Gem* 3952)

A fragment of bone carving only 6 cm high depicts a man wearing a thick military cloak, the *paludamentum*, which is fastened on his right shoulder and bears a series of horizontal press-folds. His powerful cannonball head is turned to his left, giving a great vitality to the tiny figure. His face is very carefully and sensitively modelled with its fleshy forms running down from nose and mouth. There are two vertical ridges at the bridge of the nose and two incised lines furrowing the forehead. Creases also run off from the corners of the eyes. The hair is shown cut short, but the strands are separately worked.

The man's left arm seems to project forwards at the elbow, but the curves of the laminate structure of the bone make it clear that the arm itself must have been made as a separate piece and inserted into a socket. As with the arm, although the full diameter of the bone has been used for the figure, it is possible that there were additional elements attached on either side. Indeed, there is a pin hole in the top of his left shoulder that is perhaps best understood as helping to fix another element or figure to the left of our man, rather than as the raised arm of the figure itself. In addition, there is also the trace of some element rising from the figure's other shoulder. The back of the head and the figure are finished flat and the whole must, therefore, have been attached to a flat backing as relief decoration. It is, in fact, quite possible that this fragment was part of a decorative frieze of several figures.

There is a coating of red all over the figure – the hair, the face and the drapery. It is likely that this was a bole or fixative for gilding and that the whole figure was covered in thin gold foil. The strong individuality of the face suggests that it might have been intended to be a portrait of a powerful soldier. Its high value and date, the middle of the third century AD, make one wonder if it could have been a representation of one of the soldier emperors, perhaps Valerian (AD 253–60). If there were other figures next to him, one might have been Valerian's son and joint ruler, Gallienus.

Glass cup

Roman, perhaps made in Alexandria, AD 290–325

Formerly in the collection of Lord Rothschild

Purchased with the aid of the Art Fund

Ht as restored 16.5 cm

PE 1958,1202.1

The Lycurgus cup is a deep, handleless cup made from a very special type of glass, 'dichroic', which changes colour when light passes through it – here the opaque green turns to a glowing translucent red. This is caused by the presence in the glass of minute amounts of gold and silver.

It is also the only well-preserved figural example of a type of vessel known as a 'cage-cup'. It was made by cutting and grinding the blown glass until the figures were left in high relief. Behind the main figures the interior wall of the cup has also been hollowed out to compensate for the thickness of the glass and help give an even purplish glow to the figures' bodies. The whole cup was finished by means of

'flame polishing', a very risky process but one that gave the cup a remarkably glossy finish.

The scene depicts Lycurgus, king of the Edoni in Thrace, and the wine god Bacchus with his panther and followers. Lycurgus tried to kill one of the god's followers, Ambrosia. She called for help and was transformed into a vine that entangled the king in its shoots. Bacchus taunts Lycurgus. In rage Lycurgus' muscles and thick neck bulge and his face becomes distorted as he roars. The colours of the vase have been deliberately chosen to accentuate the theme – the green of the vine leaves, the purplish red of the grapes. There is also an area of glass which is rather yellower green: this area corresponds to the body of Lycurgus, the vine and the legs of Ambrosia. With transmitted light, this area glows a more amethystine red. The craftsman who prepared the glass (*vitrearius*) must have explained this to the glass cutter (*diatretarius*) so that he could make Lycurgus' rage glow even more strongly.

A gilt bronze rim and foot were attached in about 1800. The lack of weathering suggests that the cup was always above ground, perhaps in a cathedral treasury.

HISTORY OF THE BRITISH MUSEUM COLLECTION

When the British Museum was founded in 1753, it was not, as now, a collection of art and antiquity, but rather a huge assemblage of books, manuscripts and specimens of natural history. The founding collection of Sir Hans Sloane contained some classical antiquities but these were, apart from the coins and engraved seal-stones, generally of minor significance and had been purchased simply to make up Sloane's cabinet of curiosities of 'natural and artificial rarities'.

The new Museum, however, acted as a powerful magnet and by the end of the decade one of the most important classical bronzes, a fine bronze portrait head, had been donated (**88**). It had once been part of the great collection of classical antiquities formed by Thomas Howard, Earl of Arundel (1585–1646), one of the first collections of its kind in England.

The growth of the Museum's collection soon received further impetus as a result of the interests of Sir William Hamilton (1730–1803), who for more than thirty years served as British Ambassador in Naples. There he amassed a vast collection of Greek vases (**58**), bronzes, sealstones, coins and numerous other classical antiquities, which he sold to the British Museum in 1772. The Portland Vase, the most famous cameo-glass vessel from antiquity, had also been in Hamilton's collection before it was bought by the Dowager Duchess of Portland (**133**). It was deposited in the Museum by the Fourth Duke of Portland in 1810, and finally purchased from the Seventh Duke in 1945.

The Museum is particularly famous for its great array of classical sculpture. Its first major acquisition, largely of Roman sculpture, came in 1805 when it purchased the collection of the great eighteenth-century antiquary, Charles Townley (**54** and **144**). In 1814 the marble frieze of the fifth-century BC Greek temple of Apollo at Bassai was purchased for the Museum (**57**). This, the first major acquisition of original Greek sculpture, was quickly followed in 1816 by the purchase of the extraordinary collection formed by the Seventh Earl of Elgin. The Elgin collection included, besides early vases and gold jewellery, the sculptures from the Parthenon, acquired with the permission of the Ottoman authorities, as Greece was then, and had been for nearly 350 years, part of the Ottoman empire. Ever since, the Parthenon sculptures have stood at the heart of the Museum and our understanding of classical art (**52**).

The number of antiquities other than sculpture also grew. Townley's collection of smaller antiquities came in 1814, and ten years later Richard Payne Knight bequeathed his fine collection of bronzes (**122**). In the 1830s and 1840s the Museum acquired many superb Greek vases that came from Etruscan tombs in central Italy on the estates of Lucien Bonaparte, younger brother of Napoleon.

The tradition of enlightened British diplomatic representatives abroad, begun by Sir William Hamilton and continued by Lord Elgin, resulted in further acquisitions for the Museum, especially from Sir Stratford Canning, a successor of Elgin at Constantinople, through whom much of the frieze of the Mausoleum at Halikarnassos was acquired as a gift of the Sultan in 1846 (**65**).

These years were remarkable also for the excavations conducted in Lycia by Charles Fellows, with the permission of the Ottoman authorities, from which the Museum acquired in 1842 and 1844 parts of several major tombs from the Lycian capital at Xanthos (**46** and **61**). This was the first of a series of controlled excavations carried out with local permission, most of which brought important architectural sculpture to the Museum. They include those of Charles Newton in Asia Minor (1857–9: **65** and **66**), R. Murdoch Smith and E.A. Porcher at Cyrene in North Africa (1860–61: **79**, **148** and **152**), R.P. Pullan at Priene in Asia Minor (1868–9) and J.T. Wood at Ephesus (1864–74: **72**).

In 1860 it was decided to divide the old Department of Antiquities and Coins, formed in 1807, and create the Department of Greek and Roman Antiquities. The Department's first Keeper was Charles (later Sir Charles) Newton (1816–94), a distinguished and far-sighted scholar who was committed to the acquisition and display not only of major monuments and works of art but also of smaller-scale objects illustrative of daily life in the classical world.

In addition to supporting excavations in North Africa, Cyprus and Asia Minor, Newton was able to acquire a number of large collections. One of these was the stock of the important dealer Alessandro Castellani, a member of the family of jewellers in Rome famous for work in an 'archaeological' style: it included very fine ancient jewellery (**69** and **81**), important sculptures in marble and bronze, terracottas (**82**), gems (**83**), glass (**86**) and a very large collection of superb Greek vases (**44**, **45**, **49**, **70** and **74**). A second was that of the Duc de Blacas with its outstanding gems and cameos, as well as sculptures and vases: it was purchased in 1866 (**76** and **135**).

In the last decades of the nineteenth century, the growth of local museums in Greece,

Turkey and Italy, followed by national legislation to protect antiquities, meant that major acquisitions became rare and excavations a matter of sharing the finds. The finds from the British Museum's own excavations at Ephesus in 1904–5, directed by D.G. Hogarth, were divided with the new museum at Istanbul, with the consent of the Turkish government. Similarly, shares of the finds from jointly funded excavations came to the Museum, including those from the sanctuary of Artemis Orthia in Sparta which were given by the British School at Athens in 1923, with the permission of the Hellenic government, and those from the excavations of Sir William Flinders Petrie at Naukratis in the Nile Delta and of Sir Leonard Woolley at Al Mina in Syria. Such large groups of mainly fragmentary material included some objects suitable for exhibition, but their real value lay in augmenting the collection as a research tool for the future.

The last great acquisition as a result of excavation was the bronze head of Augustus from Meroë in the Sudan, which came to the Museum in 1911 (**127**). Thereafter such important acquisitions became a rarity, not least because funds during and after two world wars were limited – the Portland Vase is a splendid exception (**133**). As a result, the pattern became established of acquiring individual objects that filled gaps in the collections, enhancing their completeness and increasing their usefulness.

In the years following the UNESCO declaration of 1970, stricter criteria began to be applied to all purchases, gifts and loans. In line with this new policy, and thanks to the financial help of individuals, including the international group of supporters known as Caryatids, and of charities and agencies such as the National Art Collections Fund (now the Art Fund) and the Heritage Lottery Fund, the Department has in recent years been able to purchase objects of the greatest importance from old collections in Britain and abroad, such as the Braganza Brooch (**85**), the Warren Cup (**132**) and the Jennings Dog (**140**).

Thanks to the efforts of its curators over many generations, the British Museum's collection of Greek and Roman antiquities is one of the greatest in the world, both in quality and depth. From its resources it has mounted exhibitions around Britain and the world while offering the millions of visitors who enter its doors, whether from home or abroad, the chance to learn about their own culture and history as well as those of others, hopefully contributing to an understanding that is fundamental for human existence.

MAPS

Britain and the Western Mediterranean

Italy and Sicily

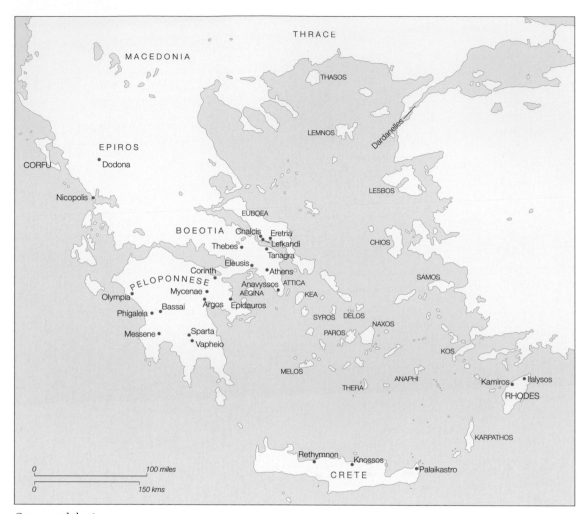

Greece and the Aegean

The East Greek world (inset)

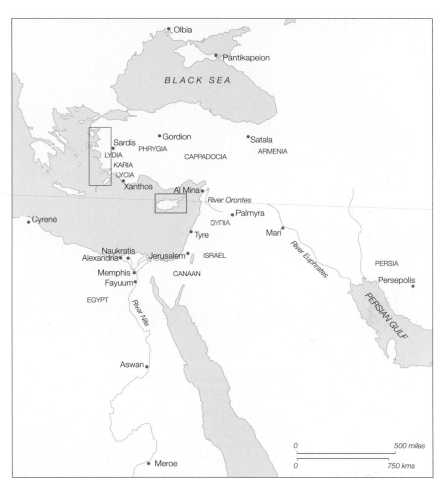

The Eastern Mediterranean

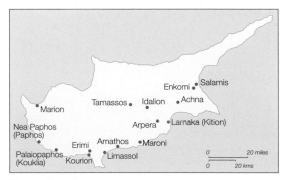

Cyprus (inset)

TIMELINES

PERIODS, RULERS AND DYNASTIES

Greek Final Neolithic	4500–3000 BC
Greek Bronze Age	3000–1100 BC
Greek Dark Age	1100–900 BC
Greek Geometric	900–700 BC
Orientalizing	700–600 BC
Archaic Greece	600–480 BC
Classical Greece	480–323 BC
Hellenistic world	323–31 BC

Roman Republic	509–31 BC
Augustus	27 BC–AD 14
Julio-Claudians (Tiberius, Caligula, Claudius, Nero)	AD 14–68
Flavians (Vespasian, Titus, Domitian)	AD 69–96
Nerva	AD 96–98
Trajan	AD 98–117
Hadrian	AD 117–138
Antonines (Antoninus Pius, Marcus Aurelius, Lucius Verus, Commodus)	AD 138–192
Severans (Septimius Severus, Caracalla, Macrinus, Elagabalus, Alexander Severus)	AD 193–235
Soldier Emperors (Maximinus Thrax, Gordian I and II, Pupienus and Balbinus, Gordion III, Philip the Arab, Trebonianus Gallus, Valerian, Gallienus, Aurelian)	AD 235–275
Tetrarchs (Diocletian, Maximian, Constantius Chlorus, Galerius, Maxentius, Licinius, Constantine the Great)	AD 284–337

KEY DATES

c. 1530 BC	Eruption of Thera
c. 1200 BC	Destruction of Mycenaean palaces
776 BC	Foundation of the Olympic Games
753 BC	Legendary foundation of Rome
594/3 BC	Solon *archon* at Athens
546–5 BC	Persians conquer Ionian Greeks and absorb Cyprus
509 BC	Last Etruscan king of Rome expelled
499–4 BC	Unsuccessful revolt of Ionian Greek cities against Persian rule
498/7 BC	Persian siege of Cypriot cities
490 BC	First invasion of Greece by Persians; Persians defeated at Battle of Marathon
480–79 BC	Second invasion of Greece by Persians; sack of Athens; Persians defeated at Battles of Salamis and Plataea
478/7 BC	Formation of Delian League, against the Persians
474 BC	Battle of Cumae; Etruscans defeated at sea by Syracusans
454 BC	Treasury of Delian League moved to Athens from Delos: the Athenian empire
444/3–429 BC	Perikles is *strategos* in Athens
431–404 BC	Peloponnesian War
430–426 BC	Plague in Athens
359–336 BC	Philip II of Macedon
334–323 BC	Alexander campaigns in the East
323 BC	Death of Alexander the Great
264–241 BC	First Punic War
218–202 BC	Second Punic War
211 BC	Roman sack of Syracuse
146 BC	Sack of Corinth and Carthage by the Romans
133 BC	Pergamon bequeathed to Rome
58 BC	Cyprus becomes a Roman province
44 BC	Assassination of Julius Caesar
31 BC	Battle of Actium
AD 79	Eruption of Mt Vesuvius
AD 122–3	Hadrian's Wall is built
AD 313	Edict of Milan – Christianity accepted across the Roman empire
AD 330	Byzantium (Constantinople) becomes capital of the Roman empire

GLOSSARY

adlocutio Roman gesture indicating formal address, especially to troops

aegis magical protective goatskin, given by Zeus to Athena

akroteria floral or figured attachments at the three angles of a pediment

alabastron (pl. *alabastra*) cylindrical perfume vessels

amphora (pl. *amphorae*) two-handled wine jar

aniconic formless object of worship

antae projecting wall-ends on Classical buildings

apex leather skull cap worn by Roman Salian priests

Aphrodite Greek goddess of love, having a special connection with Cyprus

Apollo Greek god of archery, music, culture and healing

archon Greek magistrate

Arimasp mythical one-eyed people who lived in northern Scythia (and fought griffins for supplies of gold)

ars art or technique (Latin)

aryballos small bottle for scented oil

asebia impiety (Greek)

Asklepios Greek god of healing

askos vessel in the shape of a wineskin

Athena Greek goddess of wisdom and the crafts, and patron goddess of Athens

Athenaeus Greek writer, from Naukratis in Egypt (late second century AD)

Bacchus Roman god of wine

beitel aniconic object of worship

black-figure vase-painting technique in which figures are painted in black, articulated with incision and additional red and white

bucchero black burnished pottery

cantharus drinking cup of special shape with two high-rising vertical handles (Latin)

caryatid architectural support in the form of a female figure

Centaur mythical creature, part man and part horse

chiton tunic

chlamys short cloak or wrap

Cicero Roman statesman, orator and writer (106–43 BC)

cingulum Roman soldier's sword belt

clavus vertical stripe on Roman garment

columnae caelatae sculptured column pedestals

convivia Roman banquets

deme ward or district of Classical Athens

diatretarius Roman glass cutter

dinos cauldron or bowl for mixing wine and water

Dionysos Greek god of wine

discobolus discus thrower

diskos discus

ekkyklema theatrical device on which a prepared tableau could be wheeled out on to the stage

emblema decorative feature designed to be the central element of a mosaic

erastes lover; Greek mature male lover

eromenos beloved; Greek younger male partner

Eros Greek winged youthful god of love, companion or son of Aphrodite

faience glazed frit pottery

fresco wall-painting applied to wet plaster

gorgoneion head of the monstrous gorgon Medusa

gynaikeion women's quarters in Greek houses

Hermes Greek messenger god

Herodotos Greek historian, from Halikarnassos (*c.* 485–424 BC)

himation mantle, cloak

hoplites (pl. *hoplitai*) heavily armed infantryman
hydria water jar

iynx love charm in the form of a whirling disc

kalos k'agathos beautiful and good; the striving for human
    perfection in both body and mind
kantharos drinking cup of special shape with two high-rising
    vertical handles (Greek)
kerykeion messenger's staff
kithara complex form of lyre
kline couch
klismos high-backed chair
koine shared language or culture
komos procession of drinkers from one party to another
kopis sword with a curved blade
kore (pl. *korai*) standing statue of draped female (usually
    Archaic)
kouros (pl. *kouroi*) standing figure of a naked male youth
    (usually Archaic)
krater bowl for mixing wine and water
kylikeion elaborate sideboard for display of vessels

Lapith Greek tribe, from Thessaly in northern Greece
lararium domestic shrine in the Roman house
libation offering of liquid to the gods
libertinus (pl. *libertini*) freedmen (freed slaves)
Linear A and B writing scripts used in Bronze Age Greece
louterion bowl form, usually used to hold water for washing

maenads wild women, devotees of Greek god Dionysos
    (Roman god Bacchus)
manica gladiator's defensive arm-padding
Marine Style decorative style of Greek Bronze Age pottery
    using marine motifs

Mercury Roman messenger god
metoikoi foreign residents in Athens
metopes square panels, which combine with triglyphs, to
    form part of the entablature above the columns in the
    Doric order
Minerva Roman goddess of wisdom and the crafts
ministerium set of dining implements (Roman)
Minoan term for the Bronze Age culture of Crete
Minotaur mythical creature in the Cretan labyrinth; man
    with a bull's head and tail
Mycenaean term for the Late Bronze Age culture of mainland
    Greece (*c.* 1600–1100 BC)

naiskos small temple-like structure, sometimes constructed
    over a tomb

oinochoe wine jug
omphalos raised dome in the centre of a bowl which helped
    the user hold the vessel when tipping it to pour a libation
opus vermiculatum mosaic technique using very small pieces
    of stone or glass

palmette decorative motif in the form of stylized palm leaf
paludamentum military cloak
Panathenaia Athenian festival held in honour of Athena every
    summer
pankration no-holds-barred combat sport, combining boxing
    and wrestling
patera Roman libation dish
Pausanias Greek traveller, geographer and writer, probably
    from Lydia (second century AD)
pectoral breast plate or ornament
pelike storage jar
peltai shields of crescent-moon shape
peplos tunic

Petronius Roman novelist and satirist (*c.* AD 27–66)

phallos erect penis

phiale libation bowl

Pictorial Style decorative style of Late Bronze Age Greek pottery using human figures and animals

pilos travelling hat

pithos large storage jar

Plato Greek philosopher, from Athens (428/7–348/7 BC)

Pliny Roman historian and natural philosopher (AD 23–79)

Plutarch Greek historian, biographer and philosopher, from Boeotia (*c.* AD 46–120)

Pnyx meeting place of the democratic Athenian assembly

Protogeometric stylistic and chronological term (*c.* 1050–900 BC); the style immediately prior to the Geometric

protome forepart

psykter vessel for cooling wine

pyxis trinket or cosmetic box

red-figure vase-painting technique in which the figures are left reserved in the black slip; interior details added with diluted slip

repoussé metal-working technique used for hammering out a design

rhyton vessel for aerating wine by pouring it out of a small nozzle

satyr mythical creature in the form of a man with horse's ears, tail and sometimes hooves

Sirens mythical creatures in the form of birds with women's heads, breast and arms

skyphos deep drinking cup

slip liquid clay applied to surface of a ceramic pot

sophrosyne good and measured behaviour

sphyrelaton technique of hammering metal to shape

strategos general

stylus writing implement

suttee (*satī*) Hindu practice of self-immolation by the widow on the death of her husband

symposiarchos person responsible for determining the strength of wine to be drunk at a banquet

syrinx multiple pipes or Pan pipes

techne craftsmanship

tesserae small cubes of stone or glass for mosaics

tetradrachm four-drachma coin

tholos beehive-shaped tomb (Greek Bronze Age)

Thucydides Greek historian, from Athens (*c.* 460–395 BC)

thyrsos (pl. *thyrsoi*) ivy-topped fennel staff (Greek; Latin *thyrsus*, pl. *thyrsi*)

tondo (pl. *tondi*) circular paintings or areas for painting

triclinium dining room with three couches round a square table

triglyph architectural feature with three vertical projections, part of the entablature above the columns in the Doric order

vasa murrina vessel made of fluorite (fluorspar)

vasum piperatorium pepper-shaker

Venus Roman goddess of love

vitrearius glass maker

Xenophon Greek soldier and writer, from Athens (*c.* 430–335 BC)

FURTHER READING

A select list of further reading is offered here. All the books quoted have bibliographies that will lead readers further into whatever topic they choose.

The British Museum has itself published a number of books that connect its collection with the wider field of Greek and Roman art, and these are a very good place to begin. Following this list is a selection of general books that deal with one or more periods: some give a well illustrated survey, others are more specialized. Finally there is a selection of books that provide an overview of a particular material.

L.M. Burn, *The British Museum Book of Greek and Roman Art* (London 1991)

L.M. Burn, *Hellenistic Art: From Alexander the Great to Augustus* (London 2004)

J.L. Fitton, *Cycladic Art* (London 1989)

J.L. Fitton, *Minoans* (London 2002)

J.W. Hayes, *Handbook of Mediterranean Roman Pottery* (London 1997)

I.D. Jenkins, *Greek Architecture and its Sculpture in the British Museum* (London 2007)

I.D. Jenkins, *The Parthenon* (London 2007)

I.D. Jenkins, *The Lion of Knidos* (London 2008)

E. Macnamara, *The Etruscans* (London 1990)

J. Neils, *The British Museum Concise Introduction: Ancient Greece* (London 2008)

T.W. Potter, *Roman Britain* (London 1983)

N.H. and A. Ramage, *The British Museum Concise Introduction: Ancient Rome* (London 2008)

L. Schofield, *The Mycenaeans* (London 2007)

V. Tatton Brown, *Ancient Cyprus* (London 1987)

R.A. Tomlinson, *Greek and Roman Architecture* (London 1995)

S. Walker, *Roman Art* (London 1991)

S. Walker, *The Portland Vase* (London 2006)

S. Walker, *Greek and Roman Portraits* (London 1995)

D. Williams, *Greek Vases* (2nd edn London 1999)

D. Williams, *The Warren Cup* (London 2007)

PREHISTORIC GREECE

O. Dickinson, *The Aegean Bronze Age* (Cambridge 1994)

O. Dickinson, *The Aegean from Bronze Age to Iron Age* (Abingdon 2006)

R. Hampe and E. Simon, *The Birth of Greek Art* (London 1981)

M.S.F. Hood, *The Arts in Prehistoric Greece* (Harmondsworth 1978)

EARLY AND CLASSICAL GREECE AND THE HELLENISTIC WORLD

J. Boardman (ed.), *The Oxford History of Classical Art* (Oxford 1993)

J. Boardman, *The Diffusion of Classical Art in Antiquity* (London 1994)

J. Boardman, *The Greeks Overseas* (4th edn London 1999)

J.N. Coldstream, *Geometric Greece* (2nd edn London 2003)

R. Osborne, *Archaic and Classical Art* (Oxford 1998)

J.G. Pedley, *Greek Art and Archaeology* (London 1992)

J.J. Pollitt, *Art and Experience in Classical Greece* (Cambridge 1972)

J.J. Pollitt, *Art in the Hellenistic Age* (Cambridge 1986)

M. Robertson, *A Shorter History of Greek Art* (Cambridge 1981)

S. Woodford, *An Introduction to Greek Art* (London 1986)

ITALY AND ROME

S. Haynes, *Etruscan Civilization* (Los Angeles 2000)

M. Henig (ed.), *A Handbook of Roman Art* (Oxford 1983)

F.S. Kleiner, *A History of Roman Art* (Belmont, CA 2007)

M. Pallottino, *A History of Earliest Italy* (Ann Arbor 1991)

N.H. and A. Ramage, *Roman Art* (5th edn Upper Saddle River, NJ 2008)

P. Stewart, *Roman Art* (Oxford 2004)

CYPRUS

D. Hunt (ed.), *Footprints in Cyprus* (London 1982)

V. Karageorghis, *Cyprus: From the Stone Age to the Romans* (London 1982)

V. Karageorghis, *Ancient Art from Cyprus: The Cesnola Collection in The Metropolitan Museum of Art* (New York 2000)

V. Karageorghis, *Early Cyprus: Crossroads of the Mediterranean* (Milan 2002)

MATERIALS

J. Boardman, *The History of Greek Vases* (London 2001)

J. Boardman, *Greek Gems and Finger Rings* (2nd edn London 2001)

R.M. Cook, *Greek Painted Pottery* (3rd edn London 1997)

K.M.D. Dunbabin, *Mosaics of the Greek and Roman World* (Cambridge 1999)

D.B. Harden, *Glass of the Caesars* (London 1987)

R.A. Higgins, *Greek Terracottas* (London 1967)

R. Higgins, *Greek and Roman Jewellery* (2nd edn London 1980)

G.K. Jenkins, *Ancient Greek Coins* (2nd edn London 1990)

D.E.E. Kleiner, *Roman Sculpture* (New Haven 1992)

R. Ling, *Roman Painting* (Cambridge 1991)

S. Lydakis, *Ancient Greek Painting and Its Echoes in Later Art* (Los Angeles 2002)

C.C. Mattusch, *Classical Bronzes: The Art and Craft of Greek and Roman Statuary* (Ithaca, NY 1996)

A. Stewart, *Greek Sculpture: An Exploration* (New Haven 1990)

D.E. Strong, *Greek and Roman Gold and Silver Plate* (London 1966)

C.H.V. Sutherland, *Roman Coins* (London 1974)

A.D. Trendall, *Red-figure Vases of South Italy and Sicily* (London 1989)

S. Walker and M. Bierbrier, *Ancient Faces: Mummy Portraits for Roman Egypt* (London 1997)

D. Williams and J. Ogden, *Greek Gold: Jewellery of the Classical World* (London 1994)

INDEX